VIRGINIA WOOLF:
New Critical Essays

VIRGINIA WOOLF:
New Critical Essays

edited by
Patricia Clements
and Isobel Grundy

VISION
and
BARNES & NOBLE

Vision Press Limited
Fulham Wharf
Townmead Road
London SW6 2SB

and

Barnes & Noble Books
81 Adams Drive
Totowa, NJ 07512

ISBN (UK) 0 85478 055 6
ISBN (US) 0 389 20375 0

823

W93 zcL

Printed and bound in Great Britain by
Unwin Brothers Ltd.,
Old Woking, Surrey.
Phototypeset by Galleon Photosetting,
Ipswich, Suffolk.
MCMLXXXIII

Contents

Preface

We invited these contributions with the aim of providing a communal overview of Virginia Woolf's work and some individual assessments of the nature of her achievement. With her centenary recently celebrated and her reputation still matter of heated controversy, with a few novels at best-selling level and others still more or less unknown to the common reader, with drafts and early versions of her fiction beginning to join her personal writings as part of the available literary heritage, it seemed a propitious moment to seek such general perspectives and such personal responses.

The result of our canvassing pleases us by its wide-ranging character and also by the degree to which contributors have concurred in each other's assumptions, crucial areas of interest, and even conclusions. Every essay in the book reflects awareness of Virginia Woolf's impressive stature, and of the degree to which established methods of critical assessment have so far—because she is experimental, because she is feminist, because she is oblique—failed to reach any kind of consensus about her degree or even her kind of stature. These writers have aimed to refuse the stereotyped opinions about her with which we are all so familiar; to set her in the context of her predecessors, her rivals, and her peers; to examine the sources and the nature of what is most individual in her elusive literary character, and the stages by which her unique style and methods evolved. Every one of her major fictions and many minor works receive at least some detailed attention; none is considered in isolation; fruitful and sometimes surprising comparisons are drawn.

The earlier essays in this book attempt to place Virginia Woolf in relation to other writers; the later ones consider particular aspects of her work. She is seen consistently against the cumulative tradition of English literature, which she loved with the passionate understanding of deep familiarity, but to which as a woman she could not wholly belong, and against the alternative, subversive, half-defined but rapidly forming female tradition. Patricia Clements examines her appropriation and revision of some elements in her literary inheritance, and her use of allusion (to the French symbolists, the English georgic, and classical mythology) as an integral part of the design of her narrative. S. P. Rosenbaum sets Woolf in relation to the particular combination of encyclopaedic and personal knowledge offered by her father, Sir Leslie Stephen, with his weighty philosophic interests, his repression, and his heartening advice to 'trespass'. Then she is seen in relation to Joseph Conrad, outsider and early modernist, and to T. S. Eliot and James Joyce, with whom she was so closely linked in the bringing to birth of new techniques. Shirley Neuman charts the persistent reference in her works to Conrad's image of the heart of darkness; Lyndall Gordon discusses her struggle, and Eliot's, to capture those hidden or silent aspects of the individual life which escape the trawl of traditional, Leslie Stephen biography; and Maria DiBattista, examining her responses to the challenge of Joyce—a novelist from whom she could learn, a masculine voice to which she could reply—sees her as presiding jointly with him over modern fiction.

Virginia Blain shows Woolf evolving a narrative voice that is female yet authoritative, impersonal yet not sexless. John Mepham finds one of the springs of her modernism in her need for a new elegiac expression to replace the dead forms of mourning and celebration. Tony Davenport investigates the way in which she moved towards her characteristic method of catching moment-by-moment experience, as essays stating the problem facing the modern novelist were revised and made to put forward a programme. Susan Dick analyses her use of memory to deepen her characters by extending their consciousness into the past. Isobel Grundy considers another manner of deepening and of connecting: her choice of names for her characters.

These various topics bring us back again and again to particular issues and particular areas of her life and work: the problematic nature of our experience, the artist's raw material; the difficulty we find in knowing how others perceive either the world or themselves, and our tendency to substitute fantasy for perception; the tyranny of artistic custom; the particular obscurity and the voicelessness which has invested the lives of women; the relation of the past to the present; the relation of randomness to pattern.

One writer after another turns to Virginia Woolf's search for tools with which to break the mould of fiction, to her criticism, short fictions, and diary entries about her writing in the early 1920s, to her female consciousness, to her dislike of the 'damned egotistical self', to her desire to subsume meaning in structure, life in art. These things have seemed, for us, the heart of her achievement, of her communication of her vision.

P.C.
I.M.G.

Edmonton and London, 1983

ABBREVIATIONS

We are most grateful to the Author's Literary Estate, The Hogarth Press and Harcourt Brace Jovanovich Inc. for permission to quote. Virginia Woolf's novels are cited as follows:

VO	*The Voyage Out*, 1915, 1975
ND	*Night and Day*, 1919, 1977
JR	*Jacob's Room*, 1922, 1980
MD	*Mrs. Dalloway*, 1925, 1980
TL	*To the Lighthouse*, 1927, 1982 (except in Dick, 'The Tunnelling Process')
O	*Orlando*, 1928 1978
TW	*The Waves*, 1931, 1976
TY	*The Years*, 1937, 1979
BA	*Between the Acts*, 1941, 1981

Short works and non-fiction are generally cited as follows:

RO	*A Room of One's Own*, 1929, 1954
TG	*Three Guineas*, 1938
E	*Collected Essays*, ed. Leonard Woolf, 1966–67
L	*Letters*, ed. Nigel Nicolson and Joanne Trautmann, 6 vols., 1975–80
D	*Diary*, ed. Anne Olivier Bell, assisted by Andrew McNeillie, 1977–
AWD	*A Writer's Diary*, ed. Leonard Woolf, 1953
HH	*A Haunted House, and Other Short Stories*, 1944, 1978
CW	*Contemporary Writers*, 1965
MB	*Moments of Being, Unpublished Autobiographical Writings*, ed. Jeanne Schulkind, 1976
BP	*Books and Portraits*, ed. M. Lyon, 1977
MDP	*Mrs. Dalloway's Party, A Short Story Sequence*, ed. Stella McNichol, 1978
QB	Quentin Bell, *Virginia Woolf, A Biography*, 2 vols., 1972
M and M	*Virginia Woolf, The Critical Heritage*, ed. Robin Majumdar and Allen McLaurin, 1975

1

'As in the rough stream of a glacier': Virginia Woolf's Art of Narrative Fusion

by PATRICIA CLEMENTS

Virginia Woolf shares one of her most frequently chosen images, that of the flowing stream, with practically everybody— not only with the philosophers ancient and modern, but also with some nearer literary figures, with Arthur Symons, for instance, who devised his literary impressionism for the purpose of rendering what he called 'the turbid human stream',[1] or with Conrad, who moved from his snake-like and emblematical Congo to the dark river along which Secret Agent Verloc makes his heavy way, or with Eliot, whose Thames conducted him to the horror and whose Mississippi taught him that 'Time the destroyer is time the preserver.' She shares the image with Joyce, too, who saw in the same river both the ineluctable modalities and an infinitely plural beauty. But Virginia Woolf more than once pairs her image of the flowing stream with another, its ingenious antithesis, that of the frozen, glacial stream; and this second image, which she shares with none of these contemporaries, is a complex and suggestive figure in her work. It is rich with thematic significance, for one thing: laid alongside, or behind, her emblem for flux and the fluidity of things, it undermines her expansive investigation of the fugitive moment by locking the personal, the historical and

11

the pre-historical in a chilly embrace. But it also serves as an emblem for two aspects of Woolf's own practice—the glacially accumulating procedure by which, characteristically, she seizes, reshapes, and carries along in the powerful movement of her own prose elements of an inheritance not always intended for her; and her central myth of transformation. And what the image suggests at the metaphorical surface of Woolf's prose is reflected also as a structural characteristic in her fictions. 'I insubstantise,' she wrote (*D*, ii, 248); but the fact is that she substantizes, too: in her prose, the turbid human stream is bound to return, perhaps just a few paragraphs after its first appearance, as a crystallized solid; and in the characteristic narrative movement of her mature work, what appears first as free or fluid form will reappear shortly as figure. The movement between freedom and form creates the excitement and pathos, the freedom and fatality of Woolf's prose. In its relation to the flowing stream, her river of ice, that glacial solidity, reminds her reader of the daringly explicit, ambiguous, and steadily renewing contest in her work between randomness and order, and it keeps the text charged with an expectation of the always-possible transubstantiation. Her river of ice, therefore, the transformed and transformable stream, also suggests a steady making and crumbling of aesthetic order. What I want to examine in this essay are some of the ways in which Woolf layers her treatment of the antithetical values that are implied in the flowing and frozen stream and some of the ways in which she fuses into a seamless structure the various elements of verisimilitude, metaphor, allusion, feminism and narrative design.

The 'brilliantly hyperbolic description'[2] of the Great Frost dominates the 'biography' in which it is located. It is so vivid an experience for a reader of *Orlando* that J. J. Wilson summons it to regret that the book is 'too easily dismissed as a *jeu d'esprit*, ice/escapade'.[3] And there is no doubt that the carnival of language that attends this Great Frost begins at the surface, in the biographer's attempts to reconcile truth with the protean realities of her subject's life. But the frozen Thames that dominates *Orlando* is solid to a depth of twenty fathoms, and the great carnival on its surface is supported by an echoing literary activity below. In the apparently still depths of the ice,

Woolf embeds a series of literary allusions and transformations that contend with the dazzlingly metamorphic reality at the surface. These, it is true, hold further plays and parries in the *jeu d'esprit*, but they also hint at some darker truths.

In the account of the Great Frost, Orlando's biographer struggles with the subject, striving for granite against the overwhelmingly anarchical presence of rainbow. The restrained redundancies of style and exaggerated orthodoxies of genre attempt to balance the lush and fetterless language of the subject himself. By the law of comic reversal, it is the fantasy that supplies the granite, and the biographer is constrained to report a sudden super-abundance of it: 'Birds froze in mid-air and fell like stones to the ground', we read. 'It was no uncommon sight to come upon a whole herd of swine frozen immovable upon the road.' Canvassing the historical accounts, the biographer reports sudden petrifactions across the land: 'At Norwich a young countrywoman started to cross the road in her usual robust health and was seen by the onlookers to turn visibly to powder'; in Derbyshire, the 'great increase in rocks . . . was due to no eruption, for there was none, but to the solidification of unfortunate wayfarers who had been turned literally to stone where they stood' (33–4). The frozen Thames is only the most arresting of the surprising solidifications, and while the Church does not bless it as a relic, as it does some of the rural petrifactions, the king declares it a 'park or pleasure ground', and all of the life of London contracts upon it, as though it were the single street in the city. Love and business and diplomacy are conducted on its surface, on which fire burns without effect, and it is on the river that Orlando encounters the 'melon', 'pineapple', 'olive tree', 'emerald', 'fox in the snow' with whom he falls in love in three seconds. ('Images, metaphors of the most extreme and extravagant twined and twisted in his mind' (36).) Sasha belongs to the river—skating into Orlando's life over its surface and sailing out over its liberated waves—and the transformation of Frost echoes the transformation of love. Looking across 'the boars' heads and stuffed peacocks', Orlando 'laughed, but the laugh on his lips froze in wonder' when he looked at Sasha, and when he looked more 'the thickness of his blood melted; the ice turned to wine in his veins; he heard the waters flowing and

13

the birds singing' (39). The change in Orlando, the biographer reports, 'was extraordinary' (40). The riot of metaphor, unquelled by the biographer's analytical 'pause' (37), equals the riot of metamorphosis.

The emblem for this richness of twining and twisting is, paradoxically, the frost-bound Thames. While all of this protean change goes on at its surface, it has itself, apparently, been rendered impervious to ordinary change. No matter how fiercely the fires burn on its surface, 'the heat was not enough to melt the ice which, though of singular transparency, was yet of the hardness of steel' (35). The singular transparency of the Thames, however, discloses a singular spectacle. (It is this image that stays most vividly in the mind.)

> So clear indeed was it that there could be seen, congealed at a depth of several feet, here a porpoise, there a flounder. Shoals of eels lay motionless in a trance, but whether their state was one of death or merely of suspended animation which the warmth would revive puzzled the philosophers. Near London Bridge, where the river had frozen to a depth of some twenty fathoms, a wrecked wherry boat was plainly visible, lying on the bed of the river where it had sunk last autumn, overladen with apples. The old bumboat woman, who was carrying her fruit to market on the Surrey side, sat there in her plaids and farthingales with her lap full of apples, for all the world as if she were about to serve a customer, though a certain blueness about the lips hinted the truth. 'Twas a sight King James specially liked to look upon, and he would bring a troupe of courtiers to gaze with him. (36–7)

The visual pointing to the old bumboat woman is striking, and her truth-hinting lips are given the only colour in the passage, which, in spite of the singular transparency that is being wondered at, is visually imprecise. The line that drops through the twenty fathoms of frozen water is intended to go straight to the bumboat woman, who, with her apples in her lap, suggests an altogether different dimension of time from that engaged at the horizontal surface of the river. The old bumboat woman, who has much in common with the other old but timeless women in Woolf's novels who take us back to beginnings, is crucial. Her lips hint the truth. Furthermore, in the book's future, she becomes inseparable, in Orlando's memory, from the Great Frost.

14

The Great Frost is central to the design of *Orlando* chiefly because it confirms in the character the figure of desire and betrayal.[4] (It is not irrelevant to remember that Stendhal, in what John Middleton Murry called 'that curious book *De l'Amour*', names 'crystallization' that psychological process by which Venus becomes entirely attached to her prey.)[5] The Frost is the basis for the book's important repetitions and rebirths. When the transformed Orlando returns to a transformed London, for instance, after leaving the gypsies, it is 'Sasha the lost, Sasha the memory' that she first encounters. When, Captain Bartolus at her side to name, among other monuments, Mr. Wren's new cathedral, she weeps to think, 'Here . . . had been the great carnival. Here, where the waves slapped briskly, had stood the Royal Pavilion. Here she had first met Sasha.' And she goes on to make the inevitable association: 'About here (she looked down into the sparkling waters) one had been used to see the frozen bumboat woman with her apples on her lap' (151). And when, much later, shopping by motorcar in Oxford Street, Orlando is deceived by a whiff of scent, she thinks:

> Time has passed over me . . . this is the oncome of middle age. How strange it is! Nothing is any longer one thing. I take up a handbag and I think of an old bumboat woman frozen in the ice. Someone lights a pink candle and I see a girl in Russian trousers. (274)

The old bumboat woman, her lips hinting at subsurface truth, is carried along as the essential companion of the 'Sasha!' 'Faithless!' to whom Orlando calls through the centuries.

One of the truths the old bumboat woman hints at is death, of course, and, as the necessary partner of 'Sasha the memory', she hints at betrayal and loss in love: her blue lips suggest the real, the human changes underlying the fantasy. But I suggested earlier that the image of the frozen stream is an emblem of Woolf's own literary procedure, and the lips of the frozen bumboat woman hint at that, too. Her literary lineage, embedded with her in the ice, is both witty and thematically resonant. It leads by a plunge to the beginnings of the tradition in which the poet of 'The Oak Tree' writes, and by a return to Vita Sackville-West, whose feeling for Violet Trefusis supplies

15

the material for the Sasha episode.[6]

Woolf's bumboat woman, and several of the other details in her account of the Great Frost, are drawn from John Gay's *Trivia: or, The Art of Walking the Streets of London* (1716), the 'roving Muse' of which gives some forty-five lines in response to an appeal to

> recal that wond'rous Year,
> When Winter reign'd in bleak *Britannia*'s Air;
> When hoary *Thames*, with frosted Oziers crown'd,
> Was three long Moons in icy Fetters bound.

Gay details the effects of the frost:

> The Waterman, forlorn along the Shore,
> Pensive reclines upon his useless Oar,
> Sees harness'd Steeds desert the stony Town;
> And wander Roads unstable, not their own:
> Wheels o'er the harden'd Waters smoothly glide,
> And rase with whiten'd Tracks the slipp'ry Tide.
> Here the fat Cook piles high the blazing Fire,
> And scarce the Spit can turn the Steer entire.
> Booths sudden hide the *Thames*, long Streets appear,
> And num'rous Games proclaim the crowded Fair.
> So when a Gen'ral bids the martial Train
> Spread their Encampment o'er the spatious Plain,
> Thick-rising Tents a Canvas City build,
> And the loud Dice resound thro' all the Field.

Those details appear, much enlarged, in *Orlando*, but it is what follows in Gay's poem that is of greatest interest, the 'Elegiac Lay' in which he relates the tale of Doll, the apple-woman.

> *Doll* ev'ry Day had walk'd these treach'rous Roads;
> Her Neck grew warpt beneath autumnal Loads
> Of various Fruit; she now a Basket bore,
> That Head, alas! shall Basket bear no more.
> Each Booth she frequent past, in quest of Gain,
> And Boys with pleasure heard her shrilling Strain.
> Ah *Doll!* all Mortals must resign their Breath,
> And Industry it self submit to Death!
> The cracking Crystal yields, she sinks, she dyes,
> Her Head, chopt off, from her lost Shoulders flies:
> Pippins she cry'd, but Death her Voice confounds,
> And Pip-Pip-Pip along the Ice resounds.

The applewoman is a direct ancestor of Woolf's bumboat woman. But Gay is only one stage down in the geological layering of the frozen Thames of *Orlando*: he supplies the next backward step himself, making it perfectly clear that his Doll is a parodic transformation:

> So when the *Thracian* Furies *Orpheus* tore,
> And left his bleeding Trunk deform'd with Gore,
> His sever'd Head floats down the silver Tide,
> His yet warm Tongue for his lost Consort cry'd;
> *Eurydice*, with quiv'ring Voice, he mourn'd,
> And *Heber*'s banks *Eurydice* return'd.[7]

Gay's *Trivia* is Virgilian, mock-georgic, and Virgil provides the epigraph to his poem. It is back to *The Georgics*, then, that Woolf's well-connected bumboat woman sends us. There Proteus, having 'Transformed himself into miraculous shapes/ Of every kind—a fire, a fearsome beast,/ A flowing stream', to evade shackling by Aristaeus, must now speak the truth about Orpheus. After the second death, Proteus recounts, Eurydice, 'now cold, was crossing in the Stygian barque', and Orpheus, 'for seven whole months on end', wept.

> And sang his tale of woe, entrancing tigers
> And drawing oak-trees.[8]

The transformations below the surface of the frozen Thames, though of a quite different kind from those above, nevertheless contend with them. In 'Street Haunting', on which she was working when she was struck with the idea for *Orlando* (*L*, iii, 343), Virginia Woolf chose to write of winter evenings, with their 'champagne brightness of the air and the sociability of the streets' (*E*, iv, 155), and she chose, too, to dwell on the antithetical relation of surface and depths. The eye, she says, 'is not a miner, not a diver, not a seeker after buried treasure. It floats us smoothly down a stream; resting, pausing, the brain sleeps perhaps as it looks' (156). The depth she discovers in that essay is the dwarf who prompts her to ask 'In what crevices and crannies . . . did they lodge, this maimed company of the halt and the blind?' (159). In *Orlando*, when the eye is forced to dive, what is discovered is a series of literary transformations: Virgil's tragic Orpheus becomes by literary metamorphosis Gay's parodic applewoman, who, by Woolf's transformation, becomes

17

the bumboat woman frozen into Orlando's imagination as part of the design of loss. Orlando's cries for 'Sasha, the lost' have a mythic and tragic echo and the bumboat woman's suggestion of death is three times confirmed. But Virgil's forlorn Orpheus, who consoles his woe by enchanting oak-trees, also returns us to 'the present time', since Orlando's 'Oak Tree', as is well known, is Vita Sackville-West's *The Land*. That poem, too, is georgic, headed by two lines from Virgil's Book Three:

> Nec sum animi dubius, verbis ea vincere magnum
> quam sit et angustis hunc addere rebus honorem.[9]

Victoria Sackville-West did not see any of *Orlando* until it was in print, but when she 'looked into the mirror held up for her by her friend,' Joanne Trautmann writes, 'she recognized enough details to be flattered. Some of them were private, signs between the two.'[10] *The Georgics* of Virgil may have fallen into the category of private signs, but the echoing cry of Orpheus, which shapes the text, is not only private. Victoria Sackville-West would certainly have recognized some of the petrifactions of the Great Frost as Virgilian, since Book Three includes description of the frozen river on Mount Rhodope and of a cold so severe that

> Beasts perish, frozen stiff huge shapes of oxen
> Stand starkly round, and huddling herds of deer
> Lurk paralysed beneath fresh drifts of snow.[11]

When Vita Sackville-West observed, as she must have, that the title of her book is inscribed *in* the title of Woolf's, she may also have noticed that by the layering of literary allusion in the image of the frozen Thames Virginia Woolf had connected the Hawthornden Prize poem for 1927 with its generic originator and that she had given to the prize-winning, female, poet the lyre of Orpheus.

When Virginia Woolf made the frozen Thames dominate the surface and complicate the depths of *Orlando*, she had already made a similar image do important work in her account of Elizabeth Dalloway's afternoon in London. Here,

18

as in *Orlando*, Woolf makes the frozen river accumulate and powerfully reshape elements from a literary past and present, but this short passage also demonstrates clearly the ways in which the image is an integral part of the whole. Woolf's layerings in the Elizabeth section of *Mrs. Dalloway* are of more than one kind, and before considering the allusive strata of this passage I want to examine the ways in which the glacial stream is implicated in its narrative design.

Elizabeth Dalloway's afternoon in London occupies fourteen paragraphs about two-thirds of the way through the novel, between the scene of tea with Miss Kilman and the scene of Rezia and Septimus that ends in his death (148–54). In these paragraphs, Elizabeth boards a bus ('competently'), climbs to the upper deck, and travels down Whitehall to the Strand, then up the Strand toward St. Paul's. She gets off the bus at Chancery Lane, wanders in the Temple, passes a church (it would be St. Mary-le-Strand or St. Clement Danes), looks up Fleet Street and walks up it 'a little way toward St. Paul's, shyly, like some one penetrating on tiptoe, exploring a strange house by night with a candle'. She hears some 'military music; as if people were marching', and then she turns back down the Strand to go home, so joining the rest, who, Woolf said when she planned the book, 'must converge upon the party at the end'.[12] She is, in this, 'a pioneer, a stray, venturing, trusting'.

The passage mirrors the text in which it is located—or it might be said that it stands in a relation to the whole which is like that suggested by the figure of the 'vast nest of Chinese boxes all of wrought steel turning ceaselessly within one another' in 'Kew Gardens' (*HH*, 39). It reflects both forward and back, and some of its connections with the rest of the novel issue simply from its action. When Elizabeth Dalloway climbs to the upper deck of the bus, for instance, she prepares, in a curious reversal of chronology that makes the daughter's action prior to the mother's, for a connection with the Clarissa of Peter's memory, who, in just a few pages, will, on top of an omnibus, expound her 'transcendental theory' (168). And, when Elizabeth strikes off on foot, 'venturing', she is closely linked with the fantasizing Peter Walsh, who, in his pursuit of the young woman across Trafalgar Square, across Piccadilly, and up Regent Street, is, like her, 'an adventurer, reckless', making an escape (60). When she hears the martial music, furthermore, her Homeric afternoon is linked even more closely to his, since it is when he hears the marching steps that his own step is animated and that he is reminded of his age. (Elizabeth, too, thinks of death when she hears the music: but of an anonymous, female death.) Even these actions, then, which tie Elizabeth Dalloway firmly to the world outside the book, are, by the echoes, made remarkably into aesthetic elements and so deflected from their claim (which is, however, still maintained) to be mimetic.

Other elements in the account contend more heartily with the realism, over which Woolf lays a series of defining, aestheticizing patterns. In the first place, the movement of Elizabeth Dalloway's *fugue* is shaped by the images of the flowing and frozen stream, and it is by development of the metaphor of changes in state of water that Woolf effects the beginning and the end of this section and both the transition to and the opening of the next. When Elizabeth takes her place on top of the bus, her fantasy transforms the scene:

> The impetuous creature—a pirate—started forward, sprang away; she had to hold the rail to steady herself, for a pirate it was, reckless, unscrupulous, bearing down ruthlessly, circumventing dangerously, boldly snatching a passenger, or ignoring a passenger, squeezing eel-like and arrogant in between, and then rushing insolently all sails spread up Whitehall.

Whitehall and the Strand (whose name confirms the image) are by that fantasy converted into flowing streams and Elizabeth, having escaped from Miss Kilman (who has, we know, 'lurched' appropriately through the counters of the Army and Navy Stores as a 'battleship' on her way to the Abbey), is 'delighted to be free'. The white, spreading sails image her freedom. When her freedom ends, Woolf transforms the image:

> Forgetfulness in people might wound, their ingratitude corrode, but this voice, pouring endlessly, year in, year out, would take whatever it might be; this vow; this van; this life; this procession; would wrap them all about and carry them on, as in the rough stream of a glacier the ice holds a splinter of bone, a blue petal, some oak trees, and rolls them on.

20

Like the dolphin on Mrs. Dalloway's mantelpiece, Fleet Street has been crystallized: Elizabeth's jaunt is over, and when she turns back, Woolf abandons her, moving now to Rezia and Septimus. But Woolf does not abandon the passage's preoccupation with an imagery derived from changes in state of water, and, shifting from earth to sky, she complicates the metaphor as follows:

> A puff of wind (in spite of the heat, there was quite a wind) blew a thin black veil over the sun and over the Strand. The faces faded; the omnibuses suddenly lost their glow. For although the clouds were of mountainous white so that one could fancy hacking hard chips off with a hatchet, with broad golden slopes, lawns of celestial pleasure gardens, on their flanks, and had all the appearance of settled habitations assembled for the conference of gods above the world, there was a perpetual movement among them. Signs were interchanged, when, as if to fulfil some scheme arranged already, now a summit dwindled, now a whole block of pyramidal size which had kept its station inalterably advanced into the midst or gravely led the procession to fresh anchorage. Fixed though they seemed at their posts, at rest in perfect unanimity, nothing could be fresher, freer, more sensitive superficially than the snow-white or gold-kindled surface; to change, to go, to dismantle the solemn assemblage was immediately possible; and in spite of the grave fixity, the accumulated robustness and solidity, now they struck light to the earth, now darkness.

This passage (which I have quoted at length because I shall need to refer to it later) wittily makes the transition to Septimus into a plunge: when he is discovered by the narration he is undersea; and it also suggests how deeply the change-of-state metaphor is implicated in the narrative design. The preparation for this transition is steady and developing, and it is carried throughout the passage by the metaphor. In the description of the pirate ship, the narrator is submerged in the character's fantasy; in the description of the glacial stream, the voices of character and narrator are blent; in the description of the misty pyramids, the voice is the narrator's alone. The distance is signalled by the stages in the development of the metaphor, which also represent three temporal orientations. The narrating voice, which becomes progressively more distant from the character as it changes its temporal orientation, and which, by an almost Hardyesque retreat from human perspective, moves to omniscience, is itself transformed in its metaphor of transformation.

Woolf supports the dominant, shaping image of hardening in this passage—the flowing stream become glacier—by another, which she attaches specifically to Elizabeth. This one occurs at the end of the description of the pirate ship:

> And now it was like riding, to be rushing up Whitehall; and to each movement of the omnibus the beautiful body in the fawn-coloured coat responded freely like a rider, like the figure-head of a ship, for the breeze slightly disarrayed her; the heat gave her cheeks the pallor of white painted wood; and her fine eyes, having no eyes to meet, gazed ahead, blank, bright, with the staring, incredible innocence of sculpture.

For the moment, what is most interesting about this transubstantiation of Elizabeth Dalloway is that it duplicates the movement of the whole section. This single sentence moves from its account of freedom and movement to its final fixed image in just the way that the section as a whole moves from its opening account of freedom to its final fixity, by an expansion and a contraction: it progressively narrows the metaphor, peels away from the last static detail everything capable of movement, and closes in its transmutation to hardness. The sentence, like the passage as a whole, accumulates and then relinquishes elements in its comparison. All of the motion of Elizabeth's freedom is given up for the final image of her transformed eyes (which, though they do not move, are carried along), just as the whole turbulence of the street is renounced for the splinter of bone, blue petal, and oak trees that are frozen into the moving glacier.

Since what occupies Elizabeth Dalloway's mind during the episode is the question of what she will become, the imagery of hardening perfectly embodies the character's emotional development. During the course of these fourteen paragraphs, she moves from her enchanting, childish fantasy of the pirate ship to her choice of a profession, and the decision, we are told in the mixed voice of narrator and character, will have its effects 'forever'. Her plunge into the city has had the power to perform what learned or pious teaching and preaching have not, that is,

> to stimulate what lay slumbrous, clumsy and shy on the mind's sandy floor, to break surface, as a child suddenly stretches its arms; it was just that, perhaps, a sigh, a stretch of the arms, an impulse, a revelation, which has its effects forever, and then down again it went to the sandy floor.

That the flowing stream should harden to fixity in this passage of identification is thus perfectly appropriate: a permanent change has been laid into the flux and the Elizabeth who sets out on this quest is not the Elizabeth who returns. She, too, has experienced a crystallization.

The process by which Elizabeth achieves her self-identification links her remarkably to Woolf's feminism, since it hangs on Miss Kilman's insistence that 'every profession is open to the women of your generation', and it involves a clear differentiation between the traditional spheres of activity of women and men. Riding up the Strand, Elizabeth identifies herself (though not in these terms) with the traditionally masculine: 'The feet of those people busy about their activities, hands putting stone to stone, minds eternally occupied not with trivial chatterings . . . but with thoughts of ships, of business, of law, of administration.' Her identification with that tradition links Elizabeth by association and echo with her father: 'She would become a doctor, a farmer, possibly go into Parliament if she found it necessary', she thinks. And when Richard crosses in front of Buckingham Palace on his way home to see Clarissa, the statue of the Queen makes him reflect, as his daughter does here, on tradition: 'he liked being ruled by the descendant of Horsa; he liked continuity; and the sense of handing on the traditions of the past' (129). That comfort in continuity is carried over from *The Voyage Out*, in which Richard, considering, as Clarissa puts it, 'what one means by London', adds to his 'sententious' reply—'It's the continuity'—a 'vision of English history, King following King, Prime Minister Prime Minister, and Law Law' (53).

But when Elizabeth walks up Fleet Street, she is associated, by inheritance, with an expressly female tradition. The four sentences in which the association is achieved are brilliantly

ambivalent, attached by their beginning to Clarissa's consciousness and by their end to Elizabeth's, imitating in that
the very idea of inheritance:

> In many ways, her mother felt, she was extremely immature,
> like a child still, attached to dolls, to old slippers; a perfect baby;
> and that was charming. But then, of course, there was in the
> Dalloway family the tradition of public service. Abbesses,
> principals, head mistresses, dignitaries, in the republic of
> women—without being brilliant, any of them, they were that.
> She penetrated a little farther in the direction of St. Paul's.

While Elizabeth thinks of the republic of women, penetrating
towards that mystic centre, which reminds Orlando of the
brow of a poet and on the steps of which, in *The Years*, Sara
meets Crosby's God,[13] Miss Kilman is in the Abbey, and
Clarissa is at home, like a nun in familiar veils. When Elizabeth
explores Fleet Street in the direction of the Cathedral, the
imagery is domestic, the labyrinth of streets converted to the
mystery of staircases. But, since, 'In short, she would like to
have a profession', Elizabeth appropriates the masculine
tradition, and by that act she firmly declines sanctuary and
associates herself with the Strand: 'She would become a
doctor, a farmer, possibly go into Parliament if she found it
necessary, all because of the Strand.'

'The Introduction', one of the stories that grew out of the
Mrs. Dalloway material, has an illuminating relationship to this
section of the novel, since in it Woolf develops a similar subject
(*MDP*, 37–43). Lily Everit, like Elizabeth Dalloway, is moving
from girlhood to womanhood, is, like her, wholly engaged in
the attempt to discover a personal identity, and is, like her,
confronted with the 'burden' of social sexual roles. She comes
to Mrs. Dalloway's party (her first) with a sense of her own
identity that depends on the three stars she has for her essay
on Dean Swift and on a rapturous experience of nature: 'this
was, until tonight, her ordinary being, by which she knew and
liked herself and crept into the heart of mother and father and
brother and sisters.' Like Elizabeth, Lily faces the fact of
separate male and female traditions, perceiving on the one
hand 'this orderly life where all was done already; high towers,
solemn bells, flats built every brick of them by men's toil,

24

parliaments too; and even the criss-cross of telegraph wires', and, on the other, the whole cluster of female frailties, beauties, and deferences. 'What had she', Lily wonders, 'to oppose to this massive masculine achievement?' For her, the female tradition consists in filling a place in the 'orderly life' of the patriarchy, and she 'accepted the part which was now laid on her, and naturally, overdid it a little, as a soldier proud of the traditions of an old and famous uniform might overdo it'. In this story, Woolf's feminism is all at the surface, and what she details is the death of the soul, the process by which Lily becomes someone other than herself. Here, the 'orderly life' falls first 'like a yoke about her neck, softly, indomitably, from the skies', and then 'the yoke that had fallen from the skies onto her neck crushed her.' The exclusion in this story is partly exclusion from the literary tradition—since how, wonders the virginal and humble Lily, could her essay on Dean Swift compare to the direct descent from Shakespeare that she attributes to the young man who is the other partner in the introduction. The tone of the story is acid, and in the closing comments Woolf is roughly and powerfully ambiguous. The character who makes the final remark—that Lily looked ' "as if she had the weight of the world upon her shoulders" '—has no appreciation of its truth, even though the defeated character does: 'this civilisation, said Lily Everit to herself depends on me.' 'The Introduction' carries its examination of female exclusion in an imagery of intense, and sexual, violence: the stars on the essay burn, at the end of the story, with a 'terrible lustre, no longer clear and brilliant, but troubled and bloodstained'. Like Elizabeth Dalloway, Lily Everit moves to a personal change that will last 'for ever and ever', but the metamorphosis that we are led to expect in a sugary passage about butterflies and womanhood is wholly denied: 'there are no sanctuaries, or butterflies . . . said Lily Everit to herself, as she accepted the kind compliments of old Mrs. Bromley on her appearance.'

Woolf treats Elizabeth Dalloway very differently, not only by giving her a blessed absence of the sense of duty to the old uniform, but also by suffusing in the texture of the account the feminism that confronts us on the angry surface of 'The Introduction'. Here, as in *Orlando*, the glacial stream suggests a literary accumulation, and here, too, Woolf embodies her feminist perspective in her reshaping of what she accumulates, counting on myth and allusion to play against the smooth, even lyrical, surface.

Like Lily Everit, Elizabeth Dalloway is at the outset identified with nature. When she starts on her jaunt, the imagery is pastoral: she is delighted to be out of doors, though not to be in London, since what she really likes is 'being alone in the country with her father and the dogs'. (We have heard about the dogs before—'better poor Grizzle than Miss Kilman', Clarissa thinks on her way to buy flowers, 'better distemper and tar and all the rest of it than sitting mewed in a stuffy bedroom with a prayer book!' (14)—and we shall hear about them again, when, at the end of the book, Elizabeth has joined her father but is aware of her 'poor dog . . . howling' (213).) And Elizabeth is in flight, at the beginning of this section, pursued just recently by Miss Kilman and now aware of general pursuit: 'People were beginning to compare her to poplar trees, early dawn, hyacinths, fawns, running water, and garden lilies; and it made life a burden to her.' 'Every man fell in love with her,' we hear from Clarissa, 'and she was really awfully bored.' It is under these conditions, and in a passage in which the gods are in conference above the world, that Elizabeth Dalloway becomes a statue. The country and the dogs, the flight, the assemblage of divinities, and the transformation identify a familiar myth. It is Ovid's *Metamorphoses* that are invoked in this passage, and the transformations of metaphor, point of view, and character that the passage records and enacts are supported by the myth of metamorphosis itself.

Elizabeth Dalloway is one of Diana's nymphs: when she is changed into the figurehead, she is saved from pursuit, and her 'fine eyes, having no eyes to meet, gazed ahead, blank, bright, with the staring, incredible innocence of sculpture.' While the dogs and the country link her to Diana the huntress, her flight and transformation (together with the fact that, earlier, Clarissa has connected Miss Kilman with the satyr) connect her with Syrinx (who, though she 'envied, imitated/ The virgin attitudes of Queen Diana', was pursued by Pan, and changed, on appeal to 'the sisters of the stream', to a reed). It makes her a close relative, too, of Daphne, 'the child of Peneus, kindly tyrant of the river', who begged her father to 'make her an eternal virgin, [to]/ Do what Diana's father did for her', and who, pursued by Apollo, is changed into a laurel.[14] Elizabeth Dalloway, although she intends to appropriate the masculine professions of doctoring or farmering, is nevertheless in Diana's train. It is remarkable that in her the virginity theme of the book is sublimated, while in Clarissa it is treated explicitly and as an item in her self-knowledge. Clarissa, it will be recalled, reflects that she has preserved 'a virginity . . . through childbirth' (36).

In *Orlando*, Woolf represents the myth of Daphne and Apollo on the arras in the great hall of the family house, and there she makes the motif on the arras echo the motif in the ice. Orlando's darker loss is embodied in the allusion to Orpheus, its comic transformation in the figuration of Apollo, who, if she still flees, must still pursue. In *Mrs. Dalloway*, the metamorphic story of Syrinx and Pan is predicted not only in Clarissa's evocation of the satyr (15), but also in Peter Walsh's fantasizing pursuit of 'the very woman he had always had in mind'. That pursuit is linked to Elizabeth's flight partly by its emphasis on the rejuvenation of Peter Walsh—'I haven't felt so young for years! thought Peter, escaping (only of course for an hour or so) from being precisely what he was, and feeling like a child who runs out of doors' (59)—and partly by its presentation of the theme of metamorphosis. 'She moved; she crossed; he followed her', Woolf reports. 'He pursued; she changed.' (60)

While Woolf was working on *Mrs. Dalloway*, Roger Fry was still engaged in his passionate labour of so many years, the translations of Mallarmé.[15] Since Virginia and Leonard Woolf intended to publish these, she was closely familiar with their texts: 'I think the translations are extremely interesting', she wrote to Fry as early as August, 1920, '—also very difficult. The difficulty may be partly that I've left my Mallarmé in London, and thus can't compare them with the French. But I've no doubt at all that they're very good, and give one the same strange feeling as he does' (*L*, ii, 439). When she wrote her biography of Fry, Woolf recalled that 'Almost any guest invited to dine with him about 1920 would find him, manuscript in

27

hand, seeking the right words with which to fill a gap in the translation of Mallarmé', and she quotes a letter by Clive Bell, in which he, too, jokes affectionately about Fry's preoccupation: 'after dinner just runs through a few of Mallarmé's poems, which he is translating word for word into what he is pleased to consider blank verse,' Bell writes. 'He had to start early this morning in order to lunch with Lady Colefax. But, while I am dressing, I hear him shouting to Julian through the ground-floor window—"I think before I go we've just time to run through *L'Après-Midi d'un faune*"' (pp. 239, 288).

Fry's translations of Mallarmé provide another dimension in Woolf's reshaping of the Pan and Syrinx myth. Mallarmé appears in *The Years* as the subject of Tony Ashton's lecture at Mortimer House (282); he was at one stage intended to make an appearance in *Jacob's Room* as one among 'all those Frenchmen' read by Bonamy (71)[16]; and it seems to me that he is present also in Woolf's portrait of Elizabeth Dalloway, whose afternoon in London, we are told, is the afternoon of a 'fawn'.

To believe that Woolf was alluding to the poem that was compelling such an intense attention from Fry, it is necessary to believe that she is making a bilingual pun when, twice, she calls Elizabeth a 'fawn'. But that is made easier than it might otherwise be by Woolf's report of Miss Kilman's emotional state after Elizabeth's departure, in which, playing upon the fact that in French an *éclair* can be not only the product of the high art of cuisine but also the result of atmospheric electrical discharge, she writes: 'She had gone. Miss Kilman sat at the marble table among the éclairs, stricken once, twice, thrice by shocks of suffering' (146). (In *Orlando*, *Our Lady of Purity* proclaims herself as 'the guardian of the sleeping fawn', while *Our Lady of Chastity* identifies herself as 'she whose touch freezes and whose glance turns to stone' (124).)

Mallarmé's poem makes of the Pan and Syrinx myth an allegory of poetic creation, but it is also a monument of conventional male fantasy, since, as Wallace Fowlie puts it, 'Satyrs are convenient actors or projections of our more primordial instincts and visions.' Mallarmé makes his faun's desire ambiguous: the opening line—'Ces nymphes, je les veux perpétuer'—'might be said brutally by an aroused faun or meditatively by a meticulous artist'.[17] In either case, or both,

Mallarmé's poem, like the myth, is a dream of the conquest of virginities. For his faun, Syrinx the chaste becomes the 'instrument des fuites', 'maligne'.[18] Of course Woolf knew Mallarmé's poem, probably very closely indeed, and it is difficult to believe that when she constructed the Elizabeth Dalloway section of her novel as, partly, a revision of the myth of Pan and Syrinx, she did not have his faun poem in mind, too. If she did, she would have been well aware of placing her nymph (doctor or farmer-to-be) in a line of echoes of Mallarmé that includes Huysmans' *A Rebours*, Debussy's *Prélude à l'Après-Midi d'un faune*, and Nijinsky's ballet,[19] as well as the translations she was trying to tease out of Roger Fry. Elizabeth Dalloway, like the bumboat woman, has a distinguished literary ancestry, and, like her, she is part of a feminist appropriation, a precise and witty adjustment both in 'this orderly life' and in the 'ideal order' of the 'existing monuments'.[20]

The glacial stream in *Mrs. Dalloway* is an emblem of transformation, as is Elizabeth Dalloway herself. In these fourteen paragraphs, Woolf refocuses Richard's love of continuity, reshapes Clarissa's confrontation with death and her long-preserv'd virginity, inverts Peter's satyrical pursuit of the fantasized woman, reforms into action Miss Kilman's insistence that professions are for women, and, in an act of egalitarian literary politics, redistributes some items in the literary inheritance. But in this the Elizabeth section of *Mrs. Dalloway* merely reflects the whole: although she is the most striking instance of Ovidian metamorphosis, Elizabeth is not the only one. Clarissa thinks of Peter's Daisy as a 'statue' (51); Peter Walsh is delighted to think that Aunt Helena (who shocks him by coming alive at the party) 'should turn to glass' (178); and Clarissa herself is said to be 'like iron, like flint, rigid', 'petrified' (72). (Most interesting in connection with Elizabeth is the fact that Clarissa's virginity is associated with her 'woodenness' (68).) And though the Elizabeth section provides a remarkably clear instance of the movement in Woolf's narrative from freedom to figure, it is in this, too, only a reflection of the whole.

These glacial streams embody Woolf's characteristic ambivalences: they suggest at once movement and arrest, identity and transformation, continuity and departure, creation and the crumbling of order. The change-of-state metaphor they imply enfolds her central myth of transformation (connecting it, in both of these cases, to classical roots); their geological metaphor suggests not only her preoccupation with literary tradition but also the process of accumulation by which she shapes her own material into pattern; and their crystalline structure, which is always under threat of destruction (since, as Orlando learns to his horror, ice melts), underlines the ambivalent status in her work of the aesthetic image. For her, achieved aesthetic order, the crystalline structure, denies finality; and if, by the metamorphic rule, characters must turn into statues, 'gazing from white eyes'[21] and butterflies take up the shape of marble columns (*HH*, 38), it is also true that by the same rule all of these assemblages are ready 'to change, to go, to dismantle'. The magnificent conversation near the beginning of *Between the Acts* (36–40), in which Bart consults the Encyclopedia and Mrs. Swithin and Isa discuss fish, exemplifies the same self-reversing movement that is suggested by the freezing: Mrs. Swithin's closing summary, in this conversation in which the 'problem' is neither fish nor dentists but randomness and aesthetic order, both closes the pattern and sends us back to the beginning, recreating. The last line of *Mrs. Dalloway* hangs in a similar doubleness: it confirms, on the one hand, the shift from weaving present to woven past, the final aesthetic petrifaction[22]; but since the 'there' of the sentence points back into the text, this crystal, too, dissolves.

NOTES

1. 'Prologue', *Days and Nights* (1889), pp. [1]–4.
2. James Naremore, *The World Without a Self* (1973), p. 213.
3. 'Why is Orlando Difficult?' in *New Feminist Essays on Virginia Woolf*, ed. Jane Marcus (1981), p. 170.
4. See Maria DiBattista's fine discussion of *Orlando* in *Virginia Woolf's Major Novels: The Fables of Anon* (1980), pp. 111–45.
5. *The Problem of Style* (1922; repr. 1952), p. 146.
6. See Joanne Trautmann, *The Jessamy Brides: the Friendship of Virginia Woolf and V. Sackville-West* (University Park, Pennsylvania, 1973).
7. John Gay, *Trivia*, ii, 357–98, in *Poetry and Prose*, ed. Vinton A. Dearing and Charles E. Beckwith (Oxford, 1974), i. 153–54.

8. Virgil, *The Georgics*, transl. L. P. Wilkinson (1982), pp. 139–42.
9. V. Sackville-West, *The Land* (1926; repr. 1929), p. [2]. 'I'm well aware how great/ A task it is by mastery of words/ To invest such humble things with dignity' (*Georgics*, transl. Wilkinson, p. 108).
10. Trautmann, *The Jessamy Brides*, p. 40.
11. *Georgics*, p. 111.
12. *MDP*, 15. Stella McNichol quotes this remark from 'The Berg manuscript which contains Virginia Woolf's compositional notes for *Mrs. Dalloway*.'
13. See Joanna Lipking, 'Looking at the Monuments: Woolf's Satiric Eye', *Bulletin of the New York Public Library*, 80. 2 (Winter, 1977), 141–45.
14. Ovid, *The Metamorphoses*, transl. Horace Gregory (New York, 1958), pp. 43–4, 51–2.
15. Virginia Woolf wrote to Fry about his translations for the first time in August 1920 (*L*, ii, 438), and in 1922 she wrote to urge him, teasingly, to finish: 'Several books are emerging; and I may point out that we've sold several copies of Mallarmé by Roger Fry' (*L*, ii, 565), but, as the editors of the *Letters* say, 'The proposal to publish Roger Fry's translations of Mallarmé was postponed from year to year, and they were not published until 1936, after Fry's death' (*L*, ii, 439n). In her biography, Woolf reports that 'The manuscript was stolen, probably under some misapprehension, by a luggage thief in Paris. But it rose from its ashes at St. Remy' (*Roger Fry* (1940), p. 239). Allen McLaurin, in *Virginia Woolf, The Echoes Enslaved* (Cambridge, 1973), has argued for the importance of the combined influence of the symbolists and Fry in the composition of *Mrs. Dalloway* and especially of the idea of the 'symbolic keyboard' that Charles Mauron mentions in his introduction to Fry's translations. What I am arguing above is much more specific. Woolf may have stitched into this text other allusions to the French symbolists: Clarissa thinks of 'flowers of darkness' (33), and the sky-writing aeroplane suggests Rimbaud's 'Voyelles'.
16. Beverly Ann Schlack, *Continuing Presences, Virginia Woolf's Use of Literary Allusion* (1979), p. 160: 'In Part I of the holograph MS, Woolf had attempted to enumerate: "~~Mallarme,~~ [sic] Baudelaire, Mallarme." '
17. *Mallarmé. With drawings by Henri Matisse* (Chicago and London, 1953; repr. 1970), pp. 151, 152.
18. Mallarmé, *Oeuvres complètes* (Paris, 1945), pp. 50–3.
19. Wallace Fowlie, p. 157.
20. T. S. Eliot, 'Tradition and the Individual Talent', *Selected Essays* (New York, 1932, new ed., 1950), p. 5.
21. Virginia Woolf, ' "This is the House of Commons" ', in *The London Scene* (1975), p. 37.
22. The phrase that provides my title is not present in the MS version of Elizabeth's afternoon (which may be abbreviated, pointed and formalized in revision), but the glacier image is present from the outset, in a marginal addition: 'like fragments, gentian, sticks ~~petrified~~ wooden fragments—in some slow Eternal glacier' (BL MS Add. 51045, p. 96).

2

An Educated Man's Daughter: Leslie Stephen, Virginia Woolf and the Bloomsbury Group

by S. P. ROSENBAUM

> But let us bear in mind a piece of advice that an eminent Victorian who was also an eminent pedestrian once gave to walkers: 'Whenever you see a board up with "Trespassers will be prosecuted", trespass at once.' (*E*, ii, 181)

> You certainly are very like your Father. With great differences, of course. What I mean is that if he had been a 'Georgian' and a woman, just so would he have written.—Max Beerbohm to Virginia Woolf on *The Common Reader*[1]

In the radical polemics of her later feminism Virginia Woolf argued that the lack of capital and education—the prime characteristics of the middle-class—had declassed bourgeois women. They were not middle-class, they were merely 'educated men's daughters' (*TG*, 10–12, 265). Virginia Woolf always considered herself to be uneducated. Partly for reasons of health she never attended school, and she regretted all her life that she had never competed with other children, had never compared her abilities with theirs (*MB*, 65). The advantages for a genius of not having her abilities determined by competition in an educational system may have been considerable, but surrounded by highly educated men, she felt intellectually deprived. Vanessa Bell agreed with Virginia that they were both uneducated,

> if by education is meant learning things out of books. If she had none, however, I had less, for she did at least teach herself or get herself taught Greek, and was given books to read by my father which may, for all I know, have had educational value.[2]

The dryness of Vanessa's qualification should not obscure the enormous value of having Leslie Stephen and his books as one's teacher and library of English literature and history. Virginia recalled for her father's biographer Stephen's reading to the family of such writers as Robert Louis Stevenson, Hawthorne, Shakespeare, Thackeray (he broke off in the middle of *Vanity Fair* because it was 'too terrible'), Carlyle, Austen, and especially Scott; and for poetry there was Milton, Wordsworth, Arnold, Meredith, Kipling, and others. Stephen's capacity for memorizing poetry was extraordinary and his daughter could not separate many great English poems from her memory of him: 'I hear in them not only his voice, but in some sort his teaching and belief.'[3] As for her own reading at home, she remembered her father saying, 'Gracious child, how you gobble!' when she would ask for another volume and be reminded that anything worth reading was worth reading twice (*L*, iv, 27). She ate her way through eighteenth- and nineteenth-century English writing and sampled the sixteenth and seventeenth centuries as well.[4] Being the uneducated daughter of Leslie Stephen was clearly an extraordinary inheritance for a would-be writer.

T. S. Eliot regarded Virginia Woolf as having 'a kind of hereditary position in English letters',[5] and Leonard Woolf, another outsider, recalled how her father's talk 'enabled one to catch a last glimpse of that incredibly ancient London literary world of ladies and gentlemen which went right back to Thackeray and Dickens, to Mr. and Mrs. Carlyle, to Mill and Huxley'.[6] As editor of the *Cornhill* Stephen first published Henry James's *Daisy Miller*, *Washington Square*, and 'An International Episode', Thomas Hardy's *Far from the Madding Crowd* (slightly bowdlerized) and *The Hand of Ethelberta* (though his editorial timidity lost his magazine *The Return of the Native*), as well as essays by Stephen himself, Matthew Arnold, Stevenson, John Addington Symonds, and poetry by Browning, Meredith, and Henley.[7]

Stephen's first wife was Thackeray's daughter. James Russell Lowell stood as an agnostic equivalent of godfather to Virginia. Meredith portrayed Stephen as the austere Vernon Whitford—'Phoebus Apollo turned fasting friar'—the least egoistic of the characters in *The Egoist*.[8] And Thomas Hardy, who Virginia Woolf thought had written the truest and most imaginative portrait of him (*L*, ii, 58), compared Stephen to the Schreckhorn, which he was the first to climb, finding the mountain like Stephen's personality 'In its quaint glooms, keen lights, and rugged trim'.[9]

It is the glooms more than the lights or the trim that mark the image of Stephen's personality for readers who know him only through the often misinterpreted portrait of Mr. Ramsay in *To the Lighthouse*, from Virginia Woolf's recollections in the first published version of 'A Sketch of the Past', or through Stephen's own grief-stricken autobiography, *The Mausoleum Book*, that he wrote for his children after the death of his second wife. Almost no one mentions that his daughter's first portrait of him in Maitland's biography begins (p. 474) with the recollection of the 'perfectly equal companionship' between him and his children. And in a recently discovered revised draft of 'A Sketch of the Past' Virginia Woolf clarified her thoroughly ambivalent feelings toward her father by distinguishing between three kinds of father: there was 'the writer father' that she can always get a critical hold of through his books, 'the sociable father' that she never really knew, and 'the tyrant father' that she and Vanessa suffered from for seven years.[10] The tyrannical father is the one that still dominates most discussions of Leslie Stephen's influence on his daughter. Because it is a memoir, even the revised 'Sketch' focuses less on Stephen as a writer—'the man's Leslie Stephen' Virginia Woolf calls him (p. 82)—and more on the tyrant who was the daughters' Leslie Stephen. Yet in the revised draft Virginia Woolf makes, as we shall see, some important observations about the significance of her father's criticism for her own. The full importance of Leslie Stephen for the writing of Virginia Woolf cannot be properly understood apart from his work, which she could approach directly all her adult life, without the mediations of memory. She was, after all, the writer-father's writer-daughter.

Since the rediscovery of Virginia Woolf as a major modernist, little attention has been paid to her literary and intellectual heritage by the interrelated kinds of proliferating criticism devoted to her. Formalist analyses of her fiction continue to be mainly synchronic in their assumptions; psychological investigations, for all their biographical scrutiny, take place in largely ahistorical contexts; and feminist criticism for the most part shuns the principal traditions of literature and ideas in which she developed because they were masculine. Though these critical emphases have provided considerable understanding of Virginia Woolf's art, life, and thought, they have also served to diminish her achievement by treating her work as if literary and intellectual history were irrelevant to it. That the daughter of the leading Victorian intellectual and literary historian should have her writing so insulated from that history by her critics is ironical. Yet understanding how Leslie Stephen's deeply ambivalent daughter responded to her father's work is not easy. The personal dimensions of 'that immensely important relationship' are likely, as she said, to queer the angle of vision (Add. MS. 61973, p. 2). She did not write very much directly about her father's work, and brief comparisons of the extensive critical and biographical essays that both wrote are not likely to take us very far beyond the kinds of generalities Max Beerbohm produced in his amusing letter on *The Common Reader*.

There is available, however, a wider context in which at least some of the meanings of Leslie Stephen's work for his daughter's can be examined. Stephen's grandson once described him as 'in a sense the father of Bloomsbury'.[11] He would have been horrified at this twist of history, yet he can be seen as the father of that extended family of writers and artists which formed around his children and is now known as the Bloomsbury Group.[12] In Bloomsbury the daughters of Leslie Stephen were the sisters, sisters-in-law, wives, and loving friends of educated men. The work of Stephen was part of their education as it was

Virginia Woolf's, and it influenced not only her criticism, biographies, and polemics, but also the literary and historical writings of Leonard Woolf, the biographies of Lytton Strachey, the essays of Keynes, the criticism of MacCarthy, and the biographical and critical writings of Forster. The writer-father was significant for Bloomsbury and his daughter as a Victorian philosopher and historian of ideas, as a literary historian and critic, and—perhaps most important—as a biographer. Each of these aspects of Stephen's achievement deserves to be considered separately if his complex intellectual and literary legacy is to be appreciated. The continuities and discontinuities that emerge from such a survey may also clarify developments from Victorian to modern English literature. The topic is a wide one and the discussion of Stephen's work in relation to Bloomsbury's will be unavoidably general. But for once it may be worthwhile trying to view Virginia Woolf and the Bloomsbury Group from some of the perspectives that Leslie Stephen's philosophical, historical, literary, and biographical ideas offer.

    Leslie Stephen's moral philosophy permeates his literary work. He valued literature most for its expression of ideas and its revelation of the author's character. The intellectual and biographical concern for literature is continued in much of Bloomsbury's writing, but with differences that can be better appreciated first by looking at some of Stephen's ethical ideas.
    Stephen began adult life as a Cambridge don and a clergyman. He soon rather painlessly lost his faith over the problem of evil. 'The potter has no right to be angry with his pots', he wrote later. 'If he wanted them different, he should have made them different. The consistent theologian must choose between the Creator and the Judge.'[13] With his loss of faith, Stephen had to resign his fellowship, so he came to London to be a man of letters. Some years later, shortly after the death of his mother, he decided to resign formally the office of priest in the Church of England by signing an official document. How symbolic for the literary history of Bloomsbury that Stephen asked not a close friend, relative, lawyer, or philosopher to witness his signature, but a contributor to the *Cornhill* that he was then editing. Thus it happened that on 23 March 1875

36

Thomas Hardy ceremonially witnessed Leslie Stephen's re-nunciation of the priesthood.[14]

As an essayist in London Stephen followed Huxley and championed agnosticism, which for him meant that 'the natural man can know nothing of the Divine nature.'[15] The content and form of Stephen's philosophical essays are well described by the title he gave to a collection of them: *Essays in Freethinking and Plainspeaking*. These were qualities Bloomsbury valued and displayed in their writings. Though they were atheists more than agnostics, they nevertheless cared for religious emotion more than Stephen, who seems to have experienced it only in the mountains. Stephen's arguments for the limits of our knowledge were familiar truths to Blooms-bury, yet neither he nor his heirs were really sceptics. It was the scepticism of believers about the common-sense workings of the world that he exposed in a characteristic essay.[16] Stephen's writing clearly belongs to that English and Scottish tradition of humane science identified by Keynes as having a continuity of both feeling and matter and extending from Locke and Hume to Russell and Moore.[17]

Though Stephen's loss of faith caused him little suffering, his agnosticism was sorely tried by grief. The tombstone of his father, Sir James Stephen, bore the inscription, 'Be strong and of good courage; be not afraid, neither be thou dismayed: for the Lord thy God is with thee withersoever thou goest.'[18] His son was certainly strong, courageous, unafraid, but the deaths of his wives dismayed him terribly; he knew he could not know whether the Lord God was with him or not. Bloomsbury were aware they lacked the awesome energy of the Victorians but at least they were able to accept death without the sentimental excesses of nineteenth-century grief which they grew up with. Yet there was also something admirable in this grief. After reading Maitland's biography of Stephen, Lytton Strachey quoted to Keynes as magnificent what Stephen had written after the death of Virginia's mother. Stephen wrote,

> I have often thought, in reading about Swift, for example, that the saddest of all states of mind was that in which a man regrets that he has loved because his love has brought sorrow. That is 'the sin against the Holy Ghost'—to blaspheme your best affections, which are your Holy Ghost. . . .[19]

For Bloomsbury, too, one's best affections were one's Holy Ghost.

It was Wordsworth, Stephen recorded in *The Mausoleum Book*, who taught him the transmutation of sorrow into strength.[20] 'The great aim of moral philosophy,' he said in his famous essay on Wordsworth's ethics, 'is to ... end the divorce between reason and experience.'[21] Wordsworth had suggested to him how this might be done through transforming primitive instincts into reasoned convictions. Here Stephen thought he had found the beginnings of an ethical philosophy that could reconcile the great rival nineteenth-century schools of ethical thought, the Utilitarians and the intuitionalists. In *The Science of Ethics*, a book he hoped would be his *magnum opus*, Stephen tried to expound this reconciliation. His sympathies were largely with the Utilitarians. He considered himself a follower of Mill, who of course had also derived profound consolation from Wordsworth's poetry. 'Read Mill' was the injunction of his Cambridge friends to the unenlightened,[22] just as 'Read Moore' was in Bloomsbury's Cambridge. Stephen could not follow Wordsworth in assuming that there was a divine order regulating the growth of our early impulses into rational understanding, though he certainly agreed that our obedience to the 'stern lawgiver' Duty was required for this change. Stephen found the basis of duty in Darwin rather than God. From Darwin he took the idea that duty, a fundamental concept for the intuitionalists, could be fitted into Utilitarianism through the idea of evolution. The individual's growth from instinct to reason resembles society's evolution, and the chief vehicle for this change in the individual is that 'immediate and primitive relation which holds men together'—the family.[23]

Victorian and modern English moral philosophers have pretty well demolished *The Science of Ethics*. Henry Sidgwick noted that all the problems of Utilitarian ethics re-emerge in Stephen's ethical goal of maximizing the general welfare of society, and that Stephen had not offered adequate reasons for concluding that society's welfare necessarily coincides with the individual's maximizing of his happiness. Most relevant for Virginia Woolf and Bloomsbury, Sidgwick also objected that many highly cultivated pleasures, such as aesthetic ones, have little or nothing to do with the social evolution on which

Stephen based his ethical science.[24] Moore does not mention Stephen in *Principia Ethica* but his attack on Herbert Spencer's evolutionary ethics applies equally to Stephen's. There is no record of anyone ever having read *The Science of Ethics* in Bloomsbury. Moore's combination of consequentialism and intuitionalism is very different from Stephen's. And Bloomsbury quite rejected Stephen's family-centred ideal. Something of the distance between Stephen's notion of the family as the 'immediate and primitive relation which holds men together' and Bloomsbury's non-monogamous idealization of personal relations, familial and otherwise, can be estimated from an essay on Godwin and Shelley where Stephen discusses that 'anti-matrimonial theory' in Shelley's poem *Epipsychidion*—a poem that gave E. M. Forster the title and one of the organizing ideas for his novel, *The Longest Journey*. Stephen described the lines in which Shelley attacked

> that great sect
> Whose doctrine is that each one should select
> Out of the world a mistress or a friend,
> And all the rest, though faire and wise, commend
> To cold oblivion

as 'the shrill tones of a conceited propagator of flimsy crochets proclaiming his tenets without regard to truth or propriety'.[25] Stephen's own shrillness here, together with his criteria of truth and propriety, makes him remote from Bloomsbury.

Leslie Stephen's familial science of ethics also included, however, the liberal ideal of individual freedom that connects him directly with Bloomsbury. The proprieties of personal conduct in the family and society limited one's freedom, Virginia Woolf recalled in the only essay she published devoted to her father:

> Yet if freedom means the right to think one's own thoughts and to follow one's own pursuits, then no one respected and indeed insisted upon freedom more completely than he did. (*E*, iv, 79)

(But this did not mean sons and daughters were to be allowed the same amount of freedom; Stephen was not prepared to follow Mill all the way on the question of the subjection of women.) The liberal tradition that Leslie Stephen's work embodied for Bloomsbury is clearly illustrated in the contrast of his brother's thought. James Fitzjames Stephen is still read today as a conservative critic of Mill's *On Liberty*. His *Liberty, Equality, Fraternity* is perhaps more widely known than any single work of Leslie's. Fitzjames insisted that the imperfectibility and inequality of man required a cohesive society with more restrictions on liberty and individualism than Mill or Leslie Stephen allowed for.

Leslie Stephen's liberalism was also characteristic of his literary criticism. In 'Thoughts on Criticism by a Critic' he argued that the critic must show a liberal toleration, though he should never be an aesthetic sceptic.[26] Here the difference becomes clearer between the tradition of humane science described by Keynes that links three centuries of English philosophical thought and that other tradition of literary and philosophical criticism going back to Samuel Johnson and continuing through Coleridge to Carlyle, Ruskin, and also Matthew Arnold. Both traditions influenced Bloomsbury, but the Group is unusual in the history of modern English literature in having their intellectual attitudes formed more by the first than the second. But the differences here are not simple or absolute. Stephen's biographer the great historian Maitland called his subject a Thackerayan, because of his worship of the family and his somewhat cynical attitude toward other matters (pp. 169–70). (Stephen signed a series of articles for the *Cornhill* as 'A Cynic'.) Noel Annan, Stephen's intellectual biographer, called him a Wordsworthian.[27] But he was a Millian and a Darwinian as well. His respect for Carlyle as a man was greater than that for any other of his contemporaries, including Mill whom he found a little unmanly; yet Carlyle's attacks on what he called the Utilitarian 'pig philosophy' did not, Stephen characteristically observed, 'represent my own prejudices'.[28] Although Carlyle influenced Stephen's practice as a biographer, his reactionary puritanism repelled Leslie, though not Fitzjames, whom Carlyle made his executor. Because of Stephen's aesthetic insensibility, Ruskin meant less to him than Carlyle, but Stephen was grateful for Ruskin's writings about the Alps. Arnold, of course, was an important critical influence, but it was his poetry that Stephen really admired. He thought 'Philistine' a name given to mankind by a prig.[29]

The change from Stephen's moral earnestness and Darwinian social faith to Bloomsbury's celebration of personal relations and aesthetic experiences has been widely noticed and frequently deplored. But it is arguable whether this was a greater change than that from the devout providential belief and government service of Sir James Stephen to the agnosticism and literary work of his son Leslie. Certainly in terms of literary history, Bloomsbury owed more to Leslie Stephen than he inherited from his ancestors and their Clapham Sect circle.

It was in literary and especially intellectual history that Stephen's interests in philosophy, literature, and biography came together. His two-volume *History of English Thought in the Eighteenth Century* and his three-volume *The English Utilitarians* remain important analytic expositions of two centuries of English philosophical, religious, and political ideas. Leslie Stephen was not just a practising liberal Utilitarian philosopher, he was the historian of that philosophy, and in his intellectual histories Bloomsbury could find a record and an example of the intellectual tradition they descended from. For Stephen the interest of this tradition was in its relevance for his agnosticism, and his history of eighteenth-century ideas has been called a tract for the times in its investigation of how the limits of that century's free thinking prepared for the advent of evangelicalism.[30] For Bloomsbury Stephen's advocacy of the eighteenth century was an important legacy; it was the century, he wrote,

> as its enemies used to say, of coarse utilitarian aims, of religious indifference and political corruption; or, as I prefer to say, the century of sound common sense and growing toleration, and of steady social and industrial development.[31]

Bloomsbury preferred to say that too but they were prepared to accept more of that century's literary expression than Stephen's Victorian susceptibilities allowed him to.

John Maynard Keynes in some of his essays and Leonard Woolf in *After the Deluge* wrote intellectual history in the wake of Stephen's work. Stephen was the historian of an intellectual

41

tradition in which Keynes located his own work and the lives of the economists he wrote about. Leonard Woolf, whose work and temperament resembled Leslie Stephen's more than did any one else's in Bloomsbury, tried in his intellectual history to describe the connections between communal ideas and actions in Europe between the French Revolution and the First World War. Because of its poor reception the work is unfinished, and one of the reasons for that reception is that Leonard Woolf's analysis of what he called 'communal psychology' is confined too much to the ideas of individuals instead of the functions of class structures; in this he was following Stephen's practice, though not his theory.[32] Stephen had argued in the introduction to the *History of English Thought in the Eighteenth Century* that the immediate causes of change in the history of ideas 'are to be sought rather in social development than in the activity of a few speculative minds'.[33] Stephen did not write such a history; he was concerned with changes in logical conditions rather than social ones, but he recognized the limitations of his account, as one might expect in a follower of Darwin.

Though he was a historian of philosophy, Leslie Stephen was not a philosopher of history, nor was Bloomsbury much interested in a subject that seems to attract philosophical Idealists and Materialists rather than Realists. A good deal of history was read, early and late, in Bloomsbury. MacCarthy, Forster, Bell, and Strachey all specialized in history at Cambridge and Virginia Stephen read it extensively under her father's tutelage, chose historical subjects (religion, women) for her early writing, and even taught the subject briefly at a college for working men and women (*QB*, i, 202–4). But basically, the interest in history for Bloomsbury was biographical and, in two different senses of the word, literary. 'Human beings are too important to be treated as mere symptoms of the past', Lytton Strachey proclaimed in the preface to *Eminent Victorians* (1918). 'They have a value which is independent of any temporal processes—which is eternal and must be felt for its own sake' (p. viii). This Bloomsbury conviction, derived from among other things Moore's ethics, led the Group to recognize Leslie Stephen's most important contribution to English historiography as the *Dictionary of National Biography*.

Literary history for Bloomsbury meant literature as history as well as the history of literature, which they saw as essentially the history of writers. Strachey wanted all history to approach the conditions of literature, and his models were historians like Thucydides, Tacitus, Gibbon, and Michelet. But when he comes to write his manual of French literary history, Strachey seems more under the influence of Macaulay than anyone else, as he groups the landmarks of French literature around the antitheses of rhetoric and realism.[34] Forster shared Strachey's conviction that history was a branch of literature, but literary history he dismissed as usually an evasion of the arduous necessity of coming to terms with texts. His ahistorical view of the novel is an aspect of Bloomsbury's formalism, which meant that the Group was uninterested in many of Stephen's essays in literary history. Clive Bell wrote to Lytton Strachey after reading his father-in-law's most important single work of literary history, the late lectures on eighteenth-century English literature and society, that he wondered what Stephen thought literary artists were trying to do.[35] Yet *English Literature and Society in the Eighteenth Century* may well have helped Virginia Woolf to realize how social conditions shaped literature.[36] Stephen said his interest in the history of literature was both philosophical and social: to appreciate a great writer fully it was necessary to distinguish between his individual characteristics and those resulting from his times and their 'existing stage of social and intellectual development'.[37] The evolution of English literary history accorded well with Stephen's Darwinian ideas, and Virginia Woolf was not slow to see the feminist implications of a theory of literary history that was at least rudimentarily aware of the conditions affecting literary production. In works like *A Room of One's Own*, where she explores the social and intellectual conditions affecting the development of women's writing, Virginia Woolf seems to owe something to her father's ideas. But how much she owes can be overstated. The context of Virginia Woolf's literary criticism is more often the socially anonymous common reader rather than the socially conditioned writer, and this takes us to the significance of Leslie Stephen's criticism for Bloomsbury.

*   *   *

43

> To read what one liked because one liked it, never to pretend to admire what one did not—that was his only lesson in the art of reading. To write in the fewest possible words, as clearly as possible, exactly what one meant—that was his only lesson in the art of writing. All the rest must be learnt for oneself. (*E*, iv, 80)

Leslie Stephen's teaching in the arts upon which literary criticism depends, as described by Virginia Woolf on his centenary in 1932, appropriately emphasizes his integrity and lucidity as a critic. He set moral and rhetorical standards not just for his daughter but for all the writers of the Bloomsbury Group. But 'all the rest' that had to be learned by oneşelf included a great deal that inevitably led to profound differences between Stephen's criticism and Bloomsbury's.

The most fundamental of these differences had to do with the nature and value of aesthetic experience. In Bloomsbury it was part of the *summum bonum* both for its own formal sake and also in combination with other kinds of experience. Yet to Stephen art for art's sake was a canting doctrine,

> which would encourage men to steep themselves in luxurious dreaming, and explicitly renounce the belief that art is valuable, as it provides a worthy embodiment for the most strenuous thought and highest endeavour of the age.[38]

Stephen attacked Pater's claim at the end of *The Renaissance* that art proposed only to give the highest quality to our moments for the sake of those moments, and he argued that art could not be independent of moral concerns.[39] But Stephen did not, as is sometimes claimed, equate moral and aesthetic standards; he only said they were not independent of each other.[40] Pater, of course, is a moralist in *The Renaissance*, especially with his recommendations about what success in life ought to be. Stephen's quarrel with him—and with Bloomsbury, could he have known it—was first of all a moral not an aesthetic one. They differ over the value of aesthetic contemplation. 'To recommend contemplation in preference to action is like preferring sleeping to waking', Stephen wrote in 'Wordsworth's Ethics'.[41] Pater might have agreed with this preference; Bloomsbury would not have. Yet Bloomsbury did not disagree with Stephen that literature could have instrumental moral value, though they thought its intrinsic worth was more important.

There are, nevertheless, deep aesthetic disagreements between Leslie Stephen's literary criticism and Bloomsbury's. At the end of his life, with a dozen or so volumes of literary biography and criticism to his name, Stephen expressed his dislike of the whole business:

> In some sense I am ready to admit that all criticism is a nuisance and a parasitic growth upon literature. The most fruitful reading is that in which we are submitting to a teacher and asking no questions as to the secret of his influence.[42]

Criticism had evolved, Stephen went on, from the judicial to the historical, the aspect of criticism he was most interested in. Bloomsbury would have added that criticism then evolved into the aesthetic. (And after that one might argue it became analytic.) 'The whole art of criticism', Stephen wrote earlier of the judicial critic Dr. Johnson, whom he loved, 'consists in learning how to know the human being who is partially revealed to us in his spoken works.'[43] The historical critic, by exploring the intellectual and social background of literature, helps the reader to know the author. So little did Stephen regard aesthetic, analytic criticism, that he was even willing in theory to do away with literature. Replying to Matthew Arnold's criticism of his essay on Wordsworth's ethics, Stephen wrote,

> literature may be sufficiently regarded as simply one form of personal intercourse. It is a subordinate question whether I know a man through his books or hear him discourse to me *viva vôce*, or talk to him in ordinary society. . . .[44]

For all their valuing of personal relations, Bloomsbury never went that far. The highest praise that Stephen can give an author is to say he is 'lovable'—and it always seems to be a 'he'. 'Manly' echoes through his criticism as a term of praise; female authors can be charming and are sometimes praised for being feminine but they really could not be considered lovable by Stephen. And at least twice in his criticism, Stephen expresses the urge to horsewhip his authors—Laurence Sterne for his behaviour and Jonathan Edwards for his sermons.[45]

The critical implications of Stephen's personal conception

45

of literature appear in his concern with the biographical, social, intellectual aspects of literature and in his avoidance, for the most part, of technical or affective literary analyses. As a critic of poets Stephen almost always defers to his predecessors for discussions of their poetry; with writers of prose he is more willing to talk about style, characterization, narration, and setting. But even here he remains very general. Lytton Strachey in an essay on Matthew Arnold that anticipates *Eminent Victorians* saw the essential weakness of the Victorian age as 'its incapability of criticism':

> When Dryden or Johnson wrote of literature, they wrote of it as an art; but the Victorian critic had a different notion of his business. To him literature was always an excuse for talking about something else. From Macaulay, who used it as a convenient peg for historical and moral disquisitions, to Leslie Stephen, who frankly despised the whole business, this singular tradition holds good.[46]

This complaint can also be levelled to some extent against Bloomsbury themselves. When it is not about writers, Bloomsbury's literary criticism is often about readers, but there is comparatively little attention given to analysing the writing itself. Strachey, for example, was in agreement with Stephen about the greatness of Sainte-Beuve, who sought literary understanding by focusing on the backgrounds of authors. But in one important respect Bloomsbury critics were capable of talking about literature far more than Leslie Stephen was, and that had to do with feeling.

The experience of aesthetic emotion is as central to Bloomsbury's thinking about art as their formalism is. Indeed it is the confirmation of the value of form. Stephen, like his father, thought of himself as a skinless man yet was almost incapable of discussing feelings; he was a sentimentalist and suffered from that English inhibitedness anatomized by Forster as the undeveloped heart. Virginia Woolf thought Cambridge had atrophied her father's sensibility, and connected his unaesthetic attitude with his agnostic lack of imagination (*MB*, 126; *D*, iii, 246). She owes much to her father's literary criticism, to its historical range, its style, its integrity, and its emphasis on literature as the expression of personality and character, but as a reader valuing the imaginative expression of feeling she owes him little. 'I always read a *Hours in a Library* by way of filling out my ideas say of Coleridge; if I'm reading Coleridge,' she wrote in the revised typescript of 'A Sketch of the Past', 'and always find something to fill out; to correct; to stiffen my fluid vision.' After this important statement of an indebtedness, which extended to Stephen's biographical studies and dictionary articles as well, Virginia Woolf proceeded to generalize about her ambivalence toward her father as a writer. (She said she had been reading Freud and the quasi-sexual metaphor of Stephen's influence might support this.) His was not a subtle, imaginative, or suggestive mind, but it was a strong one whose limited view of the world's humbug vices and domestic virtues she admired and even envied. Her father was not the kind of writer she had a natural affinity for,

> yet as a dog takes a bite of grass, I take a bite of him medicinally, and there often steals in, not a filial, but a reader's affection for him; for his courage, his simplicity, for his strength and nonchalance and neglect of appearances.[47]

These last qualities have not had much attention paid to them in discussions of Stephen's influence or lack of influence on Virginia Woolf, yet they are part of the lessons he gave his daughter in the arts of reading and writing.

Desmond MacCarthy once defended Stephen from the disparagement of Arnold Bennett and maintained that the virtue of his criticism was 'that there is so much intellectual hard work in it. . . . His criticism was never impressionistic and he never relied on his sensibility alone.'[48] But this made for critical limitations as well, as MacCarthy pointed out in the Leslie Stephen lecture that he gave on Stephen himself in Cambridge in 1937. There MacCarthy called Stephen 'the least aesthetic of noteworthy critics':

> deficient in the power of transmitting the emotions he had derived from literature; he seldom, if ever, attempted to record a thrill. But he excelled in describing the qualities of authors, whether he summed up for or against them; and this is a most important part of the critic's function.[49]

MacCarthy's lecture was basically sympathetic to Stephen, but nevertheless it brought down the wrath of *Scrutiny* in the form of a rejoinder by Q. D. Leavis, who described MacCarthy as a leftover decadent from the '90s who thought critics should record thrills instead of analysing literary works.[50] *Scrutiny's* polemics belong to the literary history of Bloomsbury in the '30s, but in considering Leslie Stephen's significance as a critic for Bloomsbury it is worth noting that the difference between Stephen's and Bloomsbury's literary criticism is not one of analyses versus thrills. Certainly Virginia Woolf, Forster, Strachey, and MacCarthy were more concerned with aesthetic feeling in their criticism than Stephen, but to a disinterested observer it should be clear that Stephen's unanalytic interest in literature as an expression of personality is more closely related to Bloomsbury's literary criticism than to the Leavises'. Stephen's overriding moral judgements in his criticism do, of course, make it part of the Victorian critical tradition which *Scrutiny* celebrated and sought to continue; but his dislike of critical analyses does not. Here he is closer to the conclusions of E. M. Forster, for example, who maintained at the end of his career that there was no 'first-class *raison d'être* for criticism in the arts'—only love could provide that, and love not for the artist (that Stephen was willing to give) but for the art.[51] Like so much of Bloomsbury's criticism, Forster's conclusion is both moral and aesthetic. MacCarthy's too was as much concerned with moral judgements as with aesthetic experiences. The relation of a work of literature to life, 'the extent to which it ministered, in one way or another, to all human good', that he identifies as Stephen's critical criterion was also his own.[52] MacCarthy's respect for Stephen's work as a model of criticism was such that, according to his biographer, he once disbanded a collection of critical articles because it fell below the standard Stephen set in *Hours in a Library*.[53]

Two other features of Leslie Stephen's literary criticism connecting him with Virginia Woolf and Bloomsbury remain to be mentioned: like Stephen the Bloomsbury critics were primarily critics and almost exclusively writers of prose, and very prominent among the forms of prose they criticized and wrote was biography. The preference for prose is one reason why Bloomsbury criticism focuses on the same two centuries of writers that Stephen does; Strachey and Virginia Woolf were, perhaps, more sensitive to sixteenth- and seventeenth-century writing than Stephen, and of course they wrote about the literature of their own century, but nevertheless there is a critical continuity between Stephen's and Bloomsbury's criticism of eighteenth- and nineteenth-century novelists, historians, essayists, autobiographers, and especially biographers. And it was in the practice of biography that may be found the most enduring part of Stephen's heritage for Bloomsbury.

The separation of Leslie Stephen's achievements as a critic and a biographer is one that Bloomsbury would have made sooner than Stephen. There are no clear methodological differences between the essays he published under the title *Hours in a Library* and those called *Studies of a Biographer*. Yet by distinguishing between Stephen's critical and biographical essays we can see how, beyond the disagreements about the social morality of authors or the aesthetic character of their work, Bloomsbury continued Stephen's strongly biographical interest in literature. As much as Stephen they studied what MacCarthy called the 'Natural History of Authors'.[54] The biographical essays of Virginia Woolf, Forster, Strachey, MacCarthy, and Leonard Woolf are usually shorter than Stephen's because of the changed conditions of periodical journalism, and as a result they appear more neatly turned and even contrived than Stephen's more judicious and sometimes prolix studies. (Keynes's biographical essays written for journals rather than newspapers are closer in form to Stephen's.) In an essay on biography Virginia Woolf began with the definition by Sidney Lee—her father's successor as editor of *The Dictionary of National Biography*—that biography is 'the truthful transmission of personality', which she symbolized in the images of granite and rainbow (*E*, iv, 229). There is more granitic truth in Stephen's leisurely essays and more rainbow personality in Bloomsbury's briefer lives. But despite the differences in form and emphasis, there is from time to time a noticeable similarity in tone between Stephen's essays and some of the longer ones of Lytton Strachey that were also written for journals or as part of *Eminent Victorians*. In yet another Leslie Stephen lecture on Leslie Stephen, the next one to be delivered after MacCarthy's, J. Dover Wilson pointed out how 'the limpid style, the irony, the appetent smile with which Strachey exhibits to the reader the moral tumour before he lances it, all are to be found in essay after essay of Leslie Stephen's volumes.'[55] If Strachey is the debunking father of modern biography, Stephen is one of the grandfathers.

In *English Literature and Society in the Eighteenth Century* Stephen described the British essay as a lay sermon (p. 44). It continued to be so for Stephen and also for Strachey, Forster, Leonard and Virginia Woolf, though the doctrines preached were of different religions. As a Victorian and an admirer of Carlyle, Leslie Stephen was a hero-worshipper. He used Carlyle's life of Sterling as a model for his full-length biographies of Henry Fawcett and Fitzjames Stephen, but with those two exceptions his biographies were not lay saints' lives. Of the twin plagues of biography that he once identified as hagiography and iconoclasm,[56] Stephen was more susceptible, though not as much as Bloomsbury, to the second. He was— to use a metaphor of his daughter's that comes at the end of one of her last important essays—an eminent Victorian trespasser whose example was to be followed, especially in literature. Bloomsbury biographers happily followed him, but to see this more clearly it is useful to distinguish between the four kinds of biographical genre that Stephen wrote in. There is the periodical essay, the man-of-letters monograph, the full-dress authorized life, and the biographical dictionary article. We have been discussing mainly the first of these. The second has no parallel in Bloomsbury's work, though the Group were familiar with Stephen's studies of Johnson, Pope, Swift, George Eliot, and Hobbes. The biographies of Fawcett and Fitzjames Stephen are in the same genre as Forster's *Goldsworthy Lowes Dickinson* and Virginia Woolf's *Roger Fry*. None suffers from that third plague of Victorian biography, elephantiasis. All are lucidly written and organized. In each there is that close personal relationship between author and subject that has made much of the best English biography into a form of autobiography. But for Stephen the closeness of the relationships makes emotional demands that the inhibited biographer cannot meet. His biographies of his friend and his brother are utterly reticent lives. Fitzjames's private life is treated with such decorum that it comes as a surprise to find him suddenly with a wife and seven children. Yet reticence is a problem too with Forster's and especially Virginia Woolf's modern biographies; they are far closer to Stephen's in the absence of any explicit discussion of their subjects' sexuality than they are to the full frontal biography of today. What Bloomsbury felt as a necessary constraint, however, Stephen experienced more as a comforting decency.[57] But the main difference between Stephen's and Bloomsbury's full-length biographies lies in their moral purpose. The sole stated aim of *The Life of Henry Fawcett* is to bring his character to bear on the reader's. 'Sympathetic appreciation . . . is essential to satisfactory biography', Stephen wrote in the preface to his brother's biography[58] (he is described as Fitzjames's brother on the title page) and this is true of Forster's and Virginia Woolf's biographies too, but they are more detached, more detailed about the feelings if not the emotional experiences of their subjects. The pieties of Victorian friendship have gone underground in their books, along with the moral purpose.

The arts of Victorian biography, as found in the works of Leslie Stephen, impinged most pervasively on the consciousness of Bloomsbury through the *Dictionary of National Biography*. The *D.N.B.* was begun the year of Virginia Woolf's birth, and she liked to joke about what it cost her nervous system: 'It gave me a twist of the head. . . . I shouldn't have been so clever, but I should have been more stable, without that contribution to the history of England', she wrote in her diary in 1923 (ii, 277). Year by year, from 1884 until 1900, the future members of the Group grew up with this vast serialized biographical chronicle of England. As its first and most important editor, in addition to writing some 378 lives for it, Stephen 'set the stroke' in Maitland's metaphor (p. 371). He tried to keep down the number of clergymen of one kind or another in the dictionary, for example; several saints like Alban and Asaph had to wait for the supplement to get in. And the first editor was sorely tried by 'the susceptibilities of a most fretful and unreasonable race of men, the antiquaries'.[59] Most of the biographical essays on writers in the original edition were written by Stephen, and he thought the *D.N.B.* would make a pretty good introduction to English literary history when it was finished.[60] By his critical lights it is, and his lives of the poets, novelists, and essayists are long on moral and short on aesthetic analysis. (In thirty-six columns on Alexander Pope, for instance, there is no mention of his art of the couplet.)

Stephen's stamp on the *D.N.B.* is a matter then, of emphasis, treatment, tone, as well as selection of subjects and their biographers. In announcing the beginning of the *Dictionary of National Biography*, he put its ideal of style as follows:

> I have been asked whether anything in the way of 'literary style' is to be admitted. If style means superfluous ornament, I say emphatically, No. But style, and even high literary ability, is required for lucid and condensed narrative, and of such style I shall be anxious to get as much as I can.[61]

He would have got a good deal from Bloomsbury, could they have contributed. The unofficial motto for the dictionary, suggested by one of its contributors and accepted by Stephen, was 'no flowers by request', and Thoby Stephen, as a child, is supposed to have described it as the 'contradictionary'.[62] In the words of his own biographer, Leslie Stephen established in the *D.N.B.* a school of portraiture in black and white, and thus a major Victorian source for modern critical biography. Lytton Strachey called it 'one of the most useful books in existence', while Stephen himself thought it 'one of the most amusing works in the language'.[63] Virginia Woolf mocked the *D.N.B.* along with other aspects of biography in *Orlando* (275) but kept her father's set in her workroom and used it repeatedly for her essays. Indeed all of Bloomsbury used it for their critical and biographical writings. It is the most important work in the Victorian backgrounds of the Group and epitomized Leslie Stephen's achievement for them, drawing as it does on his skills as an editor, critic, intellectual historian, essayist—and trespasser.

Hugh Kenner has suggested that Murray's great *Oxford English Dictionary* is the nineteenth-century equivalent to Gibbon's eighteenth-century epic, *The Decline and Fall of the Roman Empire*.[64] The *Dictionary of National Biography* is a closer analogue. The similarities are in story and moral rather than structure or style. For Bloomsbury the *D.N.B.* became a kind of Victorian epic tracing prophetically, if unknowingly, the development and decline of the British empire whose fall

Bloomsbury lived through and wrote about in their own biographies, essays and novels. For Virginia Woolf the *D.N.B.* also traced the decline of the patriarchy, whose fall she regretted not witnessing; it demonstrated again that the 'history of England is the history of the male line, not the female', as she wrote in 'Women and Fiction' (*E*, ii, 141). 'The lives of the obscure' were also excluded, almost by definition, from the *D.N.B.*, which gave the editor's daughter an opportunity to include a few among the essays of the common reader that she saw herself to be.

Little mention has been made in this sketch of Leslie Stephen as a literary intellectual father-figure for Bloomsbury or his importance for Virginia Woolf's fiction. There is a sense in which the most useful thing he did for her in fiction was not to write any of it. Virginia Woolf's was a prose inheritance. Among the major English and American novelists who were her contemporaries—Lawrence, Joyce, Faulkner, Hemingway, Fitzgerald—she was the only one to have written no poetry as such, outside the loose verse in her last novel. There is, very surprisingly, no evidence even of any juvenile attempts at verse; her earliest writings appear to have been historical and critical, like her father's. The novel was her great prose opportunity, and she made it her poetic one as well. She brought to it everything she learned as the daughter, wife, sister, friend of educated men. Their significance extends beyond the portraits of Leslie Stephen in *The Voyage Out* and *To the Lighthouse* and beyond the representation of the Bloomsbury Group in *Night and Day, Jacob's Room* and *The Waves*. It extends to the basic agnostic, Utilitarian, evolutionary, and liberal assumptions of those books and to their critiques of Stephen's patriarchal ethics and unaesthetic critical values. Ultimately Stephen's most enduring legacy for Virginia Woolf's fiction may have been in the way he thought rather than felt about literature. His lucid, moral, rational, commonsensical conception of literature was a logically necessary though emotionally insufficient precursor of her own.

In that extraordinary fusion of fiction and non-fiction, *A Room of One's Own*, the composite writer-narrator who both is and is not Virginia Woolf goes, after being chased off the college grass, to the famous college library to look at the manuscript of *Henry Esmond*. What takes her there is a meditation centring on the eighteenth-century style of the novel—is it an affectation of Thackeray's or natural to him? Will the alterations in the manuscript indicate they were made for style or sense? But then what is meaning and what just style? This chain of questions is characteristic of Stephen's literary historical reasoning. But it is never completed. Again the narrator is regarded as a trespasser and driven away because she is unaccompanied by a fellow of the college and has no letter of introduction (*RO* 11–12). The manuscript of *Henry Esmond* is preserved at Trinity College, Cambridge—Thackeray's old college—and it was presented to the library by his son-in-law, Leslie Stephen. For that part of the narrator that is Virginia Woolf, it appears that even the gifts of manuscripts to college libraries by educated men cannot be read by their unaccompanied, uneducated daughters.

NOTES

1. Unpublished letter, 30 December 1927, quoted by kind permission of Mrs. Eva Reichmann, the copyright holder, and the library of the University of Sussex.
2. Vanessa Bell, *Notes on Virginia Woolf's Childhood* (New York, 1974), (p. 8).
3. Frederic William Maitland, *The Life and Letters of Leslie Stephen* (1906), pp. 474–76.
4. Katherine C. Hill, 'Virginia Woolf and Leslie Stephen: History and Literary Revolution', *P.M.L.A.*, 96 (1981), 351–62.
5. 'Virginia Woolf', *Horizon*, 3 (1941), repr. *The Bloomsbury Group*, ed. S. P. Rosenbaum (1975), p. 203.
6. Leonard Woolf, *Coming to London*, ed. John Lehmann (1957), p. 34.
7. Oscar Maurer, 'Leslie Stephen and the *Cornhill Magazine*, 1871–82', *Texas Studies in English*, 32 (1953), 67–95.
8. Maitland, pp. 318, 423.
9. Hardy, *Complete Poems*, ed. James Gibson (1976), p. 322.
10. The typescript, now Add. MS. 61973 in the British Library, is a revised version of pp. 107–37 of 'A Sketch of the Past' in *MB*; it also contains an additional 27-page section on Stephen and Hyde Park Gate. The page numbers cited are those originally typed on the tss., not those added by

hand later. The typescript is quoted by kind permission of Professor Quentin Bell.

11. Quentin Bell, *Bloomsbury* (1968), facing p. 16.
12. The generalizations about the Bloomsbury Group that follow are based on assumptions about the identity and nature of the Group that I have tried to explain in 'Preface to a Literary History of the Bloomsbury Group', *N.L.H.*, 12 (1981), 329–44.
13. Stephen, *The Science of Ethics* (1882; repr. 1907), p. 267.
14. Florence Emily Hardy, *The Early Life of Thomas Hardy* (1928), pp. 105–6.
15. Stephen, *An Agnostic's Apology and Other Essays*, 2nd ed. (1903), p. 8.
16. *Apology*, pp. 42–85.
17. John Maynard Keynes, *Collected Writings* (1971–), x, 86. For a more general discussion of the intellectual setting of Leslie Stephen's importance for Bloomsbury, see my 'The Intellectual Origins of the Bloomsbury Group', *T.H.E.S.*, 29 October 1982, 14–15.
18. Leslie Stephen, *The Life of Sir James Fitzjames Stephen* (2nd ed., 1895), p. 170.
19. Maitland, p. 430.
20. *Mausoleum Book*, ed. Alan Bell (Oxford, 1977), p. 71.
21. Stephen, *Hours in a Library*, 3rd series (1899), ii, 279.
22. Stephen, *Some Early Impressions* (1924), p. 76.
23. *Science of Ethics*, p. 128.
24. Sidgwick, *The Methods of Ethics*, 7th ed. (1907), pp. 471–73.
25. *Hours*, iii, 87.
26. Stephen, *Men, Books, and Mountains*, ed. S. O. A. Ullmann (1956), pp. 250–51.
27. *Leslie Stephen: His Thought and Character in Relation to his Time* (Cambridge, Mass., 1952), p. 83.
28. Stephen, *Studies of a Biographer* (1898; repr. 1910), iii, 109.
29. Maitland, p. 170.
30. John W. Bicknell, 'Leslie Stephen's *English Thought in the Eighteenth Century:* A Tract for the Times', *Victorian Studies*, 6 (1962), 103–20.
31. Stephen, *English Literature and Society in the Eighteenth Century* (1904; repr. 1963), p. 58.
32. See Noel Annan's *The Curious Strength of Positivism in English Political Thought* (Oxford, 1959), and his introduction to Leslie Stephen, *Selected Writings in British Intellectual History*, ed. Annan (Chicago, 1979). Leonard Woolf's work is not specifically discussed but Annan's criticisms clearly apply to it.
33. 3rd ed. (1902), i, 8, 13.
34. *Landmarks in French Literature* (1912), pp. 201–2.
35. Unpublished letter, 4 June 1908, now with the Strachey Papers in the British Library.
36. Hill, *P.M.L.A.*, 351–62.
37. *English Literature and Society*, pp. 1, 5.
38. *Apology*, p. 124.
39. Stephen gave his views on literature and morality clearly in two unreprinted essays. 'Art and Morality' (*Cornhill Magazine*, 32, 1875, 91–101)

was written shortly after the publication of Pater's *The Renaissance*. 'The Moral Element in Literature' (*Cornhill Magazine*, 43, 1881, 34–50) was a defence of his ideas in 'Wordsworth's Ethics' that Matthew Arnold had criticized.

40. *Hours*, i, 100.
41. *Hours*, ii, 293.
42. *English Literature and Society*, p. 4.
43. *Hours*, ii, 3.
44. 'The Moral Element', 39.
45. *Hours*, i, 311; iii, 148.
46. Strachey, *Characters and Commentaries* (1933), pp. 188–89.
47. Add. MS. 61973, pp. 81–2.
48. MacCarthy, *Humanities* (1953), p. 195.
49. *Leslie Stephen* (Cambridge, England, 1937), pp. 11, 45.
50. Q. D. Leavis, 'Leslie Stephen: Cambridge Critic', *Scrutiny*, 7 (1939), 404–15.
51. *Two Cheers for Democracy*, ed. Oliver Stallybrass (1972), p. 118.
52. MacCarthy, *Stephen*, p. 47.
53. *D.N.B.*, 1951–60, ed. E. T. Williams and Helen M. Palmer (Oxford, 1971).
54. MacCarthy, *Stephen*, p. 46.
55. *Leslie Stephen and Matthew Arnold as Critics of Wordsworth* (Cambridge, England, 1939), pp. 20–1.
56. *Hours*, iii, 341.
57. Stephen's letters to his wife, now in the Berg Collection of the New York Public Library, reveal him to be unhappy about omissions he felt forced to make in his biographies, and in his *D.N.B.* account of his grandfather James Stephen he concealed the parentage of an illegitimate son.
58. *Henry Fawcett* (1885), p. 468; *Fitzjames Stephen*, 2nd ed. (1895), p. vi.
59. *Mausoleum Book*, p. 86.
60. *Men, Books, and Mountains*, p. 32.
61. 'A New Biographica Britannica', *Athenaeum*, 23 December 1882, 850.
62. *Some Early Impressions*, p. 163; Elizabeth French Boyd, *Bloomsbury Heritage: Their Mothers and Their Aunts* (1976), p. 35.
63. Maitland, p. 372; Strachey, 'A Frock-Coat Portrait of a Great King', *Daily Mail*, 11 October 1927, 10; *Studies*, i, 12.
64. *The Pound Era* (Berkeley, California, 1971), p. 366.

3

Heart of Darkness, Virginia Woolf and the Spectre of Domination

by SHIRLEY NEUMAN

During the summer of 1923, Virginia Woolf wrote an appreciation of Joseph Conrad for the *Nation*. In it, she initiated most of the observations she would make in a more serious and valedictory mood for the *Times Literary Supplement* on Conrad's death a year later. Both articles mildly criticize Conrad's later novels in which Marlow 'does all the talking' (*E*, i, 311). Both stress Woolf's preference for the 'early books': *Youth, Lord Jim, Typhoon*, and *The Nigger of the 'Narcissus'*. Neither essay mentions *Heart of Darkness* (1899), the novella Conrad published between *Youth* (1898) and *Lord Jim* (1900).

The intent of the omission—if intent it was—will doubtless remain consigned to the fields of night. Perhaps the 'omission' is no more than the use of *Youth* as a generic title meant to include *Heart of Darkness*, for both stories had been republished by Dent (along with *The End of the Tether*) under the general title *Youth*. That volume Woolf had reviewed for the *T.L.S.*, already making her major point that Conrad 'in these stories . . . gives us the most complete and perfect expression of one side of his genius—the side that . . . is not so subtle or so psychological as the later mood.'[1] Or the omission may have been a decision not to direct any flash of light on her own work. For Woolf reserved for *Heart of Darkness* a tribute greater than discussion in the *Nation* and *T.L.S.*: the tribute of allusion, debate, and transformation in her own novels. Allusions to Conrad's tale are pervasive and central in *Mrs. Dalloway*, the novel Woolf was working on when she wrote the Conrad appreciation and obituary article. But they had already surfaced in *The Voyage Out* and they would persist through the last pages of *Between the Acts*.

That, by allusion to both Greek and Christian ritual, Septimus is a scapegoat, that he experiences Clarissa's death for her and returns her to life, has been the liturgy chanted by most critics of *Mrs. Dalloway*. But that not all the birds Septimus hears sing in Greek, that Woolf places Septimus's reluctant assumption of his role in the context of *Heart of Darkness*, has been a melody less heard. Septimus inwardly protests against this function as 'the scapegoat, the eternal sufferer' (*MD*, 29) just before Maisie Johnson asks directions to Regent's Park Tube Station. In the midst of the 'gently trudging, vaguely gazing, breeze-kissed company' (*MD*, 30)—which, Peter Walsh will think, does to represent 'civilisation, after India' (*MD*, 79)—Kurtz's summation erupts: Maisie 'positively felt she must cry Oh! . . . Horror! horror!' (*MD*, 30–1).[2] The moment recognizes Septimus's earlier terror, watching the motor-car, at 'this gradual drawing together of everything to one centre before his eyes, as if some horror had come almost to the surface and was about to burst into flames' (*MD*, 18). Later, Septimus and Rezia returned to their room, he observes his 'prostrate body which lay realising its degradation' (*MD*, 101) and we know him deathbound as surely as is Kurtz, for, behind the phrase, we can hear Marlow's invocation of Kurtz's 'exalted and incredible degradation' (*HD*, 67).[3] That allusion opens what becomes the most sustained reference to *Heart of Darkness* in *Mrs. Dalloway*. Septimus goes on to cite Holmes as a specific instance of 'Human nature, . . . the repulsive brute, with the blood-red nostrils' (*MD*, 102) in an echo of Marlow's description of the devils that drive men. Having named his demons, Septimus knows 'an isolation full of sublimity; a freedom which the attached can never know' (*MD*, 103): a freedom Kurtz has found by having 'kicked himself loose of the earth' (*HD*, 67).

Both freedoms are madness, but, however numerous and explicit the allusions to *Heart of Darkness* in *Mrs. Dalloway*, they do not invite us to read Kurtz's madness of the soul and Septimus's madness of the mind as equivalent. Kurtz succumbs to 'brutal instincts', 'gratified and monstrous passions' (*HD*, 67) where Septimus, a world war further on mankind's return to the night before roads were made, panics because he imagines he feels nothing. Kurtz dies remorseless where Septimus imagines his 'crimes' (*MD*, 101) jeering round his head. Kurtz dies with a voiceless double summation—of Africa and of Europe, of savagery and of civilization—that, chambered in Marlow, that apologist for 'restraint', echoes through time and across continents, even into the salon of one of the most benighted guardians of civilization's 'saving illusion' (*HD*, 77). Septimus dies in defiance of Proportion and with a Dantean vision[4] of Rezia:

> all her petals were about her. She was a flowering tree; and through her branches looked out the face of a lawgiver, who had reached a sanctuary where she feared no one; . . . a miracle, a triumph, the last and greatest. (*MD*, 163)

Marlow affirms that Kurtz's summation is a victory because it strips away civilization's illusions and embraces death. Septimus dies affirming life—'Life was good. The sun hot' (*MD*, 164).

Marlow invokes 'restraint' and 'surface reality' against the darkness Kurtz affirms. While Mrs. Dalloway might well judge with Marlow that such proportion has its use in keeping one from going ashore for a howl and a dance—could she imagine such a landing—she, like Marlow, must learn that Proportion has kindred in darkness. In a passage that, Stephen Trombley has now shown us, owes much of its anger and vigour to Woolf's own medical experiences,[5] Woolf describes that 'less smiling, more formidable' sister of Proportion, a sister who toils in 'the mud and swamp of Africa, the purlieus of London, wherever, in short, the climate or the devil tempts men to fall from the true belief which is her own' (*MD*, 110–11). That sister sounds remarkably like Conrad's Europeans colonizing the Congo, 'bearing the sword, and often the torch' (*HD*, 4), and taking 'a high seat amongst the devils of the land'

(*HD*, 50): she 'is even now engaged in dashing down shrines, smashing idols, and setting up in their place her own stern countenance. Conversion is her name and she feasts on the wills of the weakly, loving to impress, to impose, . . . disguised as brotherly love', she 'offers help but desires power' (*MD*, 111). In Woolf's vision, however, Proportion has no need to voyage to the heart of a dark continent; 'she' can establish her dominions by colonizing the weak at home, beginning, Trombley reminds us, with Lady Bradshaw herself who, 'quick to minister to the craving which lit her husband's eye so oilily for dominion . . . cramped, squeezed, pared, pruned, drew back and peeped through' (*MD*, 112), but no longer fished for salmon.

Remembering *Heart of Darkness* and its ironic reading of the traditional male quest in Marlow's voyage, Woolf further ironizes Conrad's plot to emphasize the colonized over the conquerors, to accommodate the apparently more limited and superficial circumstances of an inveterate hostess. Clarissa, 'lolloping on the waves and braiding her tresses' (*MD*, 191), is indeed far too mannered for Marlow's grim descent beneath the surface of things. But in *Mrs. Dalloway* that descent is displaced and discredited. It is made symbolically by Peter Walsh in his dream, but the 'knowledge' it yields has already been invalidated by Clarissa's memories. As Clarissa will later feel that her 'triumphs . . . had a hollowness' (*MD*, 192), so Peter, a Conradian 'pilgrim', leaves Clarissa's 'feeling hollowed out, utterly empty within' (*MD*, 55). On a bench in Regent's Park, he falls into sleep, the unconscious, and *Heart of Darkness*. Marlow, we should recall here, is greeted in the Brussels office which sends him to the Congo by two 'fateful' women 'knitting black wool as for a warm pall', one 'introducing continuously to the unknown' those who set out on their voyage, 'the other scrutinizing' them with 'swift and indifferent placidity' (*HD*, 11). So too the sleeping Peter is watched over by a knitting nurse who seems 'like the champion of the rights of sleepers'. In his dream, the 'solitary traveller' passes through a forest of hemlock and fern, then 'advances down the village street where the women stand knitting and . . . the evening seems ominous; the figures still; as if some august fate . . . were about to sweep them into complete annihilation'. The voyage metaphor, the primeval, vegetation-choked forest, the knitting nurse, the analogy to Lachesis drawn by the words *ominous* and *fate* (words shared with Conrad in the comparable passage), the use of *august* (a word common in Conrad and rare in Woolf): all suggest, in Peter's journey into the unconscious, darkness, and death, an allusion to Marlow's. Peter *seems* to dream, in Conradian terms, Clarissa's dream. His awakening provides the conscious corroboration of his unconscious judgement of an event from their mutual past: 'the death of her soul' (*MD*, 63–6).

However, Woolf allows neither Peter's dreaming nor his waking judgement to speak for Clarissa. Instead, she shows him too given to 'ticketing the moment' (*MD*, 66); with too large a share of an undiscriminating colonizing spirit—'All India lay behind him; plains, mountains; epidemics of cholera; a district twice as big as Ireland' (*MD*, 54); and altogether too shallow, romantic and complacent about 'civilisation' in his unwitting and unwittingly ironic epitaph for Septimus: 'One of the triumphs of civilisation, Peter Walsh thought . . . as the light high bell of the ambulance sounded. Swiftly, cleanly, the ambulance sped to the hospital, having picked up instantly, humanely, some poor devil' (*MD*, 166). Woolf's satire warns us to read sceptically Peter's judgements of Clarissa's rigidity and superficiality; he has, after all, taught her the words like *sentimental* and *civilized* (*MD*, 41) in which she encases herself.

Against Peter's dream, Woolf sets Clarissa's memories. *Clarissa* remembers Sally's kiss—'the most exquisite moment of her whole life' (*MD*, 40)—and the intrusion on her ecstasy of Peter's facetious question, an intrusion she experiences as physical and sexual violence erupting through the surface of 'civilized' conversation: 'She felt only how Sally was being mauled already, maltreated; she felt his hostility; his jealousy; his determination to break into their companionship' (*MD*, 41). *Mauled*, one of those words we have transferred from predatory animals to predatory people, and the accusation of jealousy, reveal the sexual nature of the quarrel. The kiss is charged with sexuality, not only in itself but in Clarissa's association of her excitement at Sally's visit with Othello's joy at seeing Desdemona in Cyprus.[6] Clarissa remembers Othello's phrase again when thinking that Septimus had 'plunged holding his treasure' where she had 'defaced, obscured' it in her own life (*MD*, 202); thus Othello's short-lived happiness becomes the motif marking the moment of shattered ecstasy as the turning point in her life. Clarissa's remorse at having 'failed' her husband has, in fact, precipitated her memory of Sally's kiss, for it has led her to acknowledge 'sometimes yielding to the charm of a woman' (*MD*, 36), an acknowledge-ment made in images of tumescence and female orgasm. Clarissa has learned young the consequences of forcing the soul, for the craving for dominion concealed beneath Peter's trite remark has been a decisive factor in her violation of her own sexual integrity, has been the 'granite wall' (rougher even than Mr. Dalloway's cheek seemed to Rachel in *The Voyage Out*), stopping the natural expansion of her sexual feeling. Years later, she expresses her perception of the violence of such dominion and of the use of superficially 'civilised' behaviour to force her own sexual choices by the yoking of 'love and religion' as the destroyers of 'the privacy of the soul' (*MD*, 140). Her immediate perception is Conradian: 'All this she saw as one sees a landscape in a flash of lightning. . . . "Oh this horror!" she said to herself' (*MD*, 41).

In *The Voyage Out* Woolf had already borrowed the plot of Marlow's journey into the unknown to represent a young woman's growing sexual knowledge. Critics have noted the markedly Conradian structure of this first novel: like *Heart of Darkness*, it opens with an outgoing ship in the Thames estuary, with London, its lights emblematic of civilization, behind it; its protagonist voyages across an ocean (seeing signs of the military might of nations along the way) to a jungle town or 'station' that is a microcosm of the society left behind, then proceeds upriver, through silence, to encounter disease and death.[7] But the structural similarities of the two novels weigh less than the thematic link Rosemary Pitt has labelled 'the exploration of the self': 'Rachel, like Kurtz, is venturing too far into unknown areas of the self and experience and has to pay through extinction.'[8] That 'the horror' in *The Voyage Out* is sexual knowledge is the import of Rachel's nightmare after being kissed by Mr. Dalloway: Rachel dreams of a womb and a vagina, a 'vault' and a 'long tunnel', the walls of which 'oozed with damp' and within which she is trapped with a 'deformed', 'gibbering', animalistic man with cruel fingernails (*VO*, 86). The obvious sexual distaste and fear in the dream recur again in her parallel hallucinations, departing from Milton's description of the virgin in *Comus*, when she falls ill. Rachel's sexual experience and Rachel's death are clearly linked.

Rachel's and Terence's most fervid courtship in fact takes place on two walks into the jungle's darkness. On the first they hear 'the swish of the trees and some beast croaking in a remote world' and, on their calling each other's names, Rachel murmurs, ' "Terrible—terrible" ' (*VO*, 332), thinking of the sound of the water which is consistently the symbol for sexual drowning in the novel. In the context of the pervasive allusion to *Heart of Darkness*, we cannot help but hear Kurtz's summation behind that murmur. The second walk, during which Terence declares himself 'lustful' (*VO*, 343) and during which the marriage question is resolved, culminates in a passage which departs from the highly referential language of the rest of the novel. In it, either Rachel feels as if Helen were rolling her over and over in the grass, or, indeed, Helen is; then Rachel sees Helen, above her, kiss Terence in congratulation.[9] In this moment which constitutes the couple's announcement of the sexual choice, Rachel's reaction is hardly conventional for fiancées. She experiences Helen's gesture as punishment: Helen's 'hand dropped abrupt as iron on Rachel's shoulder; it might have been a bolt from heaven'; the grass whips and suffocates her; she is 'almost without sense'. Reawakening from this dream of guilt or fear, 'sitting up, she too realised Helen's soft body, the strong and hospitable arms, and happiness swelling and breaking in one vast wave' (*VO*, 347). The awakening to Helen, not to her lover, and the use of an image for happiness, which, if not as precise as that for the 'charm' Mrs. Dalloway finds in certain women, is nonetheless susceptible in the context of association with orgasm, suggest that not only an unwillingness to face the sexual implications of marriage but an unresolved ambiguity about her sexual choice may be the basis of the fact that, in making the socially acceptable female choice—marriage—Rachel has 'ventured too far'.

Heart of Darkness is Marlow's story even more than Kurtz's.

Returning from the unknown, he interprets it. He begins by speaking about London: 'And this also . . . has been one of the dark places of the earth.' Out of the darkness of his experience, he defines civilization: 'Light came out of this river since . . .? Yes; but it is like a running blaze on a plain, like a flash of lightning in the clouds. We live in the flicker—may it last as long as the old earth keeps rolling! But darkness was here yesterday' (*HD*, 5). Marlow's introduction, like his lie to Kurtz's Intended, defines the individual's relation to his society and to the history of civilization. The analogies with *Heart of Darkness* in *The Voyage Out* imply no such expansion of Rachel's experience. Rachel's incapacity to integrate sexual knowledge may suggest her incapacity for the marriage behaviour her society expects, but Rachel herself does not put the matter so rationally or so contextually. The allusions to *Heart of Darkness* in *The Voyage Out* remain attached to character; even when Rachel uses a phrase reminiscent of Marlow's definition of civilization—'And life, what was that? It was only a light passing over the surface and vanishing, as in time she would vanish' (*VO*, 145)—the phrase remains attached to her person. This is equally true of the single allusion to *Heart of Darkness* in *Night and Day*[10] which occurs in the final (unspoken?) conversation between Katharine and Ralph where it refers to separateness that necessarily must exist between people, to what Mrs. Dalloway would later call the 'little independence' (*MD*, 10) necessary in marriage.

Woolf's glances back to *Heart of Darkness* in her first two novels help identify her plot; our recognition of the quest plot means that we can also see the impasses it yields when women are its protagonists, when the end of the hero's quest (the discovery of identity and reintegration into the community) is recast as the end of the heroine's quest, particularly as it is posited in the nineteenth-century novel: marriage.

But even given the structural similarities of *The Voyage Out* to *Heart of Darkness*, Woolf's initial adaptation of the Conrad plot remains comparatively limited. The voyage into sexual knowledge and marriage, the heart of darkness in which we remain integral and separate even in our most intimate relationships: these do not yet gather in, in the manner of Marlow's introduction to his dark tale, the full moral reach of the history of Western civilization. Woolf claimed the furthest historical and cultural reaches of Marlow's remarks for her own in *Mrs. Dalloway* only after her reassessment of Conrad for her 1923 and 1924 articles.

Finding historical analogies for Kurtz's experience, Marlow chooses the point of view not of Kurtz or of some similar 'trader' but of a commander of a trireme, of 'a decent young citizen in a toga', 'ordered' to follow 'in the train' of a Roman tax-gatherer. 'To face the darkness' 'without thinking much about it either' is the job of the soldier in modern as in ancient Britain. To think too much about it is to understand the 'abomination' (*HD*, 6), to go mad as, each in his own way, do Kurtz and Septimus. What Maisie recognizes in Septimus as 'horror' is such insanity, born of the experience of war and leading to disbelief in the 'idea' which, Marlow thinks, 'redeems' the 'conquest of the earth' (*HD*, 7). That idea is defied by Septimus and is satirized by Woolf in the persons of Lady Bruton, Peter Walsh, Drs. Bradshaw and Holmes, and Miss Kilman. Like Maisie, Rezia shares Septimus's experience in another variation on Marlow's metaphors. Speaking aloud while thinking of her husband, she imagines her words fading like a rocket: 'Its sparks, having grazed their way into the night, surrender to it, dark descends, pours over the outlines of houses and towers' (*MD*, 27). Anticipating the 'downpouring of immense darkness' (*TL*, 195) that opens the war in 'Time Passes', the passage makes words emblematic of civilization, that 'running blaze on a plain'. 'I am alone; I am alone!' Rezia continues in still another Conrad variation, 'as perhaps at midnight, when all boundaries are lost, the country reverts to its ancient shape, as the Romans saw it, lying cloudy, when they landed, and the hills had no names' (*MD*, 28).[11]

A pattern emerges in Woolf's fiction by which the Conradian vision is granted to and reinterpreted by those who resist Conversion, in which the resisters are some women (Clarissa, Eleanor, La Trobe) and homosexuals (Septimus, Nicholas) who, presumably, have nothing to gain by dominating women. The pattern begins to emerge soon after Clarissa rejects what she terms 'the idea' of Miss Kilman which had become 'one of those spectres who stand astride us and suck up half our lifeblood, dominators and tyrants' (*MD*, 15). It emerges more fully at Clarissa's and Septimus's sight of the motor-car with its imagined 'greatness' within—whether 'Queen, Prince, or Prime Minister nobody knew' (*MD*, 19)—firmly associated with Conversion and War: the audience 'had heard the voice of authority; the spirit of religion was abroad with her eyes bandaged tight and her lips gaping wide' (*MD*, 17); 'strangers looked at each other and thought of the dead; of the flag; of Empire', and 'seemed ready to attend their Sovereign, if need be, to the cannon's mouth' (*MD*, 21). Septimus sees no 'mystery' but only 'horror' here and Clarissa suggests the novel's implicit historical reach by elegiacally imagining

> the ruins of time, when London is a grass-grown path and all those hurrying along the pavement this Wednesday morning are but bones with a few wedding rings mixed up in their dust and the gold stoppings of innumerable decayed teeth. (*MD*, 19)

Yet, in spite of her rejection of the 'idea' of Miss Kilman, Clarissa straightens a patriotic spine this Wednesday morning. Her more stringent Wednesday evening reaction against the death-dealing of Conversion results from the conjunction of two moments: that in which she first remembers having, in a moment of illumination like Marlow's 'flash of lightning', seen beneath Peter's assault the 'horror' of civilization's 'dominators', and that in which she rejoices at Septimus's preservation of what 'mattered' and sees the old woman opposite (*MD*, 202). The second moment is an inversion of the first; where the first has produced retreat, and 'the terror . . . this life, to be lived to the end' (*MD*, 203), the second conjoins to 'terror' Clarissa's original 'ecstasy' (*MD*, 39, 213). Where the first is, symbolically, death by domination, the second is life, the 'mystery' of 'here was one room; there another' (*MD*, 141).

Conrad concentrates no similar life-giving vision in his female characters. Marlow does characterize women as the guardians of civilization, but theirs is also a benighted world which demands a lie to maintain its 'saving illusion'. A saving illusion remains nonetheless an illusion, and the listeners on the deck of the *Nelly*, facing a 'luminous estuary' at the beginning of Marlow's narrative, cannot 'see' halfway through it, and at its end find themselves looking out into 'the heart of an immense darkness' (*HD*, 3, 28, 79). No ecstasy here; no birds sing, even in Greek.

Woolf extends Marlow's 'idea' of civilization and makes it positive by setting against his 'saving illusion' of women an authentic spiritual recognition by women: Sally, the old woman opposite, and the singing woman outside Regent's Park Tube Station all contribute to Clarissa's final 'ecstasy' and her recuperation from her discovery of the 'horror' beneath Peter's hostility. The singing woman provides the link between Sally and the old woman opposite and refutes Peter's dream judgement on the 'death' of Clarissa's soul. At first, this wretched figure seems to offer little to gladden the heart. Explicitly associated with Death in the comparison to 'a wind-beaten tree for ever barren of leaves', she calls to mind the woman whom the 'solitary traveller' of Peter's dream sees in the trees 'at the end of the ride' (*MD*, 63); she also recalls Clarissa's having felt 'herself suddenly shrivelled, aged, breast-less' before the 'blowing, flowering of the day' (*MD*, 35). Yet she remains the most cheering figure in the novel, for if she is Death, she is also Life, her voice 'an ancient spring spouting from the earth' (*MD*, 90), and, though unheeded by Peter, a vigorous reproach to his judgement about the 'death' of Clarissa's soul. As Life, she is explicitly connected with Clarissa through the narrator's description of the endurance of her song, a description which echoes Marlow's evocation of the swamps the Romans discovered on reaching Britain, and which recalls Clarissa's musings about the 'ruin of time'. Where Clarissa imagines London a 'grass-grown path', the narrator tells us this woman has been singing 'Through all the ages—when the pavement was grass, when it was swamp' and will not stop until 'the pageant of the universe would be over' (*MD*, 90–1). However 'battered', she persists to sing of her *lover*, or, applied to Clarissa, of Sally, not of Richard or of Peter. She sings, J. Hillis Miller has proved, of resurrection. Miller identifies the red asters, the speaking of love, the May day, the phrases ' "give me your hand and let me press it gently" ' and ' "if someone should see, what matter they?" ' (*MD*, 91) as paraphrase and translation of 'Aller Seelen', Richard Strauss's song for All Soul's Day when the dead rise to come, in Miller's reading, to Clarissa's party.[12] The narrator's description of the singing does indeed associate it with that resurrection imagery connected with spring and Persephone's return from the underworld: 'As the ancient song bubbled up . . . , still the earth seemed green and flowery; still, though it issued from so rude a mouth, a mere hole in the earth.' Then the imagery becomes orgasmic, the hole in the earth, a vagina: 'muddy too, matted with root fibres and tangled grasses, still the old bubbling burbling song, soaking through the knotted roots of infinite ages . . . streamed away in rivulets over the pavement . . . fertilising, leaving a damp stain' (*MD*, 91). What strikes one about the passage is that the fecundation is achieved without any male presence. In its effacement of the model of domination and submission, and in its orgasmic language, it re-evokes Clarissa's sexual response to Sally. The connection of resurrection and rebirth imagery with Clarissa's ideal of love denies Marlow's assessment of civilization as founded on the practical rapacity of men legitimized and made inescapably grotesque by women's love, based on 'saving illusion', for them.

For in *Mrs. Dalloway*, Woolf represents non-possessive love, whether particular and erotic (Clarissa and Sally), or whether general and the effect of mutual and respectful recognition of 'independence', as a genuine resurrection from 'horror', whether particular (Peter Walsh's domination) or general (the War). As Peter Walsh and the Smiths pass out of sight of the singing woman, the 'barren' tree flowers: 'Cheerfully, almost gaily, the invincible thread of sound wound up into the air like the smoke from a cottage chimney, winding up clean beech trees and issuing in a tuft of blue smoke among the topmost leaves' (*MD*, 92). This domestic and pastoral simile may complete the *Cymbeline* allusion that so many critics have noted in Clarissa's 'Fear no more the heat o' the sun', the dirge sung over an Imogen later to be resurrected from the dead. Cymbeline ends the play and the war of Romans and Britons with a call to peace:

> Laud we the gods;
> And let our crooked smokes climb to their nostrils
> From our blest altars. Publish we this peace
> To all our subjects. (V, v, 476–79)

68

I suspect the allusion here is filtered through *Ulysses* (1922), in which Stephen ends his discussion of Shakespeare with the first sentence of Cymbeline's speech, glossing it, 'Cease to strive'.[13] The old woman sings, for Clarissa and Sally, in opposition to strife, to the 'dominators', Peter included, of the novel; sings in opposition to Peter's dream of Clarissa, a figure of death at the top of trees; sings in opposition to the war which has 'smashed' Mr. Brewer's 'plaster cast of Ceres' (*MD*, 95).[14] She makes her final surrogate appearance, diminished and domesticated but nonetheless vital, in the old woman opposite.[15] Clarissa's vision of her emphasizes necessary separateness and 'privacy of the soul', even in love. That vision, joined to her understanding of Septimus's resistance to the 'dominators' through the 'gift' of his life, conjoins her original 'ecstasy' to 'terror' as Clarissa again stands before Peter. Her regained wholeness through the double recognition of Septimus and the old woman is no 'saving illusion' but genuine corrective to the 'horror' of dominion for, this time, Peter recognizes and respects their necessary independence: 'For there she was' (*MD*, 213).

Woolf's allusions to *Heart of Darkness* would not be so frequent or so precise again until she came to write *Between the Acts*, the only other of her novels in which war is so immediately present in the thoughts of the characters. In *To the Lighthouse*, the symbolism associated with *Heart of Darkness* is generalized beyond the confines of specific allusion. Mrs. Ramsay takes as 'her' stroke the third and longest stroke of the lighthouse beam but remains aware that it is preceded and succeeded by darkness. She also resumes the earlier image of darkness for the isolation of the individual self in her wedge-shaped core of darkness. The real darkness of this novel, of course, is 'Time Passes'. Snuffing the candle on his reading of Virgil, Mr. Carmichael effectively puts the light out on European civilization. With Europe sinking into war, an 'immense downpouring of darkness' effaces the house that sheltered poet and painter, philosopher and scientist, the woman who ordered the candles lit, and her children. As World War II approached, Woolf faced the spectre of domination even more directly in *The Years*, *Three Guineas*, and *Between the Acts*, all of which respond to the imminence of war.[16] In the first, the allusions to *Heart of*

Darkness are only two,[17] but they are attached, significantly, to Peggy and North, the generation of those who, like Septimus, will have to, willing or not, defend the Empire, and they are used in a pattern consistent with that established in *Mrs. Dalloway*. Listening to the sounds of London and the distant Thames traffic, Peggy associates 'the heart of darkness . . . the depths of night' with 'Death; or worse—tyranny; . . . the fall of civilization' (*Y*, 418) and sees no light on the plain. North feels himself 'in the middle of a jungle; in the heart of darkness' and wants to push through 'the briar-bush of human . . . wills' to the 'fruit, the fountain that's in all of us' (*Y*, 444). The fountain he has just opposed to the spirit of Conversion:

> For him a life modelled on the jet . . . , on the spring, of the hard leaping fountain; another life; a different life. Not halls and reverberating megaphones; not marching in step after leaders, in herds, groups, societies. . . . Not black shirts, green shirts, red shirts . . . but . . . the stream and the bubble— myself and the world together. (*Y*, 442–43)

The ideal, in face of the reality of contemporary events, is lightly mocked by Woolf who lets us see the image of bubbles arise from North's look into his champagne glass; nonetheless, the heart-of-darkness allusion remains contrasted to the life-giving spring associated with the singing woman in *Mrs. Dalloway*, and to the fecund fountain of Mrs. Ramsay with-standing the warlike scimitar of her husband's egotism. Transformed and pushed deep beneath the surface, that image becomes the lily pond of *Between the Acts*, a 'symbolic center' to which, Stephen Fox demonstrates, all the main characters and themes of the novel are directly or indirectly linked.[18]

North's rejection of 'black shirts, green shirts, red shirts' anticipates Woolf's forthright identification, in *Three Guineas*, of 'masculine' values with tyranny, and of Fascism with the conviction that it is 'the essence of manhood to fight' (*TG*, 326). There she also argued that the 'tyrannies and servilities' of the private relations of men and women necessarily become the 'tyrannies and servilities' of a war-mongering state (*TG*, 258). The equation provides part of the structure of *Between the Acts*, which opens and closes with quarrels between man and wife, in which Lucy suffers two blows to her faith struck by her brother and in which Isa imagines a girl beating the soldiers assaulting her over the head with a hammer. Cutting across the private violence twice come the bombers; underneath it runs the thread of conversational allusion to the War— '. . . If the worst should come—let's hope it won't—' (*BA*, 231). If the equation urges us to a political reading of *Between the Acts*, the framework of the novel connects that reading once again with *Heart of Darkness*. For *Between the Acts* not only moves forward and outward from quarrel to quarrel, it recedes from darkness to darkness. The first of its many parodic histories returns us yet again to the Romans: 'From an aeroplane . . . you could still see . . . the scars made by the Britons; by the Romans; by the Elizabethan manor house' (*BA*, 8). Its last moment places civilization in the context provided by Marlow, looking back to 'night before roads were made, or houses' (*BA*, 256). By a series of embeddings, the pageant of England's literary history viewed between scenes of violent emotion, the cultural context represented by the entire festival day, England between the wars,[19] and the novel itself become an interval, a 'flicker' before the dark redescends.

The pageant itself picks up the themes of Money, Dominion, and Conversion we find in *Heart of Darkness* and in other Woolf novels. Conrad's narrator remembers the 'men of whom the nation is proud, from Sir Francis Drake' (*HD*, 4); in La Trobe's pageant, England comes of age when Drake heaps his riches on his Queen's dock. The parody of literary history is affectionate, comic, elegiac; it also sharply observes that literature often chronicles the conquest of other people's money or spirit. Money, Dominion, and Conversion run through the pageant: the gramophone recalls the dispersed audience with a reminder that 'The King is in his counting house/ Counting out his money'; Lady H. H. catalogues the wealth she schemes to get; Budge wields his truncheon over 'thought and religion; drink; dress; manners; marriage too', and over 'the purity and security of all Her Majesty's minions; in all parts of her dominions' (*BA*, 189–90); Miss Eleanor Hardcastle longs 'to convert the heathen' (*BA*, 194).

Much has been written to prove that—in this novel in which Greek oracles and crepe soles find themselves contiguous—

71

the pageant unifies. But not only does the gramophone stop on *dis*(persal), not only do the audience and the family disperse, but the actors, the writer (in her own opinion at least) and the audience prove inadequate to its 'idea' of civilization. The actors' words are lost on the breeze and the audience mis-quotes or fails to remember almost every literary allusion in the novel. The megaphontic voice does indeed ask us to examine that civilization by comparing 'bomb droppers' with builders of view-destroying villas (*BA*, 218), by suggesting an equation between 'the great wall . . . civilization' and 'kindness to the cat' (*BA*, 219), the equation of *Three Guineas* between private and public life. But North Pargiter and *Three Guineas* have taught us to mistrust the megaphontic voice; the gramo-phone's affirmation is delayed by a 'hitch' in which, among other wrong records, 'Rule Britannia' turns up; beneath the music's 'measure' meant to produce from 'chaos and caco-phony' a final resolving and uniting, we still hear 'the warring battle-plumed warriors' (*BA*, 220–21); the audience dispersed, the *Heart of Darkness* becomes the novel's final metaphor.

In keeping with the affectionate mockery of the literature *Between the Acts* chronicles, it is Old Flimsy who introduces Marlow's historical reach. Her *Outline of History* is actually cribbed from G. M. Trevelyan's *History of England*, [20] but its evocation of the England of prehistoric swamp and forest has, by the end of the novel, strong Conradian overtones. Her reading of it frames the day, but it is only in the evening that, having stopped to 'voyage' into a picture and having lost her place in the book, she arrives at 'Prehistoric man' standing upright and raising the first 'great stones' (*BA*, 255) of the wall of civilization. Lucy's reading might seem to promise a new beginning for warring mankind but the prominent allusion to *Heart of Darkness*[21] two paragraphs further on makes that a dubious promise. As Giles turns out the light on the room, on the day, as he and Isa become dog fox and vixen, as the domestic quarrel with its inevitable relation to the global war begins 'in the heart of darkness' (*BA*, 256), we feel Marlow's running blaze of light that is civilization has gone out; we feel his ironic vision of a 'civilisation' founded on savagery and 'abomination' carried forward and given new vitality by the political and personal events of the novel.

But if this 'night that dwellers in caves had watched from some high place among rocks' (*BA*, 256) seems to promise only repetition of violence, the contrasts between Lucy and La Trobe make it ambiguous. Like Lucy, La Trobe voyages 'away from the shore' (*BA*, 246), but where Lucy reads the chronicles of the past and has read to the beginning of human conquest, La Trobe divines the present; her curtain rises on the scene Giles and Isa enact, on the words they speak. Set 'apart from her kind' (*BA*, 247) by lesbianism, art, and 'unladylike' behaviour, La Trobe fulfils those conditions by which, Woolf tells us in *Three Guineas*, women can 'help to prevent war': she is an 'outsider' free of 'unreal loyalties' (*TG*, 146). Lucy is told: in the beginning was prehistoric man, raising the first stones in civilization's walls. The reader of *Between the Acts* is not: the curtain rises on La Trobe's words but, for the reader, these remain in darkness and silence.

That darkness and silence is the culmination of Woolf's use of spring/fountain imagery to balance the 'horror' of domination. Before beginning her 'voyage' into the evening, Lucy stops by the lily pond. She identifies herself and her faith with the fish, not with the depths of the pond. No 'outsider' Lucy, reading her *Outline of History* and caressing her cross; for her it 'was always "my brother . . . my brother" who rose from the depths of her lily pool' (*BA*, 241). But La Trobe, voyaging into her new play, sinks beneath the surface of the pond: 'From the earth green waters seemed to rise over her' (*BA*, 246). That pond is used in the novel as 'image of the individual mind', as 'conscious thought'; its watery rings and lily pads are groups of people or couples; it symbolizes 'nature' and, in the legend about it, 'time and history'; it is 'life and death, love and fear'.[22] It is also a 'deep centre', a 'black heart' that is specifically literary in that it has a *story* connected with it. That story is restricted to the world of women and speaks silence. It tells of a lady drowned in a 'black cushion of mud' (*BA*, 54), but so little is known of her that she may be only the thigh-bone of a sheep. In this she resembles the portrait of the unknown lady that is a 'picture', unlike that of the ancestor that is a 'talk producer' (*BA*, 46). Not only the drowned Lady Ermyntrude, however, but her legend is silenced by being relegated to the world of women, dismissed by Bart's pleasantry, 'Kitchenmaids must have their drowned lady.' Among the group at the lunch table, only Mrs. Manresa can be like the kitchenmaid—'outsider' by sex and class—and believe, her belief a 'spring of feeling' bubbling 'up through her mud' (*BA*, 56–7). Only once again in the novel does a character become the depths of the lily pond; only for La Trobe does the mud become 'fertile', do words rise 'above the intolerably laden dumb oxen plodding through the mud. Words without meaning—wonderful words' (*BA*, 248). Words that, at the end of the novel, remain silent, outside the discourse of her neighbours in the pub whom war once again threatens. But words which, rising through the mud of the spring-fed lily pond, promising, perhaps, a new birth, evoke those other words 'with an absence of all human meaning' sung by the old woman with the 'voice of an ancient spring spouting from the earth' (*MD*, 90). Words that, however battered this Persephone in her return from the Underworld, however war-smashed the image of Ceres, speak to endurance and even a new fecundation and flowering.

La Trobe's 'scene', cast as it is in Conradian metaphor, makes Conrad's demands that we inquire into our 'civilisation', that we acknowledge its 'horror' and its 'heart of darkness'. Like Conrad, Woolf invokes female values to 'save' 'civilisation'. But where Marlow bows before the coercion of women's 'saving illusions', Woolf insists that no illusion can save, and demands female subversion, a conscious separateness from 'unreal loyalties' and the tyrannical 'darkness' of domination, in both private and public life. Ralph as well as Katharine, North as well as Peggy, Giles as well as Isa, are free to choose that freedom. But its image is no longer Conrad's Laura, locked in her house with her piano and her illusions, and with seven centuries of male poetics behind her. That image has yielded to the disreputable earth-goddess, to the visions communicated by the 'outsiders', Septimus and Miss La Trobe, to Clarissa's woman-centred moment of being, to the life 'modelled on the jet . . . , on the spring'. In that life, Woolf's transformation of *Heart of Darkness* implies, the words of the singing woman and of La Trobe, the legend of the lily pond, will be heard and will become meaningful, will lay new stones for a new wall of civilization.

'Heart of Darkness', Virginia Woolf and the Spectre of Domination

NOTES

1. 'Mr. Conrad's "Youth"', *T.L.S.*, 20 September 1917, 451. Volume III of the *Mrs. Dalloway* MS in the British Museum (MS. Adds. 51046) has, on the reverse of pp. 152–73, a draft of the 1924 Conrad obituary article, from which a reference to *Heart of Darkness* has been excised. Information from P. Clements.

2. Beverly Ann Schlack, *Continuing Presences: Virginia Woolf's Use of Literary Allusion* (1979), p. 143, notes that this and Clarissa's ' "Oh this horror!"' she said to herself' 'may be echoes of Conrad.'

3. Joseph Conrad, *Heart of Darkness*, ed. Robert Kimbrough (New York, 1971). This is the authoritative text of *Heart of Darkness*; all references to it have been checked for substantive difference from the Dent edition. Further references will be indicated in the essay by *HD*.

4. Jean M. Wyatt, '*Mrs. Dalloway*: Literary Allusion as Structural Metaphor', *P.M.L.A.*, 88 (1973), 440, identifies this allusion.

5. Stephen Trombley, *All that Summer She Was Mad: Virginia Woolf: Female Victim of Male Medicine* (1981), pp. 75–106.

6. Schlack, p. 63, discusses Clarissa's homosexuality in terms of the Othello allusion, and, pp. 69–71, discusses Septimus's homosexuality at length. See also Suzette A. Henke, 'Mrs. Dalloway: the Communion of Saints', *New Feminist Essays on Virginia Woolf*, ed. Jane Marcus (1981), pp. 134–36, on Clarissa and Septimus as 'repressed homosexual characters'.

7. The following critics have noted parts of this pattern: Dorothy Brewster, *Virginia Woolf's London* (1959), pp. 27–8; James Naremore, *The World Without a Self: Virginia Woolf and the Novel* (1973), p. 45; Avrom Fleishman, *Virginia Woolf: A Critical Reading* (1975), pp. 1–2; Alex Zwerdling, '*Between the Acts* and the Coming of War', *Novel*, 10 (1976–77), 224; Hermione Lee, *The Novels of Virginia Woolf* (1977), p. 34; T. E. Apter, *Virginia Woolf: A Study of her Novels* (1979), pp. 14–15; Rosemary Pitt, 'The Exploration of Self in Conrad's *Heart of Darkness* and Woolf's *The Voyage Out*', *Conradiana*, 10 (1978), 141–54, develops the only sustained argument about the parallels.

8. Pitt, pp. 141, 146.

9. Madeline Moore, 'Some Female Versions of Pastoral: *The Voyage Out* and Matriarchal Mythologies', *New Feminist Essays on Virginia Woolf*, p. 99, notes of this scene that, 'if read as Rachel's hallucination, the love object is as much Helen as it is Hewet', and that Helen and Terence are in 'competition for Rachel'. See also Mitchell A. Leaska, 'The Death of Rachel Vinrace', *Bulletin of Research in the Humanities*, 82 (1979), 331.

10. Fleishman draws attention to the phrase 'heart of darkness': 'it points to the ultimate loneliness that is aligned with the imagery of imagination and night throughout the novel' (p. 44).

11. Fleishman identifies the allusion to Conrad in Rezia's analogy (p. 2).

12. J. Hillis Miller, 'Virginia Woolf's All Souls' Day: The Omniscient Narrator in *Mrs. Dalloway*', *The Shaken Realist: Essays in Modern Literature in Honor of Frederick J. Hoffman*, ed. Melvin J. Friedman and John B.

Vickery (Baton Rouge, 1970), p. 115. Miller repeats the argument in his *Fiction and Repetition: Seven English Novels* (1982), 189–91. Henke, p. 146, argues from Miller's article that Clarissa returns to her party 'ready to offer her guests the illumination that will transfigure the gathering into a beatified communion of saints' (p. 144). I would not, myself, go so far for either Clarissa or her guests.

13. James Joyce, *Ulysses* (New York, 1961), p. 218.
14. Allen McLaurin, *Virginia Woolf: The Echoes Enslaved* (1973), p. 156, draws attention to the allusion to Ceres; Schlack analyses the Ceres connections in the novel at some length, particularly in terms of the goddess as a 'shattered-by-force, benevolent female deity' (pp. 52–3).
15. Henke sees this woman as 'emblematic of the feminine life-force that endures and creates' (p. 144).
16. The articles collected in a Virginia Woolf issue of the *Bulletin of the New York Public Library*, 80 (1977), read *The Years* as Woolf's response to politics in the 1930s. Zwerdling also reads the novel in terms of the war, though not from a feminist point of view.
17. These allusions have been previously identified by Fleishman (pp. 195, 197).
18. This argument is made by Stephen D. Fox, 'The Fish Pond as Symbolic Center in *Between the Acts*', *Modern Fiction Studies*, 18 (1972), 467–73.
19. Zwerdling, p. 222.
20. Nora Eisenberg, 'Virginia Woolf's Last Words on Words: *Between the Acts* and "Anon" ', *New Feminist Essays on Virginia Woolf*, annotates Woolf's adaptation of Trevelyan (p. 265).
21. The allusion has been noted by the following critics: Brewster, p. 28; Fleishman, pp. 195, 218; Howard Harper, *Between Language and Silence* (1982), p. 316; Jean Wyatt, 'Art and Allusion in *Between the Acts*', *Mosaic*, 11 (1978), 100; Zwerdling, p. 224.
22. The list is Fox's (pp. 469–72).

4

Our Silent Life:*
Virginia Woolf and
T. S. Eliot

by LYNDALL GORDON

'Come to lunch', Virginia Woolf invited her brother-in-law, Clive Bell. 'Eliot will be there in a four-piece suit.'[1] It was easy to caricature Eliot's respectable façade. Later, when she knew him better, she was more searching. 'How he suffers!' she noted when he came to tea on 1 February 1935.

> Yes: I felt my accursed gift of sympathy rising. . . . Suddenly T. spoke with a genuine cry of feeling. About immortality . . . he revealed his passion, as he seldom does. A religious soul: an unhappy man: a lonely very sensitive man, all wrapt up in fibres of self torture, doubt, conceit, desire for warmth & intimacy. And I'm very fond of him—like him in some of my reserves & subterfuges. (iv, 277)

In 1940 the diary again points through Eliot's 'bronze mask' to the tormented martyr: 'an inhibited, nerve-drawn dropped face—as if hung on a scaffold of heavy private brooding.'[2]

In these quick sketches, Virginia Woolf circles the essence of Eliot. Both these writers had definite ideas about the hidden essence and structure of lives which might serve, in turn, as

---

*Title from 'Hours in a Library' (*E*, ii, 37). A shortened version of 'Our Silent Life' appears as 'A Writer's Life' in *Virginia Woolf: A Centenary Perspective*, ed. Eric Warner.

guidelines for biographic studies of themselves. This kind of study would be, ideally, complementary to standard biography in that it would concentrate on the invisible moments of a writer's life that terminate in the work. Emerson said: 'The life of a great artist is always thus inward, a life of no events.'[3] I shall look at ideas for an 'inward' life in the novels of Virginia Woolf, glancing at similar ideas in Eliot, and then suggest the problems and rewards of a more imaginative approach to critical biography.

The novels of Virginia Woolf search out what she called the 'caves' of character like the beam of the lighthouse when it strikes the unknown aspect of Mrs. Ramsay. In the same way, at dinner, Mrs. Ramsay's eyes go round the table, exploring, without effort, the thoughts and feelings of her guests 'like a light stealing under water so that . . . the reeds in it and the minnows balancing themselves, and the sudden silent trout are all lit up hanging, trembling' (*TL*, 165). Her eyebeam lights up a hidden self wrapped in the artifice of manners. It is an exercise of that gift to see through all lies which the beam of the lighthouse had briefly exposed. The biographer behind her novel, the artist behind her easel, reproduce the action of the lighthouse. Lily Briscoe's painting of Mrs. Ramsay searches out the source of her authority. Seeking what is screened by the Victorian mother's arresting beauty, she pares it away and paints her as a wedge shape of darkness. Later, Virginia Woolf said that the painter Walter Sickert was the best of biographers for 'when he sits a man or woman down in front of him he sees the whole of the life that has been lived to make that face. . . . None of our biographers make such complete and flawless statements' (*E*, ii, 236).

Virginia Woolf's notion of portraiture is well-tried, but her theory of the form of biography has not yet been grasped, much less used. In 'A Vanished Generation', a 1908 review of the letters of the Knox family in the first half of the nineteenth century, she argued that 'a distinct shape' might be brought out of such material, but biographers, she predicted, would be too timid. 'To arrange . . . is considered unnecessary, or perhaps disrespectful.'[4] In a review of a biography of Maria Edgeworth, she complained of excess detail: 'turbans and chariots with nothing inside them' (*BP*, 156). Her own biographic essays on the eccentric traveller, Hester Stanhope, and on the girlhood of Queen Elizabeth, may read like spontaneous, idle shots at motives, conduct and phases in a lifespan that may seem from a historical point of view quite peripheral, but she was examining states of mind so muted that they almost defied expression. She fastened on the sources of action—the hidden moments and obscure formative experiences—and treated actions as mere consequence.

In 1909 Virginia Stephen wrote a fictional review of a biography of an imaginary Victorian writer, Miss Willat.[5] The unpublished 'Memoirs of a Novelist' provided a theoretical base for later experiments in fiction. It fulfilled her wish 'to write a very subtle work on the proper writing of lives. . . . It comes over me that I know nothing of the art; but blunder in a rash way after motive, and human character' (*L*, i, 325).

Miss Willatt, Virginia Stephen imagines, was a writer who died in 1884. Her books now lie on the topmost shelves of seaside libraries. One must take a ladder to reach them and a cloth to wipe them off. Virginia Stephen deliberately picks an unpromising subject, a not very appealing woman whose talents were less than minor. (Miss Willatt thought it indecent to describe what she knew, her family, so 'invented Arabian lovers and set them on the banks of the Orinoco.') Miss Willatt so fits the stereotype of the silly spinster that she makes the greatest possible demands on her biographer's powers of discernment.

Her fictitious biographer, Miss Linsett, has no powers of discernment. She dwells sentimentally on the balls of the 1840s, not realizing that a large, awkward creature like Miss Willatt would have wished to hide her body. Miss Linsett obscures her subject with other contemporary platitudes: tender regrets at the death of her father. Virginia Stephen (as fictitious reviewer) dismisses this twitter:

> Happily there are signs that Miss Willatt was not what she seemed. They creep out in the notes, in her letters, and most clearly in her portraits. The sight of that large selfish face, with the capable forehead and the surly but intelligent eyes, discredits all the platitudes on the opposite page; she looks quite capable of having deceived Miss Linsett.
>
> When her father died (she had always disliked him) her spirits rose. . . .

Miss Linsett makes the father's death in 1855 the end to one chapter and Miss Willatt's removal to London the beginning of the next. In other words, the biographer's plan depends, whenever possible, 'upon changes of address', which confirms the reviewer's suspicion that she 'had no other guide to Miss Willatt's character'. What Miss Linsett misses is the decisive moment in the life: Miss Willatt's sudden decision, at 36, to give up the sham of philanthropy for writing.

Miss Willatt's work among the poor provokes long accounts of charitable societies. Digression is, again, the result of a biographer's inability to discover what is interesting about a writer's life which is without public importance or historic action. Other typical fillers are the pedigree (Miss Linsett takes thirty-six pages over the history of the family, 'a way of marking time during those chill early pages') and the slow approach to the grave. Here, once more, the narrative slackens to a funeral pace. Miss Linsett lingers with relish over the excruciating details of her subject's last illness and leaves her, in the end, buried in extraneous facts.

With this early satire on literary biography, Virginia Stephen bounced herself away from a stale tradition in much the same way as Jane Austen's early satire, 'Love and Friendship', cuts free from stale sentiment. 'Memoirs of a Novelist' warns in particular against excessive detail which could blur crucial moments and, above all, against the mental slot. In the same year (1909), reviewing the Carlyles' love letters, Virginia Stephen repeats this warning: 'the more we see the less we can label' and again, 'the further we read the less we trust to definition.'[6] In 'Memoirs', the attentive reviewer can glimpse a live woman—flawed, ambitious, restless and intransigent— but cannot rescue the rest of Miss Willatt's story, for such women, in the past, 'have been rolled into the earth irrecoverably'. Here, the young Virginia Stephen is circling the potential subject on which she was to cast the lighthouse beam of her great novels: the obscure, middle-aged woman.

More or less at the same time, Virginia Woolf and T. S. Eliot began to use silence to light up the more elusive corners of experience ('the heart of light, the silence'). In *The Voyage Out* the unfledged novelist, Terence Hewet, wants ' "to write a novel about Silence . . . the things people don't say. But the difficulty is immense" ' (262). In 'Silence', an unpublished poem dated June 1910, Eliot describes how, while walking one day in noisy city streets, he sees them shrink and divide.[7] His everyday preoccupations, his past, all the claims of the future are wiped out by a commanding silence. 'Silence' is Eliot's first and perhaps most lucid description of the timeless moment. He concludes that there is nothing else beside it.

Silence, in both cases, suggests experience where language fails. In Eliot, there is the untranslatable silence of religious vision. In his early poetry, Eliot directs the reader to it with a blank space following 'some infinitely gentle/ Infinitely suffering thing' or *'Et O ces voix d'enfants, chantant dans la coupole!'* or 'Inexplicable splendour of Ionian white and gold' or the beating silence after the thunderous 'DA'. At the same time, this experience is so private and ultimately incommunicable that Eliot conceals it with the distracting chatter of literary allusions and almost consents to a cacophony of voices which break up an experience which is, anyway, rare and evanescent. Eliot injects silence so rudely that he awakens the reader to reciprocal effort. His tactic comes, I think, from an American tradition of sermon and confession which creates, anew, the reader's consciousness. The reader looks into the dots, dashes and spaces of Whitman, Dickinson and Eliot for an image of himself, and the spaces call out potentialities and powers of judgement he has never known. Eliot's silence is so painfully abrupt that it brings us to judgement. We are forced to recognize flesh as ridiculous or loathsome, if possible to be discarded. In contrast, what we see in Virginia Woolf's silence is far less pre-determined. Her silence simply circles certain characters—Rachel, Jacob, Mrs. Dalloway—and then she recedes softly, leaving 'a zone of silence' to reverberate with unstated suggestion.

In Virginia Woolf's case, silence is often used to register what is muted in women. 'I have the feelings of a woman but I have only the language of men', she quoted in a 1920 review.[8] From *The Voyage Out* on, she sees that the real future of women lies less in immediate public rights than in their hidden views, as yet unfathomed. In 1930, in an introductory letter to the writings of the working-class members of the Co-operative Women's Guild, Virginia Woolf said: 'These voices are beginning only

81

now to emerge from silence into half-articulate speech. These lives are still half-hidden in profound obscurity' (*E*, iv, 148).

George Eliot calls us to attend to 'that roar which lies on the other side of silence'. Where George Eliot used 'the secret of deep human sympathy'[9] to unlock the lives of the obscure, Virginia Woolf followed them with a slow-paced silence, pausing whenever she sensed an unvoiced intent. In *The Voyage Out*, Rachel replies to the questions of her fiancé, the potential novelist, about the nature of women with the non-verbal virtuosity of her music. 'Rachel said nothing. Up and up the steep spiral of a very late Beethoven sonata she climbed. . . . It seemed to be reserved for a later generation to discuss [the secrets of her sex] philosophically' (357). *The Voyage Out* offsets the groping novelist and the inarticulate Rachel against an articulate, sharply-marked English community. Rachel, still in the making, knocks against an ex-M.P., a don, a doctor with the crust of definition upon them.

Rachel's elusiveness could be exasperating—after all, it may signify nothing but vagueness—but her author took this risk in order to show how women must fit their experience, with its infinite subtleties, into man-made language. Whatever that language cannot express will float off, undefined. Rachel presents the same sort of challenge as Fanny Price and, in both cases, the writer almost defeats her purpose. Austen and Woolf wish to exhibit a woman of intrinsic stature who is likely to be overlooked. Rachel invites ready-made categories: she appears passive, malleable and pitifully lacking in the animation we expect from heroines. She does not look like a heroine. Though she has large, enquiring eyes, her face lacks colour and 'definite' outline. Virginia Woolf dared to make her faceless, inarticulate, incompetent and, except for her music, inactive to the point of indolence. She is not merely unformed; she is the epitome of indefiniteness.

Rachel seems blurred because she is fixed in a social structure that is unreal to her, 'reality dwelling in what one saw and felt, but did not talk about' (35). Her intelligence stirs but cannot risk exposure. She lurks obscurely beneath the sea. Her affinity is for imagined monsters of the deep who 'would explode if you brought them to the surface . . . scattering entrails to the winds' (18). In Rachel, Virginia Woolf created a character easily defaced, therefore faceless and, because we cannot *see* her, we can hear her breathe, and faintly, far off, pick up her elusive note.

As James Joyce presented the need for forging the uncreated conscience of his oppressed Irish race, so Virginia Woolf set out to generate an uncreated model of womanhood. Both perceived a stronghold guarded by language and that it is with language that it must be opposed. The Irish orator in *Ulysses* gives an exemplum of the Jews as a tribe of nomad herdsmen subject to Egypt. Only by distancing himself from the code of the dominant civilization was it possible for Moses to come down from Sinai with a new code *'graven in the language of the outlaw'*.[10]

Virginia Woolf's model originated with her mother, but her mother purified not only of the dramatic plot of her outward life and not only of the passing platitudes of Victorian womanhood but purified of the artifice of language itself. Lily, alone with Mrs. Ramsay in the dark bedroom, 'imagined how in the chambers of the mind and heart of the woman . . . were . . . tablets bearing sacred inscriptions, which if one could spell them out would teach one everything, but they would never be . . . made public.' Biographer and artist in Lily unite to ask: 'What art was there, known to love or cunning, by which one pressed through into those secret chambers?' (*TL*, 82).

A biographic problem latent in the portraits of Rachel Vinrace and Mrs. Ramsay is given explicit formulation in *Jacob's Room*. This book has something in common with 'Memoirs of a Novelist', which was intended as the first in a series of fictional biographies. Both works are less concerned with Miss Willatt or Jacob than with their biographers' problem: if the invisible life is ultimately unknowable, is not biography pointless, its failure inevitable?

All through *Jacob's Room*, his biographer talks directly to the reader. We two push ourselves forward—busy, agog, distractable—while our subject slips out of sight. The would-be biographer is 'vibrating . . . at the mouth of the cavern of mystery, endowing Jacob Flanders with all sorts of qualities he had not at all . . .; what remains is mostly a matter of guesswork. Yet over him we hang vibrating' (72). The biographic obsession is comic in its futility. The biographer confides the struggle to do an imaginative portrait from scraps of memory, fragmentary reports of friends, books fingered, scenes visited by Jacob. At moments of acute frustration, when the biographer finds Jacob's room empty, its occupant gone, in other words ungraspable, the reader is invited to share in his creation.

It is to be a modernist portrait. This much the biographer directs. We are not to draw Jacob's features but to give him a significant form, as people who had loved him had built an image, like Fanny Elmer who recognized him in the statue of Ulysses in the British Museum. The reader is given little help. The biographer supplies only the barest outlines: Jacob spent his childhood at Scarborough; he was educated at Cambridge; he worshipped the Greeks; he smoked a pipe, sat by fires, exchanged small talk. He seems to have the qualities of a hero: the way people of all backgrounds are drawn to him for no particular reason suggests a leader in the making. His blend of simple-heartedness and worldliness promise responsible action. But what exactly Jacob was to be remains a mystery. The deliberately fragmented narrative with its curt sentences, its tantalizing glimpses—Jacob lying on his back in Greece—force the reader to share in the biographer's effort and failure. What is so impressive is this honesty about failure. As 'Memoirs of a Novelist' warned against the usual mental slots, so Jacob's biographer refuses to content herself with the usual stories, the Tom Jones story, say, of the young man who couples with the plausible flirt, Florinda, or becomes besotted with an idle married woman on tour. Jacob does perform the Tom Jones routine and others, but we sense that whatever is silently furled within him would have bypassed banality with the passing of youth. The biographer, following this track or another, waits with faithful, often hopeless patience for his telling biographic moment.

Jacob's Room questions whether, if a subject is unknowable, it is not then logical to risk the act of imagination that would give to the subject a coherent form. At the same time, a biographer must be truthful enough to exhibit the broken areas, the silent spaces. At the Parthenon, Jacob gazes at marble figures whose backs were left unfinished. On this model, Virginia Woolf devised a kind of biography which refused deceptive fullness of

Our Silent Life: Virginia Woolf and T. S. Eliot

definition. This she hoped would give it the formal restraints of a suggestive art.

Virginia Woolf thought biography should leave something to the imagination. When she composes her portrait of her mother in *To the Lighthouse* she treats external biographic facts as mere punctuation (Mrs. Ramsay does die, most disconcertingly, in brackets) and strikes boldly for invisible states of mind that uphold action. She asked, first, what was her mother to herself? It was an inspired stroke to let the beam of the lighthouse catch her, in a rare moment, alone. The scene is deliberately understated, unanalysed, a model of biographic tact. Secondly, Virginia Woolf asked what was the private scene of her parent's marriage? Again, imagination had to take her beyond the child's memory.

As the portrait progressed she feared it was too made up and was relieved when her sister confirmed its accuracy when the book came out in May 1927. She wrote to Vanessa Bell:

> I'm in a terrible state of pleasure that you should think Mrs. Ramsay so like mother. At the same time, it is a psychological mystery why she should be: how a child could know about her; except that she has always haunted me. (*L*, iii, 383)

As silence circled the untried spaces of character, so Virginia Woolf plotted the hidden shape of the lifespan. Both she and Eliot marked off the lifespan by what Eliot called 'essential moments' and Virginia Woolf, 'moments of being'. Eliot was not so concerned with public circumstance as with what he called 'unattended moments'. At the end of *The Waste Land* he says that whatever is worth recording in a life will not be found in wills or obituaries, in the legal papers presided over by the lean solicitor or even in well-intentioned biography, the webs woven over the career by the 'beneficent spider'. The whole force of the career is contained in

> The awful daring of a moment's surrender
> . . . . .
> By this, and this only, we have existed.

To find these moments, the biographer must pare away the trivia of the external life for, said Eliot, in *The Dry Salvages*: 'our

85

own past is covered by the currents of action.' In the first draft of *Little Gidding*, II, he uncovers the essential moments of his own history: the agonized all-night vigils in Paris in 1911 and the emotional quickening that came to him as a young man as he sailed off the coast of Cape Ann:

> Remember rather the essential moments
> > That were the times of birth and death and change
> > The agony and the solitary vigil.
> . . . . .
> The fresh new season's rope, the smell of varnish
> > On the clean oar, the drying of the sails,
> Such things as seem of least and most importance.
> So, as you circumscribe this dreary round,
> > Shall your life pass from you. . . .[11]

Virginia Woolf for her part considered that 'there are only a few essential hours of life.' She, too, thought the biographer might shed 'the regimented unreal life' to fasten on the definitive moments. For Eliot, these moments are when, rarely, he loses himself in a religious vision. They are transforming moments, invitations to a new life. For Virginia Woolf, in contrast, the definitive moments look back into the past. 'If life has a base that it stands upon' it is a memory. Her life as a writer was based on two persistent memories: the north Cornwall shore and her unconventional Victorian parents.

Early one morning, lying in the nursery of her family's summer home at St. Ives, she heard 'the waves breaking, one, two, one, two . . . behind a yellow blind' and knew, she said, 'the purest ecstasy I can conceive' (*MB*, 64–5). Years later, she wanted the waves' rhythm to sound all through *To the Lighthouse* and *The Waves*. Is there a link between the moment in the nursery and the commanding intuition of her maturity that the rhythm of human processes, if attended to without the interference of timetables, will have something in common with the wavelike rhythms of the physical universe, waves of sound, light, the sea? That one, two, rise and crash came to represent, certainly, the recurring creative possibilities of the lifespan and its finality.

The other crucial memory, of her parents, provoked endless

analysis. There is a photograph of Julia Stephen reading with her younger children in about 1894. The photograph breathes the perfect stillness of the children's absorption. More than thirty years later there is a similar scene in *To the Lighthouse*. As the Victorian mother reads aloud, she sees a son's eyes darken, sees a daughter drawn by an imaginative word, and concludes 'they were happier now than they would ever be again' (94). The family dead haunted Virginia Woolf's imagination. 'The ghosts', she wrote in her diary at the age of 50, 'change so oddly in my mind; like people who live, & are changed by what one hears of them' (iv, 83). With these changes in understanding came the need to compose their portraits in her fictions. She said more than once that her books were not exactly novels; they were fictional elegies.

For Virginia Woolf the essential hours were concentrated in early childhood, but there were later turning points: in 1905, when, quite by chance, she may have come upon a form for the modern novel while tramping in Cornwall; in 1907–8, when she discovered the creative uses of autobiography; in 1926, when she spied 'the fin' of a submerged life that she must pursue and proclaim in its entirety in *The Waves*; and, finally, the 'soul's change' of 1932 when she resolved to speak out for her sex. Such crucial points, she noted in her diary, no biographer could guess from external events. Luckily, her bent was so continually autobiographic that the array of recently published works and the unpublished papers, taken together with the established works, do give an account of the hidden moments on which her life turned. These allow us to see Virginia Woolf not so much as she appeared to others, to her family and Bloomsbury, but as she appeared to herself.

Virginia Woolf demonstrates how to do such a life in *The Waves*. There she follows six lives simultaneously from childhood to maturity. The six lives rise on the crest of the moments with an imaginative residue: the moment of waking in the nursery, the sponge of sensation, the farewell for Percival, the blue madonna in the National Gallery, the sense of blending as one generation or one species at Hampton Court. The art of living lay in the recognition of these moments which are not the preserve of the powerful, the glamorous or the gifted but are common to all lives. The six friends fasten on crucial moments as they happen and seal them in memory. Bernard, reviewing these lives, isolates this skill of creative memory, at its peak in childhood and not measurable by any of the usual criteria of education. The six cultivated this skill outside the schoolroom, in garden or field. What made these six lives distinctive, though, was that they did not force their internal rhythms to coincide with set biographic schemes of marriage and career. Nature's masterplan rolled out with ease. Bernard's multiple-biography is original because he decides that all the Victorian stories of birth, school, marriage and death simply are not true, that lives turn on 'moments of humiliation and triumph' that occur now and then, but rarely at times of official crisis or celebration (169). Compared with this the set design of standard biography is 'a convenience, a lie' because its 'military progress' from pedigree to grave passes over the half-finished sentences and half-discernible acts on which the real life turns (181).

Bernard trusts that the lines of six lives will be coherent if he cuts out what Virginia Woolf called, in her private shorthand, 'waste' (by which she meant the appointment book, official honours and doings). Bernard assumes that a classic shape lies buried in this clutter of event. Four years later, Eliot was to write the same theory into *Burnt Norton*. He, too, used the word 'waste' for the empty stretches of the lifespan that are not worth recording in the light of a sublime moment:

> Ridiculous the waste sad time
> Stretching before and after.

Eliot was so single-minded that his life and work redefine, repeatedly, the same drama, the private search for salvation. To him, 'the life of a man of genius, viewed in relation to his writing, comes to take a pattern of inevitability, and even his disabilities will seem to have stood him in good stead.'[12] If we apply Eliot's theory to his own life, its inner coherence is obvious. His life was modelled on the set pattern of lives of saints and martyrs so that if we follow, say, his relations with women, it is curious to see how inexorably they were fed into the religious drama. Emily Hale prompted the sublime moments; Vivienne Haigh-Wood, the sense of sin and guilt, and provided, throughout that first marriage, the living martyrdom.

Later, sensible, efficient Mary Trevelyan propped Eliot's life in the '40s and early '50s. For her, their friendship was a commitment, for Eliot quite peripheral. His passion for immortality was so commanding that it allowed him to reject each of these women with a ruthless firmness that shattered their lives.

The shape of Eliot's life is one of paring down, concentration. The shape of Virginia Woolf's life is less easy to see because its pattern is inclusive. She did not drop life for art so quickly as the cerebral young man of 'La Figlia che Piange'. Her diary spurts all the time, bathing her with experience. Her proximity to life and her responsiveness is so unflagging that she had no need, like Yeats, to generate feeling through the actor's mask or, like Eliot, to break, agonizingly, through the crust of comfortable deadness. In Eliot's case, so much had to be discarded to make his life conform to the pattern of the religious life. Virginia Woolf sought, on the other hand, a pattern that could admit 'everything', every stage of the life-span with its plethora of moments. The clue to the governing pattern of her career may lie in *The Waves*. There, she divided the lifespan into stages which, her notes for the book suggest, would prove 'that there are waves . . . by wh. life is marked; a rounding off, wh. has nothing to do with events. A natural finishing.'[13] This may be the pattern of her creative life: a wave ridden to its crest, then sometimes a trough, but always another wave rising far out. She allowed each successive wave to break the previous mould: a poem-novel was followed by an essay-novel which was followed by a drama-novel.

Bernard wishes, he tells the reader, 'to give you my life' (169). It is a composed life like those of his five friends. However unconventional the theory in *The Waves*—the concentration of moments, the refusal of 'waste', the repetition of a coherent pattern—the compositional principle remains intact. Bernard restores meaning to the often humdrum process of living. His method ensures that the weight of his multiple-biography should fall on the constructive moments on which effective lives turn. It also ensures attention to the destructive moments when effort, and maybe life itself, seems pointless. For Virginia Woolf to rise from her own trough (when, engulfed in depression, she spied 'the fin'), she had to ask, through her six samples, what resources do we have against the biological or psychological minimums of existence?

In middle age, Bernard sank to his lowest point. The great wave of renewed energy that followed came through ordinary acts of imaginative sympathy that flowered in the biographic masterpiece of Bernard's old age. His creative tide rises to flood the caves of memory as he shapes figure after figure. Working from the givens of nature—the limpet clinging to a rock, the beast stamping, the nymph of the fountain—he retells memories until they take their final set. Here is another compositional principle, analagous to the statue image in *Jacob's Room*: under Bernard's expert touch, the six friends harden as statues who can outlive their time. He fixes their lives, at their very moment of pulsation, like Yeats's marbles of the dancing floor.

A third compositional principle follows from the early tactic of silence. Bernard is an accomplished phrase-maker but, as he grows older, he begins to distrust sentences that come down with all their feet on the ground because, he believes, conclusiveness falsifies truth. The reader must learn to live with 'the fin', as Virginia Woolf did, with what is unknown or barely seen. In this way, the six friends attend to one another's unvoiced intent: they—and since they comprise our species, *we*—are natural biographers and, as we exist in community, we exist by composing others.

In *Orlando*, Virginia Woolf said in her most extravagant manner: 'every secret of a writer's soul, every experience of his life, every quality of his mind is written large in his works' (189–90). Obviously, this cannot apply to all writers—Shakespeare and Austen are truly invisible—but it certainly applies to the autobiographical writer, so that would seem almost perverse for critical biography, where the centre of interest lies in the private events that are the sources of creativity, to imitate the schema of historical or political biography where the main interest lies in public action.

More is known about Virginia Woolf's own life than about that of almost any writer. Quentin Bell's biography gives a complete and candid record of her life and an immediate sense of what it was like to know Virginia Woolf day by day. Yet, Virginia Woolf has remained elusive and perhaps must always remain so. She told Ethel Smyth in 1938 that she was 'trained to silence'. In an unpublished piece she said: 'There is a silence in life, a perpetual deposit of experience for which action provides no proper outlet and our words no fit expression.'[14] For all the verbal freedom and wit with which she presided over the intellectual London of her day, she reserved, I think, a side of herself for her novels alone. The private voice of the novels is so different from the public voices of the letters, the journalism and the feminist tracts that it suggests an invisible life, parallel to but distinct from her public career. This invisible life we shall never wholly know but we can glimpse it, now and again, in the ardent letters exchanged with her husband and in the diary, and it appears very strongly in the autobiographical pieces and the novels. The death of Rachel in *The Voyage Out* and the mental solitude of Septimus Warren Smith in *Mrs. Dalloway* and of Rhoda in *The Waves* are Virginia Woolf's backward, transforming looks at her own muted side, potentially creative, potentially distorted and always threatened with extinction. To follow the history of Virginia Woolf's muted self is to follow the more muted characters in her novels.

But can we legitimately read back from the work to the life? 'Somewhere, everywhere,' said Virginia Woolf, 'now hidden, now apparent in whatever is written down is the form of a human being.'[15] To detect this is a very delicate undertaking. Eliot forbade it in 'Tradition and the Individual Talent' (1919) where he argued the writer's separation from the work. But this celebrated position he contradicted in other essays. In 'Ben Jonson' (also 1919) he declared that 'the creation of a work of art . . . consists in the process of transfusion of the personality, or, in a deeper sense, the life, of the author into the character.' In 'John Ford' (1932) he admitted that the work alone would 'give the pattern . . . of the personal emotion, the personal drama and struggle, which no biography, however full and intimate, could give us'.[16]

No biography? Yet there is a composed kind of biography, implied throughout Eliot and Woolf, that would bring us closer than any other to the sources of creativity. This writer's life would have to rock back and forth between the life and the work, coming to rest always on the work. The sequence would depend not primarily on chronology but on the sources of creativity as they emerge one after another so as to focus at all times on the development of an artist. We must look, first, at Virginia Woolf's parents as they were and then at the way she remembered them in *To the Lighthouse*, seen close up in their own time, then, after a passage of years, from the mature perspective of a modern artist. The play of actual and composed character, of actual and composed event, continues in the second stage, the long twenty-year apprenticeship. The young writer's mental solitude, her odd education and recurring illness offset a young woman's journey towards knowledge and death in *The Voyage Out*.

Then, in the third stage, Virginia Woolf's mature efforts to compose her life—her waves of renewed experiment—are balanced by the formal diagram of the lifespan in *The Waves*. Virginia Woolf composed her life as deliberately as she composed her work. She presents a case of a writer whose life is not merely a background but is a major source for her work. She turned her early losses, her memories and moments of bliss into art which, at the same time, casts its perspective on her life.

Although the autobiographical writer offers to the biographer the decided advantage of entrée to the silent life, he or she might also present a special problem. Writers who expose themselves, as do T. S. Eliot and Virginia Woolf, will inevitably erect protective façades. These the biographer will have to uncover with sympathetic caution. Eliot is particularly elusive for his façades invade, nearly take over his poems. In her letters, Virginia Woolf is a chameleon, willing to take on the colours of innumerable correspondents. The writer, again, lurks behind this dramatic versatility.

If we accept Eliot's and Woolf's premise that there is no formula for biography, each life will then offer a unique challenge. In Eliot's case, where there is the single trajectory of religious impulse, the biographer must ask where did that impulse come from and when did it quicken? In a career in which every poem redefines the position won in the previous poem, every fragment of manuscript must be dated with scholarly precision. The enormous hoard of buried criticism, say all the obscure reviews of 1921, the year he composed *The Waste Land*, must be fitted into place beside the poetry. In short, the challenge here is the quite practical one of chronology.

The special problem in Virginia Woolf's case lies in her womanhood and requires some imagination. For the greater the woman, the less possible it is to slot her feelings, thoughts and relationships into fixed categories. Although she called herself 'mad', the term 'madness' is hopelessly inadequate; so, too, the notion of frigidity.

Many writers, like Eliot, have feared curiosity and done all they could to prevent a biography. The right relation to a subject lies in finding a balance between curiosity and respect, surrender and judgement. Rampant curiosity leads to demeaning and pointless gossip. At one point the notion that Eliot had homosexual leanings gained some currency, based on a tissue of supposition. So far, there is not a shred of real evidence. On the contrary, an unpublished letter from Eliot to Conrad Aiken from London at the end of 1914 confessed quite opposite inclinations. On the other hand, if curiosity is subdued by excessive detachment, a biography will be an empty edifice of facts, equally pointless. Montaigne summed up the problem perfectly:

> A sound intellect will refuse to judge men simply by their outward actions; we must probe the inside and discover what springs set men in motion. But since this is an arduous and hazardous undertaking, I wish fewer people would meddle with it.[17]

If the biographer takes imaginative risks, he must test his findings over years to be sure of their accuracy. But, slow and hazardous as it would be, no kind of biography is more exciting, for no biography could bring one closer to the creative moment.

'I perceive', Virginia Woolf said in the second draft of *The Waves*, 'that the art of biography is still in its infancy or more properly speaking has yet to be born.'[18] What kind of book, she had asked as early as 1916, 'will stand up and speak with other ages about our age when we lie prone and silent'? And she hinted that autobiographic writers of her own time were creating almost a fresh branch of literature, a new form for the private drama, that lay yet hidden in the popular foam of triviality.[19] T. S. Eliot and Virginia Woolf propose, independently, an imaginative form for writers' lives which one might call classic as opposed to 'fullscale' or 'official' biography. The crucial method, Virginia Woolf suggests in 'The Art of Biography', is to distinguish between the barren fact and 'the fact that suggests and engenders'.[20]

NOTES

1. Clive Bell, 'How Pleasant to know Mr Eliot', *T. S. Eliot: A Symposium*, ed. Richard March and Tambimuttu (1948), p. 16.
2. Diary MS., 18 February 1940, Berg Collection, New York Public Library.
3. *Emerson in His Journals* (28 September 1839), ed. Joel Porte (1982), p. 225.
4. *T.L.S.*, 3 December 1908.
5. Holograph MS., 17 pp., Monks House Papers (University of Sussex), B. 9(a). This was the first piece of fiction that Woolf submitted for publication. She offered it to the *Cornhill*, the journal her father had edited; Reginald Smith turned it down.
6. 'More Carlyle Letters', *T.L.S.*, 1 April 1909, p. 126. Unsigned.
7. Holograph notebook, Berg Collection, New York Public Library. Eliot was 21 and in his final undergraduate year at Harvard. The city streets were presumably those of Boston.
8. 'Men and Women', *T.L.S.*, 18 March 1920, repr. *Books and Portraits* (1977), p. 30. She is paraphrasing Bathsheba in *Far from the Madding Crowd*, Ch. 51: 'It is difficult for a woman to define her feelings in language which is chiefly made by men to express theirs.'
9. *Middlemarch*, Ch. 20; *Adam Bede*, Ch. 17.
10. *Ulysses* (Penguin, 1971), pp. 143–44.
11. Helen Gardner, *The Composition of Four Quartets* (1978), Appendix A, p. 228.
12. 'The Classics and the Man of Letters' (1942), *To Criticize the Critic*.
13. Notes (3 November 1930), *The Waves: The Two Holograph Drafts*, ed. J. W. Graham (1976), p. 758.
14. Monks House Papers B. 11.
15. 'Reading', *E*, ii, 29.
16. *Selected Essays* (New York, 1950), pp. 137, 180. In the 1940 essay on Yeats, where Eliot praised the autobiographical candour of Yeats's *Last*

Poems, he formally modified his doctrine of impersonality (*On Poetry and Poets*, 1957, p. 255).

17. 'Of the inconsistency of our actions', *Complete Essays*, transl. Donald M. Frame (Stanford, 1965), p. 244.
18. *Waves Holograph*, p. 684.
19. 'Hours in a Library', *E*, ii, 37–8.
20. *E*, iv, 228.

5

Joyce, Woolf and the Modern Mind

by MARIA DIBATTISTA

The modern mind—that 'queer conglomeration of incongruous things'[1]—found its speaking voice, Woolf was often forced to admit, in the work of James Joyce. For her it was not an easy nor voluntary concession, but it was a necessary, even admirable one, a victory for Woolf's public generosity over her private prejudices as a reader and writer of fiction. Her remarks on *Ulysses*, themselves often scandalous, traverse the full range of 'monstrous, hybrid, unmanageable emotions' (*E*, ii, 219) that Woolf claimed were spawned in the modern mind, in which no feeling survived inviolate and entire. Her responses, typically modern, thus issue from her uncontrolled and contradictory:

> I should be reading Ulysses & fabricating my case for & against: I have read 200 pages so far—not a third; & have been amused, stimulated, charmed, interested by the first 2 or 3 chapters—to the end of the Cemetery scene; & then puzzled, bored, irritated, & disillusioned as by a queasy undergraduate scratching his pimples. (*D*, ii, 188–89)

Woolf knew that in 1922 Joyce was 40, her own age, so that the unhappy figure of the queasy undergraduate indicates, poorly, I fear, her own attempt to identify the general audacities of the Joycean performance that seemed to her pretentious, underbred, tricky, startling—her judgement upon finishing *Ulysses* and finding it, though armed with genius, a 'mis-fire' (*D*, ii, 199). The case for and against *Ulysses*—'immense in daring, terrific in disaster'[2]—was itself a hybrid of her own mind, but with unerring instinct she felt that some case for and against must be made.

The case for and against *Ulysses* revolved on the question of method. In 'Modern Fiction', that essay which recounts the gratitudes and hostilities that inspire the living writer in the modern (then contemporary) scene, Joyce is singled out as the most notable, sincere and courageous opponent of the Edwardian materialists, Bennett, Galsworthy and Wells. The Edwardian practice, though competent in workmanship, was deficient in life. 'Constrained, not by his own free will but by some powerful and unscrupulous tyrant who has him in thrall', the Edwardian writer slavishly accedes to the demand of the novel 'to provide a plot, to provide comedy, tragedy, love interest, and an air of probability embalming the whole'.[3] Joyce is the irredentist who overthrows the powerful and unscrupulous tyranny of the reigning Edwardian fashion. He is the disenchanter who releases the world of modernity from its thraldom to convention. A curious transaction invests Woolf's criticism of the materialists and her championing of the 'spiritual' Joyce. He is the liberator of modern fiction because he refuses to provide; his is an art, it seems, of conscious deprivations and calculated improvidences. He is the writer as 'free man' who bases 'his work upon his own feeling and not upon convention' and whose fiction supplies 'no comedy, no tragedy, no love interest or catastrophe in the accepted style'. The function of his sincerity and his courage is to chronicle the movements of the 'ordinary mind on an ordinary day'. From the Joycean example she derives her famous injunction: 'Let us record the atoms as they fall upon the mind in the order in which they fall, let us trace the pattern, however disconnected and incoherent in appearance, which each sight or incident scores upon the consciousness' (*E*, ii, 106–7). It has not been sufficiently remarked that this prescription issues from an appreciative reading of *A Portrait of the Artist As a Young Man* and *Ulysses*. Her own dynamic theory of consciousness is illustrated in Joyce's 'sincere' mimesis which admits 'little of the alien and external' and discards

97

what seems to him adventitious. The extraneous and adventitious Woolf identifies with probability, coherence, or any other of 'these signposts which for generations have served to support the imagination of a reader when called upon to imagine what he can neither touch nor see' (107). Joyce penetrates the illusory stability of the material order (violating its shibboleths, probability and coherence) to reveal the unpredictable and ungovernable operations of spirit, thus restoring to the modern novel the 'light of conception' that had been obscured by the material densities of Edwardian fiction. *Ulysses*, she approvingly records, is irradiated by 'sudden lightning flashes of significance' that 'come so close to the quick of the mind' (107).

Hers was an admiration not to be sustained, a qualified advocacy. For the 'quick of the mind' revealed through Joyce's method does not seem to coincide fully with what she means by 'life', that 'semi-transparent envelope surrounding us from the beginning of consciousness to the end'. There is a gap between the sensations received into the mind and life, a gap, she implies, too easily eliminated or accounted for in the Joycean method. Joyce is the free man writing as he chooses and as he must, but it is this very freedom that Woolf finally disavows. His method she judges a relative failure, a failure laid to the comparative poverty of the writer's mind. In a subtle but interesting transposition of terms, the very negations that define the courageous originality of *Ulysses*—the exclusion of novelistic symmetries and coherences—prove to be false economies. Joyce's poverty is the poverty of the 'damned egotistical self' (*D*, ii, 14), as Woolf privately characterized it, that confines the reader's imagination in 'a bright yet narrow room'. 'Is it due to the method', Woolf enquires, a bit too disingenuously, 'that we feel neither jovial nor magnanimous, but centred in a self which, in spite of its tremor of susceptibility, never embraces or creates what is outside itself and beyond?'[4] These reservations, though posed in the interrogative mood, hardened into unchanging opinions. Woolf's characterization of the Joycean mind is singular, even distressing, particularly because she herself fails to provide an illustrative figure for this outside or beyond she desires, except to suggest where it is not—it is not inside the mind. In her reading notebook for *Ulysses*, which also contained her working notes for 'Modern Fiction', Woolf observes of Joyce's characters:

> Their minds lack quality and as you get nothing *but* their minds!—still an effort in the right direction—at least out of the first Class Carriage line. . . . The first class carriage that takes you to the best hotel in Brighton—that's true of Arnold B[ennett] though not quite so true of Wells.[5]

Ulysses directs us to an outside or beyond that it never itself attains—such is the promise, never fulfilled, of its narrative line.

Woolf's reading of Joyce, distorted through the prism of curiosity, envy, resentment and sheer befuddlement, is thus always double. Joyce is the acknowledged liberator who frees the modern novel from stifling convention. He is most of all sincere and courageous, the two writerly virtues Woolf espoused for female writers if they were to emancipate themselves from the restrictions imposed by the inherited tradition.[6] But Joyce is also limited by the self-conscious and exhibitionistic nature of his own rebellion. It is this indecorous side of his virtues that she comments on in 'Mr. Bennett and Mrs. Brown'. Her diagnosis of the modern predicament remains the same: 'At the present moment we are suffering, not from decay, but from having no code of manners which writers and readers accept as a prelude to the more exciting intercourse of friendship' (*E*, i, 334). The question of method devolves into the consideration of narrative 'manners' and she couples Joyce with T. S. Eliot in describing the 'more adult writers' of the time: 'Their sincerity is desperate; their courage tremendous; it is only that they do not know whether to use a fork or their fingers' (334). Joyce, though adult, is underbred. Lest Woolf be condemned for recommending drawing-room manners as a specific against the unmannerliness of epic literary revolutions, it should be recorded that her polite criticism is succeeded by a more startling demand for 'savagery.' Joyce's unmannerliness, the scandal of his indecency, she complains, is the 'calculated indecency of a desperate man who feels that in order to breathe he must break the windows':

> At moments, when the window is broken, he is magnificent. But what a waste of energy! And, after all, how dull indecency is,

when it is not the overflowing of a super-abundant energy or savagery, but the determined and public-spirited act of a man who needs fresh air! (334–35)

Curiously it is savagery she misses in Joyce; she desires a more kinetic display of spleen, a more violent breaking of forms. If there are to be no manners, let there at least be the exuberances of the wild heart, a recurrent and cherished figure of super-abundant life in Woolf's fiction from Sally Seton to Mrs. Manresa in *Between the Acts*. In *A Room of One's Own*, Woolf comments that Shakespeare's indecency 'uproots a thousand other things in one's mind, and is far from being dull. But Shakespeare does it for pleasure; Mr. A, as the nurses say, does it on purpose' (152). Joyce, like Mr. A, Woolf's generic name for those self-conscious 'virile' males 'writing only with the male side of their brains', is indecent on purpose. His indecency is dull because it is self-conscious and didactic, a way of taking readers to task, not offering them the pleasures to be gained in the general uprootings and upheavals of the otherwise quiescent, unreceptive mind. Joyce as dutifully public-spirited and rather underbred—Woolf's is neither an accurate nor especially compelling caricature, but it does reveal the dispositions of her own temperament. She is less interested, critically, in Joyce's tenor than in those of his narrative vehicles that can transport the modern novel out of its accustomed routes (leading to the best hotel in Brighton) and into the dark and as yet untravelled spaces of the mind. It is precisely Joyce's narrative vehicle that she would adopt in her own exploratory expedition into the ordinary mind on an ordinary day—*Mrs. Dalloway*.

Mrs. Dalloway, the product of her fortieth year, was intended, of course, to be the vindication of Woolf's own method: 'If they say this is all a clever experiment, I shall produce Mrs. Dalloway in Bond Street as the finished product' (*D*, ii, 178). Produced in Bond Street, *Mrs. Dalloway* was not to be attired in the fineries of the Edwardian materialists; she would be dressed, if not fashionably, at least suitably in the modern mode. However idiosyncratic this style might have seemed at its inception, it clearly evolved, in the composition of the novel, in response to the example—and pressure—of the Joycean method. In her early attempt to conceive a 'new form for a new novel', Woolf had become elated at the prospect of devising an entirely different approach: 'no scaffolding; scarcely a brick to be seen; all crepuscular, but the heart, the passion, humour, everything as bright as fire in the mist. Then I'll find room for so much—a gaiety—an inconsequence—a light spirited stepping at my sweet will' (*D*, ii, 13–14). *Jacob's Room* conveyed some of this spirit of gaiety and inconsequence, but in *Mrs. Dalloway* her sweet will was chastened by more bitter realizations.

In her writing notebook for *Mrs. Dalloway*, Woolf remarks on the pressing need for a 'general style . . . as one's attention is too broken':

> this to be psychology gradually increasing in tension
> all through the day.
> but the continuous style?
> must have the effect of being incessant.
> texture unbroken.[7]

The writerly will, in its sweetness (Woolf would call it its generosity), must provision itself against the dangers attending the desire for inconsequence: distraction and disassociation. In another notebook entry, Woolf records a further plan for her unfolding narrative that replicates the diurnal design of *Ulysses*:

> Hours: 10 11 12 1 2 3 4
>   5 6 7 8 9 10 11 12 1 2.[8]

Woolf's *Hours* (the working title of *Mrs. Dalloway*) appeal to the established success of Joyce's temporal orderings. For *Ulysses* had demonstrated how the very compression of a one-day chronicle could provide for narrative expanse, the room to encompass and enclose all the myriad impressions affecting the ordinary mind on an ordinary day. *Mrs. Dalloway* acknowledges the authority of the Joycean solution to the relativities of modern life by preserving, as *Jacob's Room* did not, narrative scaffolding—the regularized time-keeping that organizes the novel's day around leaden rings of sound.

Yet this narrative scaffolding is introduced into the novel less as a visible support to the reader's imagination than as a menacing, ominous structure. Those leaden rings of sound that toll the irrevocable hour bind the narrative to the ineluctable modality of the temporal, to chronicity and its certitudes: how it is certain we must die. The unbroken sequentiality of the novel thus issues out of an undeniable morbidity, a contagious emanation from the febrile temper of its 'heroine', recently afflicted with influenza, and of Septimus Smith, victimized by a darker pathology. Woolf's formal appropriation of Joyce's one-day narrative thus disclosed a marked difference in what each could imagine transpiring in an ordinary mind on an ordinary day in June. Joyce's characters enjoy the pleasures of retellings and foretellings; Woolf's suffer the irrational suspense of forebodings (like Peter Walsh's premonition of Clarissa falling where she stood (56)). Hers is more thoroughly the imagination of disaster. Only a continuous style could tranquillize the narrative susceptible to such sudden and erratic perturbations.

The search for a general and continuous style that links the discontinuous and unifies the disassociated impressions and incidents of the day bred an uncharacteristic mutation of Woolf's imagination—an actual reworking of another narrative episode. Her fiction often echoes other fictions (*Orlando* is dense with such allusive moments) but seldom by a protracted appropriation of already imagined life. Such an extensive borrowing allowed Woolf simultaneously to assume and cast off the authority of Joycean representations and permitted, eventually, the deeper affinities in their vision to emerge.

I am speaking of course of the motorcade sequence that constitutes not so much an allusion but an interpolation and criticism of the processions in 'Wandering Rocks'. 'Wandering Rocks', as is well known, is an apocryphal interpolation in *Ulysses*, since no such episode occurs in the *Odyssey*, an avoidance in the original that is confronted in the successor epic. Joyce's audacity is to introject his imagination precisely in the space vacated by Homer. A route not taken by the ancient is the peril the modern is condemned to navigate. I propose to examine in detail Joyce's and Woolf's narrative detours in order to map, through the divagations pursued by their writerly wills, the determining boundaries of their fictional realms.

Joyce's Dublin, both as a real place and as re-imagined land, is most accurately figured in the dislocations and derangements of 'Wandering Rocks'.[9] The random movements of Dublin's citizens (the dominant 'symbol' of the chapter) are juxtaposed to the apparently purposeful itineraries of Father Conmee, who initiates the wanderings, and the viceregal cavalcade, on its way to open the Mirus bazaar, that concludes it. Ambulatory symbols of Church and State thus enclose a chaotic interior as all subjugating powers subdue rebellious territory, by surrounding it. Although Joyce cunningly exiles the symbols of sacred and profane authority to the peripheries of the chapter, their usurpations shadow the consciousness of the characters confined within the apparently exitless maze that is Dublin. The design of 'Wandering Rocks' is professedly modelled on the labyrinth, but this modern maze issues into no sacred civic centre, the hidden site of truth that houses monstrosity, the hybrid minotaur. Indeed the chapter is emphatic in its deliberate decentrings; it is organized in nineteen sections that are themselves isolated by marks of division and separation, isolated asterisks on a field of white. As a printed artefact, 'Wandering Rocks' thus insists on the vacancies and divisions between its characters. Into these empty spaces rush England and Rome, for institutions, like nature, abhor a vacuum. Their presence invests the chapter with whatever 'design' it may possess, although it is a despised and contestable order they symbolize and enforce. Caritas, the moral energy of social union, the ostensible motive of Father Conmee's excursion, is a palpable absence. 'Cheerful decorum',[10] the amiable beauty of public life, its grace of manners, is ironized in the greetings that pass between the motorcade and Dublin's passers-by, saluting their allegiance to the forces of occupation.

Only Joyce, the supreme artificer, subverts the grounds of these usurping authorities by attacking the idea of order itself, not just structurally in the disposition of sections, but thematically, for example in Father Conmee's meditations on the ways of God and men as he catches a chance glimpse of a turfbarge, with a bargeman 'seated amidships, smoking and staring at a branch of poplar above him' (*U*, 221). The idle and idling become the idyllic and 'Father Conmee reflected on the

103

providence of the Creator who had made turf to be in bogs where men might dig it out and bring it to town and hamlet to make fires in the houses of poor people' (*U*, 221). Like all benevolent despots, Father Conmee (whose reign is mild) enlists a venerated argument for the justice and beauty of things as they are (or as he finds them)—the argument from design. No caritas informs his vision, only the aesthetic appreciation of the Creator's well-conceived and executed plan. Later the crumpled throwaway announcing 'Elijah is coming, the restorer of the Church in Zion' drifts through the narrative, a vagrant emblem of civic prophecy. Millenialism and the utopian vision exist in the shattered form of an eschatological discard to be retrieved, if not completely recuperated, in Joyce's own retrospective rearrangement of the events of the day in 'Circe' and 'Ithaca'. 'Wandering Rocks', beyond the reach of such imaginative reparations, remains a vivid and bitter satire of disassociation.

Joyce's urban satire is relentless, threatening to throw *Ulysses* itself permanently off course. Deprived of the guidance of an inspiriting teleology (even in the debased form of millenarian fantasy), the Joycean logos becomes vagrant and disoriented, dispersing itself aimlessly in discrete descriptions of individual minds, things, or scenes. The serpentining, ambulatory letters of H. E. L. Y.'s walking advertisement retell, at the level of the constituent word, this diaspora of signs. HELY's is a linguistic throwaway, an eye-catching advertisement for the decentred word that must be reconstituted if Zion—the place of novelistic language—is to be restored. This language itself may be a cunning design devised by the mind, a macro- and microcosm constructed on and thus concealing the void incertitude. Yet in the evolving association of letters and men, inspirited by caritas, is founded the mystical estate that is literature—the 'realm of the manners and customs of society—a spacious realm', as Stephen Hero reminds us.[11] Stephen Hero, unlike Cranly, is no cynical romanticist who holds that 'the civil life affected in no way the individual life' (*SH*, 174). An apocryphal but in many ways the most modern of *Ulysses*'s chapters, 'Wandering Rocks' details with agonizing clarity the problematic of the modern novel and the obligation of the modern artist: to articulate and thus confer meaning on the social life it represents, a meaning as yet unuttered and thus in need of creation. Only through such articulations does the novel justify itself as a legitimate social creation.

The potential errancy of the social will, and the novelistic caritas that can unite the isolated, disaffected and vagrant self into an authentic community of purpose and belief, is the thematic crux Woolf seizes upon in her own subtle transpositions of 'Wandering Rocks' in *Mrs. Dalloway*. This interpolated sequence is introduced as a radical and potentially terrifying dislocation. Clarissa has been shopping in Bond Street, musing about the contending loves and hatreds that threaten to deface her 'panoply of content', 'all pleasure in beauty, in friendship, in being well, in being loved' (15) and expose it as the defensive armature of self-love. Just as she is about to surmount the kinetic pain of hatred and division through the transfiguring waves of kindness and love, what she perceives as a pistol shot disrupts her potentially transcendent moment. The violent explosion initiates the first of many confusions in reference, false interpretations to which the sequence is prey. The violent explosion proves not to be a pistol shot, but a car backfiring. The ensuing correction of reality thus consolidates an opposition in the narrative's internal rhythms: the private, vertical rhythm striving for sublimity (taken to its extreme in the prophetic social ravings of Septimus Smith calling for the birth of a new religion) and the public, horizontal movement of the powers of this world (the temporal persistence of the collective will incarnated in the symbols of the English state, the flag and the enduring royal line). Curiously, it is this latter, horizontal movement that divulges in its passage the depths of the communal mind: 'For the surface agitation of the passing car as it sunk grazed something very profound' (21).

The profundities dredged up by the passing vehicle yield, however, a suspect tenor. It symbolizes, that is, 'the voice of authority; the spirit of religion was abroad with her eyes bandaged tight and her lips gaping wide' (17), a kind of communal blindness and idiocy. Its passage thus constitutes a questionable and paradoxical event. Its incidental appearance in the narrative transmits a shock 'trifling in single instances ... yet in its fullness rather formidable and in its common

105

appeal emotional' (21), evoking as it does the 'thought of the dead; of the flag; of Empire', that is, of the historical mission of England itself. The narrative voice is momentarily held in thrall by this fullness of reference and response. The car in its passing possesses what Clarissa herself lacks, 'something central which permeated; something warm which broke up surfaces and rippled the cold contact of man and woman' (36).[12] The power of the motorcade to evoke the variety and irreticences of human life contributes to the novel's profound social comedy. Even the narrator seems slightly chagrined that the 'deeper sources of life' could be 'unsealed suddenly, inappropriately, sentimentally, by this sort of thing' (23). That these 'deeper sources' unearthed by the 'immortal presence' figured forth in the passing vehicle constitute the novelistic material itself seriously competes with the narrator's own power to plumb the depths of the communal mind. The narrator's response is to challenge this evocative power with the authority of scepticism, questioning the identity of this invisible figure who can exercise such a formidable appeal. The face itself, barely seen, remains unknown; even its sex is in dispute. Yet the narrator is forced to admit that 'greatness was seated within; greatness was passing, hidden, down Bond Street' (19). Thus the narrator seems compelled to attend the passage of this greatness and record the contingent, irrational surfacings from the depths it provokes if the novel's social consciousness is to be fully represented.

Only Septimus conceives of this hidden greatness, converts this social comedy into a terrible fatality: 'this gradual drawing together of everything to one centre before his eyes, as if some horror had come almost to the surface and was about to burst into flames' (18). His is the reading of madness (really an over-reading), an alienation that unmasks the secret alliance struck between sentimentality and social terror. Through Septimus's readings, Woolf effects her departure from Joyce. Joyce tracks the passing of the viceregal cavalcade strictly as external, surface movement. Woolf relocates the icon of social and political authority at the centre of her social panorama, thus exposing the depths of the communal allegiance to and complicity with the social power the motorcade symbolizes.

Septimus's apocalyptic ravings thus inaugurate a contestatory movement in a narrative in danger of drowning in its own associative and affirmative rhythms, in the fatal fluency of its vagrant, often inappropriate thoughts.[13] The novel's social passages are to be arrested and redirected by a countermovement of severance and opposition initiated by the aeroplane which supersedes and finally replaces the motorcade as an object of communal observation. The aeroplane sequence introduces a new theme into the narrative, the theme of writing as a social activity that competes with the theme of political symbology and aspires to displace it. The motorcar, to the 'sane' mind, suggests 'normal' readings, limited by the firm correspondence between sign and signified: the car denotes the presence of legitimate authority, queen, Prime Minister or some other stolid 'figure'. The aeroplane is a vehicle which transports not a traditional, but an elusive tenor: the unpredictable fluidities of thought itself, unbound by any determined or easily discernible system of signs. It is the symbol of symbolization itself, of 'man's soul; of his determination . . . to get outside his body, beyond his house, by means of thought, Einstein, speculation, mathematics, the Mendelian theory' (32). The aerial apparition concentrates the will to transcendence (getting beyond the body, the house and its confinements, the beyond Joyce never fully embraced), a self-overcoming linked to the free play of representations— speculation, mathematics, the Mendelian theory.

Initially, the letters the aeroplane inscribes in the sky do not form actual words; its writing is illegible, unreadable. Even the letters are indistinguishable in their first outlines: 'A C was it? an E, then an L? Only for a moment did they lie still; then they moved and melted and were rubbed out up in the sky, and the aeroplane shot further away and again, in a fresh space of sky, began writing a K, and E, a Y perhaps?' (23–4). A spectator, Mrs. Coates, ventures 'Blaxo'; another, Mrs. Bletchley, offers 'Kreemo'—the neologisms of nonsense or commercialism. These comic readings dissolve, however, into the interpretations of Septimus for whom the skywriting is identified, not with the seemingly eternal exercise of temporal power, but with the more fugitive and transient appearances of Beauty. To him the 'smoke words' bestow 'in their inexhaustible charity and laughing goodness, one shape after another of unimaginable beauty . . . signalling their intention to provide him, for nothing, for ever, for looking merely, with beauty, more beauty' (25). Septimus, the castaway prophet, reads the smoke words not as definite signs linking him to a stable world of referentiality; for him is reserved the message of the world transmitted through the caritas of art, the inexhaustible charity and laughing goodness of the perishable word.

Joyce's exemplary naturalism and Woolf's instinctive lyricism are conflated to produce a comic venture in modern sublimity—transcendence through advertising. The perishability of the sky words lends the sequence its romantic intensity and some of its (qualified) pathos; the subsequent identification of the writing as an advertisement for toffee triggers its profound comedy, Woolf's gentle satire on the symbolizing powers of the mind. Her own writing, inferentially, succeeds as a dialectic of association and disassociation, the perpetual making and unmaking of the shapes of beauty and the forms of charity, the novelistic virtue par excellence. Woolf's resistance to the affirmations of her own continuous style never reify into the marmoreal rigidity of an eternal Logos; her mimesis in not the dutiful transcription of unalterable words. Her language is the language of mortality itself, prey to the same vanishings and impermanences.

Woolf's demystification of the spell of writing reaches even deeper. Unlike the advertisement for HELY's in 'Wandering Rocks', the commercial signs for toffee do unite her novel's community of spectators. Only the fact-recording, determinedly naturalistic, *unlyrical* side of the narrative mind resists the mystical appeal of these all too profane inscriptions. The narrator documents but refuses to participate in this communal rite of transfiguration. As the aeroplane makes its final manoeuvres, 'curving up and up, straight up, like something mounting in ecstasy, in pure delight', the narrator discerns the discrete, though temporarily obscured, plumes of 'white smoke looping, writing a T, and O, an F' (42). As a figure for the ecstasy and sublimity of the emancipated will, the aeroplane is permanently discredited. Its smoke signals, like the druidical plumes of smoke that conclude 'Scylla and Charybdis', portend a similar abdication of the will to those religious, political or commercial powers who by tradition, cunning or artful design can manipulate the depths of the communal mind.

The complicity of writing with established power is the suppressed, never fully realized subtext of *Mrs. Dalloway*, the source of the novel's deep and unresolved ambivalence towards its own representational activity. So deep does this ambivalence run that the novel cannot express the theme of writing except as the prerogative of the masculine mind. Later in the novel, for example, Lady Bruton will call on Hugh Whitbread, the perfect English gentleman, to compose a letter for her to *The Times*, a task he performs with all the ease and assurance of an inheritor. Watching his marvellous transformations, reducing her own 'tangles to sense, to grammar. . . . drafting sentiments in alphabetical order of the highest nobility', Lady Bruton wonders, rightly, 'Could her own meaning sound like that?' (121–22). This question is not rhetorical, but registers a serious epistemological doubt. Woolf's obsession with an unwritten novel[14] that would express the great unsaid of life issues from her desire to rid her own writing of such distortions of female meaning, the syntactical dominations of the masculine order (represented by that prestigious symbol of linearity, the alphabet),[15] even if that order is of the highest nobility. Women do not write in *Mrs. Dalloway*; that privileged activity is not contemplated for women until the great middle period marked by *A Room of One's Own* and its companion fiction, *Orlando*, the 'biography' of a female writer. Women's meaning is communicated through a pre-literal language of feeling, a shared code of silent utterances like those unspoken recognitions that 'went beneath masculine lunch parties and united Lady Bruton and Mrs. Dalloway, who seldom met, and appeared when they did meet indifferent and even hostile, in a singular bond' (161). Woolf does not even suggest here that this singular bond uniting her women accounts for the different rhetoric of her male and female characters; indeed there appears to be no such difference separating, for instance, Clarissa and Peter Walsh. Such discriminations are lost, sacrificed in the service of a continuous style. Nor does she venture, as she will in *A Room of One's Own* (115) any speculation about the possible differences distinguishing a male and female sentence. The sexes are divided in *Mrs. Dalloway* in the depths of the mind itself, before any language or written tradition have been constituted or learned. In writing *Jacob's Room*, Woolf had wondered, anxiously, if what she was doing was being better done by Joyce (*D*, ii, 69). *Mrs. Dalloway* demonstrates that their differences were not comparative, a matter of method or execution, but absolute, her mind awed in the exercise of the power (novel-writing) which he confidently assumed, his recoiling, as Bloom's mind recoils, from those unsayable and unfigurable realities (especially Death surprising in the midst of life) hers sought to embrace.

Woolf records in her diary T. S. Eliot's remark that *Ulysses* 'would be a landmark, because it destroyed the whole of the 19th Century. It left Joyce himself with nothing to write another book on' (*D*, ii, 203). Eliot was wrong in thinking *Ulysses* left Joyce with nowhere to go. *Finnegans Wake* is not a book about nothing, but everything, the whole cycle of human culture. But Eliot was right in proclaiming *Ulysses* a cultural monument and a monitory artefact that marked the site of a generational impasse. Woolf and Joyce were conscious of their precarious location between what the catechizer of 'Ithaca' calls the irreparability of the past and the imprevidibility of the future (*U*, 696). Envying but unable to emulate or duplicate the predictive and recuperative powers of romantic prophecy, they would settle, always uneasily, in that temporal gap in the historical continuum known as the here and now (one working title of *The Years* (*D*, iv, 181)). Joyce's attempt to represent the epiphanic instant in which words like 'foetus' could yield their spiritual significance and become entire scenes of instruction, and Woolf's meditations on the moment that can make life stand still and disclose the still places where the figures of eternity serenely abide, register their unwillingness to be confined in the present as pure presence. It is this restless hope that lies behind Stephen Hero's definition of the modern as the vivisective mode that 'reconstructs the spectacle of redemption' (*SH*, 186). Time must be set free, and with it the creative potential of the modern mind.

Perhaps nowhere is this spectacle played out with more comic exuberance than in *Orlando*, a work that I will, perhaps eccentrically, select to isolate some resemblances between

Joyce and Woolf.[16] *Orlando* is, among other things, a hybrid produced by the modern mind—parodic, rhapsodic, biographic, fantastic, prosaic, poetic. Joyce is not thanked in the prefatory acknowledgement of friends (living and dead) who assisted Woolf in the writing of *Orlando*, but his example is to be felt, not just in the novel's mixture of modes, but, more directly, in the last, modern chapter in which Orlando finds herself directly immersed in present time, 'the old Kent Road . . . on Thursday, the eleventh of October 1928', the day on which the novel ends: 'People spilt off the pavement. There were women with shopping bags. Children ran out. There were sales at drapers' shops. . . . Here was a market. Here a funeral' (275–76). The narrative description aims at Defoe's realism of detail, but it is the Joycean method that shadows her playful imitation of Defoe's convincing 'truth-telling', what Stephen Dedalus, after St. Ignatius Loyola, calls composition of place. A similar 'scenic' moment occurs in 'Scylla and Charybdis' when Stephen attempts to reimagine the 'local color' of Shakespeare's London, the living background to *Hamlet*, the Globe, the stage of the world:

> It is this hour of a day in mid June. . . . The flag is up on the playhouse by the bankside. The bear Sackerson growls in the pit near it, Paris garden. Canvasclimbers who sailed with Drake chew their sausages among the groundlings. (*U*, 188)

Joyce insists that the representing mind 'Hold to the now, the here, through which all future plunges to the past' (*U*, 186). His retellings and foretellings define the space of eternity where past, present, and future converge in the novelistic egotistical sublime. ('Give me my Wordsworth,' Stephen says, at contemplating the succession of ages (*U*, 206).) Woolf resists the allure of such Wordsworthian sublimities. She subjects *Orlando*—and her readers—to all the disorienting incoherences of the immediate present where 'Nothing could be seen whole or read from start to finish': 'After twenty minutes the body and mind were like scraps of torn paper . . . and . . . it is an open question in what sense Orlando can be said to have existed at the present moment.' Only when Orlando's mind is shielded from the glare of bright reality by a

111

'green screen' does it regain its 'illusion of holding things within itself'. Objects then appear to be 'precisely life-size', thus restoring to its representations the desired precision of realism (276).

This realism is 'the extreme psychological naturalism' Erich Auerbach admired and elegantly defined as the modern form of Western mimesis, the current destination of its odyssey of styles.[17] Woolf's narrative consciousness is a coloured screen or semi-transparency that mediates between the receptive mind and external stimuli and presents a protective surface to absorb and muffle 'the shock of time' (*O*, 288). Woolf's narrative practice is thus more traditional than Joyce's. She preserves in her fiction the figure of the author as a permeating and permeable presence. Her narrative persona, though anonymous, identifies itself through the 'continuous style' that discloses, in its unfolding, what Bernard in *The Waves* calls the 'central shadow' (207)—the shaded habitation of the Other, hypostasized in the figure of the often invisible author. Barthes admits, in *The Pleasures of the Text*, to the need for this figure: 'I desire the author: I need his figure (which is neither his representation nor his projection), as he needs mine (except to "prattle").'[18] To find the author figured forth and sublimated in the continuous style is one of the pleasures of the Woolfean text. *Ulysses* holds other entertainments.[19]

Two paintings in *Between the Acts* that hang in Pointz Hall can be seen as emblems of the two masterly styles that have come to define the modern temper: Joyce's garrulous virility and its generative improvidences, Woolf's 'feminine' reticence and its sustaining economies. One is a portrait of an ancestor with a name, a history, and an eccentric, voluble desire to have his dog Colin buried at his feet in the same grave. The other is a picture of a lady 'in her yellow robe, leaning, with a pillar to support her, a silver arrow in her hand, and a feather in her hair' who leads the eye 'up, down, from the curve to the straight, through glades of greenery and shades of silver, dun and rose into silence' (46). The male portrait is Joycean man, the producer of talk. The unnamed lady is Woolfian woman, silent, anonymous, a ghost from *limbo matrum* come to revive the feminine art of continuity and the soothing, unbroken rhythms (up, down) of the feminine mind. Joyce is the stage

Irishman, Woolf the playwright, like Miss La Trobe, who refuses to come out of the bushes.

But the portrait and the picture are not meant to compete for attention nor divide loyalties. They are placed in the novel opposite a window that looks out into the outside or beyond that Woolf thought the novel should embrace and create. They mutually define, they do not rend, this novelistic space they oversee.

NOTES

1. 'The Narrow Bridge of Art', *E*, ii, 226.
2. 'How It Strikes a Contemporary', *E*, ii, 156.
3. 'Modern Fiction', *E*, ii, 106.
4. *E*, ii, 107–8. Eliot seems to have shared this view. Woolf records a conversation with Eliot in which he remarked that there was no 'great conception' in *Ulysses*:

   > He thought that Joyce did completely what he meant to do. But he did not think that he gave a new insight into human nature—said nothing new like Tolstoi. Bloom told one nothing. Indeed, he said, this new method of giving the psychology proves to my mind that it doesn't work. It doesn't tell as much as some casual glance from outside often tells. I said I had found *Pendennis* more illuminating in this way. (*D*, ii, 203)

   I think they were both wrong.
5. 'Modern Novels (Joyce)' Holograph Notebook, unsigned and undated, iv: Henry W. and Albert A. Berg Collection in the New York Public Library (Astor, Lenox and Tilden foundations). I would like to thank Quentin Bell and the New York Public Library for permission to quote the unpublished material cited in this essay.
6. This, of course, is the concluding argument of *A Room of One's Own*.
7. *Mrs. Dalloway* Holograph Notes dated 9 November 1922–2 August 1923: Berg Collection.
8. Ibid.
9. According to Frank Budgen, 'Joyce wrote the "Wandering Rocks" with a map of Dublin before him on which were traced in red ink the paths of the Earl of Dudley and Father Conmee.' Joyce's realism triumphs in such scrupulous documentation. See Frank Budgen, *James Joyce and the Making of 'Ulysses'* (Bloomington, 1967), pp. 124–25. See also Clive Hart's meticulous and therefore useful guide to the interpolations in this episode and a chart of its spaces in *James Joyce's Ulysses: Critical Essays*, ed. Clive Hart and David Hayman (Berkeley, 1974), pp. 203–16.

10. *Ulysses* (New York, 1961), p. 22. All further citations will be to this edition, cited as *U*.

11. *Stephen Hero* (New York, 1963), p. 78. Hereafter all citations to this edition will be cited *SH*.

12. J. Hillis Miller identifies, correctly, I think, this power with the narrative voice itself. See his 'Mrs. Dalloway's All Souls Day', in *The Shaken Realist: Essays in Modern Literature in Honor of F. J. Hoffman*, ed. O. B. Hardison, Jr., *et al.* (Baton Rouge, 1970), p. 113.

13. See Geoffrey Hartman, 'Virginia's Web', *Beyond Formalism* (New Haven, 1970), pp. 71–84. Hartman has a suggestive discussion of the affirming and resisting rhythms in the Woolfian imagination.

14. 'An Unwritten Novel' was more than just the title of a short story in her first collection, *Monday or Tuesday*. It also defines, conceptually, a major if elusive part of her poetics for the novel.

15. One inevitably recalls Mr. Ramsay's travails in exploring the alphabet of thought, a singularly male construction, in *To the Lighthouse*.

16. For an extremely suggestive, if preliminary discussion of Woolf's indebtedness to Joyce in *The Years*, see Suzette Henke, 'Virginia Woolf's *The Years*: Echoes of Joyce's *Ulysses*', *Modern British Literature*, 4 (1979), 137–39.

17. *Mimesis* (Princeton, 1968), p. 538.

18. Roland Barthes, *The Pleasures of the Text*, transl. Richard Miller (New York, 1975), p. 27.

19. Hugh Kenner's appreciation of the full repertory of Joyce's many 'voices' leads him to formulate the Uncle Charles Principle that states that the narrative idiom need not be the narrator's. See his *Joyce's Voices* (Berkeley, 1978), pp. 15–38.

6

Narrative Voice and the Female Perspective in Virginia Woolf's Early Novels

by VIRGINIA BLAIN

Never was a book more feminine, more recklessly feminine. It may be labelled clever and shrewd, mocking, suggestive, subtle, 'modern', but these terms do not convey the spirit of it—which essentially is feminine. That quality is of course, indescribable. (From *TLS* review of *VO*, 1 April 1915, M and M, 49)

   A.J.: Virginia Woolf has said that it is fatal for anyone who writes to think of their sex.
   S.B.: Nonetheless, Virginia Woolf thought a lot about her own sex when she wrote. In the best sense of the word, her writing is very feminine, and by that I mean that women are supposed to be very sensitive to . . . I don't know . . . to all the sensations of nature, much more so than men, much more contemplative. (From Alice Jardine's interview with Simone de Beauvoir, transl. Ellen Evans, printed in *Signs: Journal of Women in Culture and Society*, 5 (1979), 233)

It is reassuring and at the same time disappointing to find so experienced and profound a thinker about women as Simone de Beauvoir beginning to flounder as soon as she seeks to describe 'feminine' writing in non-prescriptive terms. Of course, many would say that this is inevitable: exactly what they would have expected. Others, however, like the younger French feminist critic, Hélène Cixous, less afraid of being prescriptive, would argue that feminine or female writing has nothing to do with being more contemplative or sensitive to nature but must seek its own 'body language', rejecting what she calls 'phallogocentricism' in favour of a more appropriate morphological model.[1]

It is not my purpose here to enter into an extended analysis of the current highly controversial 'nature/nurture' debate about the true constitution of the feminine gender.[2] However, it seems to me that the view Virginia Woolf puts forward in 'Professions for Women', that our prime obligation in any such debate is to resist all attempts to contract its terms of reference, is one that still carries weight. 'I mean, what is a woman? I assure you, I do not know. I do not believe that you know. I do not believe that anybody can know until she has expressed herself in all the arts and professions open to human skill' (E, ii, 286). Although undoubtedly a feminist in the modern sense of the term,[3] Woolf always remained adept at gracefully sidestepping the moment she felt herself being steered towards the limitation of any definitive standpoint. She certainly allowed herself a human inconsistency frowned upon by sterner theorists. ('If I were still a feminist. . . . But I have travelled on' she muses in her diary entry for 17 October 1924 (ii, 318)— four years before the polemically feminist *A Room of One's Own*.) None the less, despite her resistance to marking out boundaries to female abilities and potentialities, her feminism was of the variety—once considered old-fashioned, now again, it seems, in the vanguard—that believes in '*la différence*':

> It would be a thousand pities if women wrote like men, or lived like men, or looked like men, for if two sexes are quite inadequate, considering the vastness and variety of the world, how should we manage with one only? Ought not education to bring out and fortify the differences rather than the similarities? For we have too much likeness as it is. (*RO*, 132)

Such statements support de Beauvoir's insistence upon Woolf's gender-consciousness as a writer. Despite the arguments put forward in *A Room of One's Own* for an androgynous ideal, it remains true that Woolf's novels show a radical awareness of feminist issues, and that they take up the question of 'what is a woman' from a perspective that aims to deconstruct the kind of masculine prejudices in Desmond MacCarthy's condescending praise of her for 'courageously acknowledging the limitations of [her] sex'.[4] That is, from a perspective which is unashamed to be female, and which has as its ultimate goal the ability to take its own femaleness so much for granted that the issue of gender can be forgotten, as in the hypothetical case of Mary Carmichael in *A Room of One's Own*, who had 'mastered the first great lesson; she wrote as a woman, but as a woman who has forgotten that she is a woman, so that her pages were full of that curious sexual quality which comes only when sex is unconscious of itself' (140). As Woolf herself was the first to admit, she found female intellectual shame far easier to overcome in her own case than bodily shame, largely owing to the mixed advantages and disadvantages of her peculiar temperament and upbringing. But to give voice to an even intellectually unashamed female perspective meant giving voice to a new form of the novel, and it is these most tantalizing and nebulous aspects of novelistic form—narrative voice and perspective—that I shall chiefly be concerned to explore here.

In his recent essay on the narrative form of *Mrs. Dalloway*, Hillis Miller reminds us: 'The most important themes of a given novel are likely to lie not in anything which is explicitly affirmed, but in significances generated by the way in which the story is told.'[5] In the terms of the present discussion, I would go further than this to argue that meaning can be no more and no less political than style, for in no other sense can a female perspective have meaning which escapes prescription. Style in Woolf's fiction is as much part of her 'female perspective' as it is an expression of her aesthetic beliefs. Yet it is probably fair to say that she was less concerned with evolving a 'feminine sentence' in the manner of a Dorothy Richardson who, having a dramatized first-person female narrator, used 'female' stream-of-consciousness,[6] and more concerned, as she said herself, with 'merely giving things their natural order, as a woman would, if she wrote like a woman' (*RO*, 137). This is in key with her later brilliantly open-ended definition of novelistic form as 'the sense that one thing follows another rightly' (*D*, iv, 172, 16 August

1933). More specific, and so more useful for the present discussion, are her remarks in a review of Brimley Johnson's *The Women Novelists* (1918), about the 'very difficult question of the difference between the man's and the woman's view of what constitutes the importance of any subject. From this spring not only marked differences of plot and incident, but infinite differences in selection, method and style'; 'There is the obvious and enormous difference of experience in the first place; but the essential difference lies in the fact not that men describe battles and women the birth of children, but that each sex describes itself' (*CW*, 27, 26).

'Each sex describes itself': a remark with profound implications for Woolf's own art, and one which applies with particular force to her earliest novels. It is with the first three of these that I shall be most concerned here, for each in its own way is as experimental as any of the later fiction, in the sense that each is trying out means of breaking through the barriers of inherited male conventions towards the expression of an authentic woman's voice: not the voice of Everywoman so much as the voice of Virginia Woolf as subject-of-consciousness.[7] Of course one must bear in mind in this context her Yeatsian quest for freedom from personality ('Sydney comes & I'm Virginia; when I write I'm merely a sensibility' (*D*, ii, 193)). But as so many critics have remarked, there *is* a unique Woolfian voice belonging to her novels alone. She herself was quite aware of this quality and of its desirability; by the time she had finished *Jacob's Room* she felt she had found it: 'There's no doubt in my mind that I have found out how to begin (at 40) to say something in my own voice' (*D*, ii, 186). Her first two novels have commonly been held to be much less experimental than *Jacob's Room*, but in moving mountains the first efforts make least impression upon the onlookers, although in fact requiring more courage and vision than the last.

The mountain she was moving was of course the mountain of male prejudice. When she looked back for inspiration to earlier women writers, only Jane Austen and Emily Brontë seemed to have had the 'genius [and] integrity . . . in face of all that criticism, in the midst of that purely patriarchal society, to hold fast to the thing as they saw it without shrinking. . . . They wrote as women write, not as men write' (*RO*, 112). Although

Woolf admired Charlotte Brontë and George Eliot—the latter, particularly, exerted a profound influence despite many surface differences—she felt that both of these writers had fallen foul of the current 'man's sentence . . . unsuited for a woman's use'. In a suggestively Beardsleyesque image, Woolf depicts Charlotte Brontë as one who 'stumbled and fell with that clumsy weapon in her hands', while 'George Eliot committed atrocities with it that beggar description. Jane Austen looked at it and laughed at it and devised a perfectly natural, shapely sentence proper for her own use and never departed from it' (115).

'Perfectly natural, shapely . . . proper for her own use': this statement, typically, pronounces everything and nothing about 'the' female sentence; her point being, of course, that there is no such thing. 'Sentence' in this context takes on an almost metaphoric meaning, so that Woolf suggests that a writer needs, above all, the freedom to be his or her own creator in and of language. 'I keep thinking of different ways to manage my scenes; conceiving endless possibilities; seeing life, as I walk about the streets, an immense opaque block of material to be conveyed by me into its equivalent of language' (*D*, i, 214, November 1918). Exactly thirteen years later in another diary entry she wrote: 'I think I am about to embody, at last, the exact shapes my brain holds. What a long toil to reach this beginning' (*D*, iv, 53, November 1931). In some senses all of Woolf's work can be read as a quest for an authorial self, but the early work shows on its surface more of the signs of struggle inherent in such a quest. The real bogey handed on to her from the nineteenth century, with which she engaged at this period in a life-or-death combat, was the masculine voice of the omniscient narrator.

Jane Austen simply did not use the typically Victorian omniscient narrator convention of Thackeray, Trollope and George Eliot; yet to imitate her sentence would have been as pointless as to adopt George Eliot's heavy disguise of a male persona. For an unspoken assumption among readers is that the Victorian omniscient narrator *is* a male persona; female omniscience, in a patriarchal society with an androcentric religion, is a contradiction in terms. Under the conditions of this male-dominated tradition which Virginia Woolf inherited, to adopt the all-knowing voice of omniscient narration was, in effect, to adopt a thoroughly masculine tone. It is a measure of the miracle she wrought on behalf of her sex that by the time she wrote *The Waves* she had created a linguistic territory in which a female omniscient narrator could take voice and find the freedom in which to remain sexually neutral. 'I am the seer. I am the force that arranges. I am the thing in which all this exists. Certainly without me it would perish. I can give it order. I perceive what is bound to happen.' As one of her more perceptive commentators, J. W. Graham, has remarked of this passage from the first holograph draft of *The Waves*, this 'she . . . perceives what is bound to happen; but she does not make it happen.'[8]

Graham speaks of the narrator in *Middlemarch* having 'a form of *knowledge* superior to [the characters']' whereas, 'in contrast to this effect of authorial omniscience, the narrative continuum that Virginia Woolf sought to establish might be termed "omnipercipience"' (p. 106). It is tempting to take this view as further evidence for Woolf's success in dismantling the kind of masculine prejudices endemic in the morally superior tone of the typical Victorian narrator-persona and in creating a discourse which can give voice to a morally neutral or unprejudiced female omniscience—or more accurately, as Graham says, 'omnipercipience'. Of course *The Waves* can in some senses be regarded as a special case, coming as the final ('six-sided') flowering of her 'androgynous' period of the late '20s, and in its exploration of the idea of the androgynous mind even more of a *tour de force* than *Orlando*. However necessary a path it was for her to have followed, her later novels indicate the extent to which *The Waves* proved in this regard to be a cul-de-sac. It seems to me that too much can be made too easily of Woolf's so-called 'androgynous ideal', and while we may not wish to reduce it, as one critic does, to 'a temporary metaphor, appropriate in the context of an essay on women and fiction',[9] we should perhaps remain wary of pursuing it through her works with a kind of single-mindedness that was never exhibited by their author.

A discussion of the nature of narrative voice can usefully include extended analyses of passages from the works in question, but within the scope of this essay I can only offer some suggestions towards possible new lines of enquiry. If we now look at Woolf's first three novels while bearing in mind the especially problematical nature of the 'I' for a female writer at the beginning of the twentieth century, it may help us towards a fuller appreciation of the genuinely revolutionary qualities they embody.

In a letter to Lytton Strachey written during the long composition of *The Voyage Out*, Virginia Woolf responds to his tales of the novel he will write with a characteristic blend of teasing affection and self-mocking envy: 'Why do you tantalise me with stories of your novel? I wish you would confine your genius to one department, it's too bad to have you dancing . . . over all departments of literature . . . and now fiction.' She then goes on to say: 'A painstaking woman who wishes . . . to give voice to some of the perplexities of her sex, in plain English, has no chance at all' (*L*, i, 381). On one level, this clearly continues the tone of self-mockery, but its aptness to what she was in fact engaged upon in her first novel, giving 'voice to some of the perplexities of her sex', lends it the deeper ring of truth. It is significant, too, that it is Strachey to whom she is writing in this disarmingly self-depreciating manner, since *The Voyage Out* can be read as an extended argument with those aspects of Bloomsbury most particularly represented by her earliest literary rival.

For while it is true that Bloomsbury was in many ways a strong liberating influence in Virginia Stephen's life, releasing her from the toils of respectable bourgeois hypocrisy associated with life at Hyde Park Gate, the double-edged characterization of the two Bloomsbury figures in *The Voyage Out*— St. John Hirst and Helen Ambrose—indicates the extent of their author's unease with some of the values they represent. Both appoint themselves as Rachel's educators; both regard their own attitudes to sexuality as uniquely untrammelled by conventional hypocrisy; both assume that women can have no equal share in male sexual enjoyment. When Rachel tries to explain to Helen her sense of fear and confusion at her own abruptly awakened sexual feelings after Richard Dalloway's kiss, Helen's response is dismissive.

> Men will want to kiss you, just as they'll want to marry you. The pity is to get things out of proportion. It's like noticing the

noises people make when they eat, or men spitting; or, in short, any small thing that gets on one's nerves. (90–1)

This is very similar to St. John's attitude to female sexuality: that it is virtually non-existent, and certainly has nothing to do with any notion of masculine pleasure or fulfilment. Here he talks to Hewet, who is beginning to fall in love with Rachel:

'What I abhor most of all,' he concluded, 'is the female breast. Imagine being Venning and having to get into bed with Susan! But the really repulsive thing is that they feel nothing at all— about what I do when I have a hot bath. They're gross, they're absurd, they're utterly intolerable!' (216)

This is a delightfully barbed parody of the narcissistic side of male homoeroticism; but one of its effects is to make more sinister the alliance between the female-despising Hirst and the strongly male-identified Helen. In a novel which is so largely concerned with the sexual initiation rites of a virgin girl, it is tempting to see in the characterization of these two Bloomsbury figures and their effect on Rachel a sharply personal reference to Woolf herself. However, more than enough has been written elsewhere about Virginia Woolf's relationships with her Bloomsbury friends, as well as with her father, mother, sister, brothers, half-sisters, half-brothers, brother-in-law, half-brother-in-law, to say nothing of husband, to make one almost begin to doubt whether any of her novels were 'made up' at all. Louise De Salvo's account of the genesis of *The Voyage Out* seems to hint that the earlier version, *Melymbrosia*, is the better novel, because it bears a less disguised relation to Woolf's personal experiences.[10] As a basis for evaluation this kind of reasoning is open to the objection that it refuses autonomy to the novel as fictional construct. *The Voyage Out* is not a disguised first-person novel, as such criticism implies. Although Rachel is seen from the inside, it is not her consciousness which frames the novel, but that of Woolf's narrator, whose gender-conscious ironies operate as a constant reminder to the reader of the existence of the sex-war as a kind of grim backcloth to the romantic love story.

Irony is of course an excellent substitute for masculinity when it comes to lending authority to a narrative voice, as women writers have always had reason to know. More assured in her later novels, as well as more anti-authoritarian, Woolf had less need of the interventions of an ironic narrator. Even in this novel, we find the poised witty voice of the opening—in tone a composite of Jane Austen and late George Eliot ('Each of the ladies, being after the fashion of their sex, highly trained in promoting men's talk without listening to it' (11))—to be gradually subsumed into the voices of the characters as the story draws further out from its solid anchorage in English literary tradition. It is too simple to say that the authorial voice becomes one with the heroine's: the perspectives are broader than any single viewpoint, as is beautifully illustrated by the final scene in which it is St. John Hirst, redeemed by his heroic perseverance on Rachel's behalf, who reverses her journey from this world into the unknown by coming back into the circle of light and warmth in the hotel from the darkness beyond.

One consequence of identifying Rachel Vinrace with her author has been a denigration of the novel as the product of a prudish mind. James Naremore, despite some excellent analysis of what he calls the 'submission of the narrator's ego to the world she writes about', cannot resist chiding Woolf for being 'manifestly prudish' in *The Voyage Out*.[11] In a critic who is otherwise sensitive to what he terms 'the generally erotic nature of her art', this misreading (as it seems to me) smacks of a blindness to the female perspective of this particular novel. Like De Salvo, he makes too close an association between the identities of author and heroine, and projects onto Woolf the nervousness about sexuality that is a characteristic of Rachel Vinrace. Virginia Woolf herself may or may not have been sexually nervous: the point I would wish to stress is that she is perfectly conscious, as author, of this quality in her heroine—it is not a case of an unconscious projection of her own secret fears.

Naremore (p. 22) quite rightly points to the evocative image of the old lady gardeners as one which contains overtones of both sexuality and death:

> millions of dark-red flowers were blooming, until the old ladies who had tended them so carefully came down the paths with their scissors, snipped through their juicy stalks, and laid them upon cold stone ledges in the village church. (*VO*, 28)

But this is not a generalized image of a sex/death equation: it is specifically an evocation of female castrators at work, and as such carries a resonance not only in the scene where Rachel spies the old women decapitating live chickens behind the hotel, but also in the much later dream-image of her delirium: 'Terence sat down by the bedside. . . . Her eyes were not entirely shut. . . . She opened them completely when he kissed her. But she only saw an old woman slicing a man's head off with a knife' (413). This is a recurrent dream of hers (p. 406), and, like the disgustingly oozy vaginal tunnel dream, represents an internalization by Rachel of certain male fears about women. (Particularly male homosexual fears—Terence's friendship with the homosexually-inclined St. John is left deliberately suggestive.) Naremore's misunderstanding of this important layer of meaning in the novel is underlined by the nature of his reference to Woolf's essay 'Professions for Women', which he invokes in confirmation of his 'author-as-prude' theory.

He cites a well-known passage from this essay in which Woolf confesses to having been unable, as a writer, to rid herself of inhibitions about 'telling the truth about my own experience as a body', and in a footnote (p. 44) he quotes at length from another passage which develops the image of a woman writer as a girl fishing:

> letting her imagination sweep unchecked round every rock and cranny of the world that lies submerged in the depths of our unconscious being. Now came the experience that I believe to be far commoner with women writers than with men. The line raced through the girl's fingers. Her imagination had rushed away. It had sought the pools, the depths, the dark places where the largest fish slumber. And then there was a smash. . . . The girl was roused from her dream. . . . she had thought of something, something about the body, about the passions which it was unfitting for her as a woman to say. (*E*, ii, 287–88)

Certainly, this passage describes sexual inhibition in the writer as writer; but such inhibition could have other causes than prudishness. In fact, Naremore stops quoting at exactly the point where Woolf ascribes such a cause. She goes on:

> Men, her reason told her, would be shocked. The consciousness of what men will say of a woman who speaks the truth about her passions had roused her from her artist's state of unconsciousness. She could write no more. The trance was over. Her imagination could work no longer. This I believe to be a very

common experience with women writers—they are impeded by
the extreme conventionality of the other sex. (288)

I should like to suggest that it is this very problem of a
woman's disablement by fear of condemnation by the other
sex, that is Woolf's subject in her first novel. For Naremore,
like other critics, again too simply interprets Rachel's death.
He assures us: 'For Rachel . . . there does come an ultimate
union with Hewet, which results indirectly in her death'
(p. 52). 'And ultimately, death has the power to bring about
an intense communion; at the moment when Rachel dies,
Terence feels that "their complete union and happiness filled
the room with rings eddying more and more widely" ' (p. 53).
Precisely: *Terence* feels—Terence, whose petty power struggle
with Helen over the doctor ('Unconsciously he took Rodriguez'
side against Helen') has led to a possibly fatal delay in
obtaining more trustworthy medical help, and whose jealousy
of Rachel's 'otherness' gives credence to her delirious fears of
'castrating', in the sense of emasculating, him:

> Terence . . . was looking at her keenly and with dissatisfaction.
> She seemed to be able to cut herself adrift from him, and to pass
> away to unknown places where she had no need of him. The
> thought roused his jealousy.
> 'I sometimes think you're not in love with me and never will
> be,' he said energetically. She started and turned round at his
> words.
> 'I don't satisfy you in the way you satisfy me,' he continued.
> 'There's something I can't get hold of in you. You don't want
> me as I want you—you're always wanting something else.'
> (370)

In this novel men and women are shown to share the fear
that the other sex will use them, turn them into objects. But
whereas men have an age-old common language in which to
give voice to this fear, women have no such language. In
Rachel, the fear becomes fatally internalized. Terence dismisses peremptorily and without compunction the most
important thing in her life—her music: 'that kind of thing is
merely like an unfortunate old dog going round on its hind legs
in the rain' (357). Undertones suggesting Dr. Johnson's comment on women preachers reinforce his message here, and he

remains quite insensitive to her anxiety at being exhibited as an object at the hotel tea-party after their engagement. The point is, of course, that there is no conceivable way for Rachel to object to any of this treatment, in terms a conventional male like Terence could understand, except by rejecting him outright. And rejecting a man one has attracted and to whom one has promised sexual fulfilment is in traditional male mythology tantamount to castrating him.

Despite some flaws in construction, this novel does not in my view read like the work of a writer projecting her own unconscious sexual timidity onto her heroine. Nor is it just another *Bildungsroman* detailing the metaphysical education of a heroine enacting Eliade's version of the heroic myth, who ' "returns to life a new man" ', as Avrom Fleishmann would have it.[12] Some feminist critics have been equally guilty of ignoring the impact of the female perspective in this novel. Patricia Stubbs, for instance, futilely castigates Woolf for failing to create new feminist role models in her fiction, claiming that 'she deliberately avoided [writing] at a conscious level about what it means to be a woman living in our society.'[13] 'At a conscious level'; does this mean, at the level of polemical assertion? Yet, if Hillis Miller is right, the most important themes of any novel lie not in its explicit affirmations, 'but in significances generated by the way in which the story is told.' If this is true of any novel it is surely true of *The Voyage Out*, which enacts precisely through its narrative strategies 'what it means to be a woman living in our society' and which, as the remarkably polished first work of an extraordinarily sophisticated and self-aware mind, deserves to be taken more seriously in its own right as a voicing of 'some of the perplexities of her sex'.

' "[Gibbon] has a point of view & sticks to it" I said. "And so do you. I wobble" ' (*D*, ii, 115). This snippet from a reported conversation with Strachey in 1921 once more disguises under disarming self-depreciation an important perception about the difference between Woolf's own writing and the arch-masculine style of a Gibbon or a Strachey. Her 'wobbling' is her ability to undermine the very idea of any centralized moral standpoint, any authoritarian idea of 'omniscience', by a strategy of continual modulation of tone of voice. This strategy she developed more fully in her middle period, but already in *The Voyage Out* she had taken up a distinctly combative posture toward the masculine intellectual world in general, and that of Bloomsbury in particular. By the time she wrote her next novel, *Night and Day*, she was prepared to take on the even more vexed question of woman versus family inherited from the Victorians. Here Bloomsbury was much more on her side, although the sex battle—or, more precisely, the battle for a hearing of the female view—still continues, endowing the fiction with its own intricate and comprehensive form.

Narrative subject-position has shifted radically in *Night and Day*. No longer so concerned to play with the postures of certainty, Woolf allows her viewpoint to 'wobble' in good earnest. The sense of mistiness achieved in the earlier part of the novel is profoundly effective in unsettling any mundane expectations of firm focus. Mitchell Leaska is one critic who has commented on Woolf's technique in *To the Lighthouse* of using semantic constructs containing 'it seemed', 'perhaps it was', 'it was as if'. After listing examples, he remarks:

> Supposedly, these are omniscient statements; but when we begin to notice the 'seem's, the 'perhaps's, the unspecified 'something's, and so on, we begin to question the narrator's omniscience: we sense him [*sic*] to be a little diffident; a little uneasy—uncertain.[14]

The same technique marks the much earlier *Night and Day*; here it reaches a point where 'omniscient' almost ceases to be a useful definition of the narrator's function.

The cool, observant, mildly ironic tone of the narration which opens *Night and Day* is identified at this stage with the heroine, Katharine Hilbery—or at least with that 'fifth part of her mind' (1) which is occupied with the social rituals demanded by her place within her family circle. The counter-tendency towards mistiness and lack of outline enters the novel with Ralph Denham's bemused outsider's perception of this charmed circle:

> it seemed to Mr. Denham as if a thousand softly padded doors had closed between him and the street outside. A fine mist, the etherialized essence of the fog, hung visibly in the wide and rather empty space of the drawing-room, all silver where the

candles were grouped on the tea-table, and ruddy again in the firelight. (2)

The impersonal narrating voice then takes up this counter-pointed tone which in itself suggests the possibilities of questioning the cool certainties of ironic observation: 'The smaller room was something like a chapel in a cathedral, or a grotto in a cave, for the booming sound of the traffic in the distance suggested the soft surge of waters' (7). This voice soon modulates back into Katharine's own self-perceptions, which now take on a romantic haze of their own:

> While Mr. Denham examined the manuscript, she glanced up at her grandfather, and, for the thousandth time, fell into a pleasant dreamy state in which she seemed to be the companion of those giant men, of their own lineage, at any rate, and the insignificant present moment was put to shame. (8)

There are 'seemings' of many kinds in this novel; people 'seem' to the narrator, to themselves, to other characters; but gradually outlines clarify and the definitions grow sharper. The nebulousness which characterizes many perceptions early in the novel never disappears entirely, but once a new plane of reality far removed from social 'realism' has been established— where things are indeed found to be other than they seem—the 'seemings' drop from the narrator's discourse. The antithetical values of 'Night' and 'Day' have been turned about and placed in a new relationship with one another.

One of the problems encountered in the narrative technique of *Night and Day* is that a novel which tries to show the insubstantiality of our usual notions of 'reality' by means of a form which in many respects is still that of the traditional realist novel, runs into the danger of itself disappearing into insubstantiality. As in *The Voyage Out*, Woolf's technical radicalism is here of such a subtle kind, relying for its subversive effect on shifts of vision and focus from within the citadel of prejudice, that its extent has often gone unrecognized. However, in an important recent essay Jane Marcus has argued for a feminist reading of the novel as a radically subversive re-statement of the themes of Mozart's opera *The Magic Flute*[15]—though one may wonder what we are now to make of Woolf's reaction noted during the composition of *Night and Day*: 'I went to the Magic

Flute, & thought rather better of humanity for having that in them' (*D*, i, 153–54). Marcus makes no mention of this remark, and while many of the structural parallels she locates are indeed illuminating, I cannot agree with her overall view of the novel as a simple reversal of the patriarchal patterning of *The Magic Flute*, nor do I read it as so uniformly comic in form and execution as she does.

Certainly there is a strong comic vein in the novel, introducing a note of hilarity or even farce to descriptions of Katharine's interfering aunts, the byplay between Rodney and Cassandra, and Mrs. Hilbery's sentimental excesses. But it seems to me that a great deal of the real substance of the novel concerns the growth of the relationship between Katharine and Ralph, and that this is not treated primarily as the stuff of comedy. Perhaps it would be a more successful novel if it were; part of the comparative failure of *Night and Day* as against *The Voyage Out*, in my view, springs from the imposition of a comic-romantic ending upon a story which has placed so much stress on the tragic impossibilities in life. In these terms, the novel seems not so much to illustrate successful control, by subversion, of patriarchal positions, as its own subversion by its over-rigorous, over-conscientious effort to put the masculine case fairly through the characterization of Ralph Denham.

Ralph does not appear to me to be in any meaningful sense a 'natural lower-class man . . . the agent of freedom for the upper-middle-class woman' (Marcus, p. 114). Far too intellectually-minded for either role (besides being quite solidly middle-class), Ralph finally gets the girl he deserves: not the free-minded, fine-hearted Mary Datchet, but the self-centred, vague, imperious Katharine. The complex relationship between Katharine and Ralph is made the repository for a great deal of tortuous exploration and revaluation of traditional notions of romantic love. There are some wonderfully managed passages: the sense of the importance of what is left unsaid is made very telling; but the burden of seriousness placed on Ralph sits oddly with the flashes of comedy that illuminate other aspects of the novel. On one of the rare occasions when the narrative perspective withdraws from Ralph to describe him comically from the outside, at the beginning of Chapter 25, we find a note of satire directed not only against Ralph's ideal of

129

romantic love, but also, by means of an extended allusion, against that arch-Victorian concept of the lone (male) individual upholding his love/integrity as a shield against the perfidiousness of life.

> Still, still, one goes on, the ticking seconds seemed to assure him, with dignity, with open eyes, with determination not to accept the second-rate, not to be tempted by the unworthy, not to yield, not to compromise. Twenty-five minutes past three were now marked upon the face of the watch. The world, he assured himself, since Katharine Hilbery was now half an hour behind her time, offers no happiness, no rest from struggle, no certainty.[16]

The satiric note provided by this splendid spoof on traditional masculine values is unusual in the case of Ralph, who is clearly intended to be a man well ahead of Terence Hewet in the evolution of a civilized male. As such, however, he belongs to the realm of wish-fulfilment, as does the comic happy ending of the book. The comic sight of Mr. Hilbery, the Victorian father fearfully jealous of his daughter's love and liberation from paternal control, 'the extravagant, inconsiderate, uncivilized male, outraged somehow and gone bellowing to his lair with a roar' (530), is far more artistically convincing than Mrs. Hilbery's sudden transformation into a *dea ex machina* who engineers the happy events. Here one might well bring the charge that the sentimentality of her character has escaped authorial control and is allowed to give a false shape to the action.

Woolf's most comprehensive attempt to give a hearing to the masculine point of view—and thereby to exorcize the masculinist genie—resulted in the highly interesting case of *Jacob's Room*. Modern critics have on the whole been less enchanted with the novel than were Woolf's fellow-artists Forster and Eliot, partly no doubt because of its eclipse by the major work which followed it. Leaska gives a well-balanced interpretation along traditional non-feminist critical lines, taking Jacob himself as a serious experiment in a new kind of characterization, which asks the reader the question: 'What does that looking-glass reflect of Jacob?' He concludes that Jacob's life is one which 'has been hopelessly denuded of grace', but he never verges on the kind of insight brought to the novel by a recent feminist critic, Judy Little, who finds it to be a parody of the *Bildungsroman* form, primarily comic in intention and effect.[17] (It is perhaps more than a coincidence that both *Jacob's Room* and *Night and Day*, the novels in which Woolf explores the male psyche most conscientiously, have been interpreted by feminist critics as comedies.) Yet, while I find much of Little's reading persuasive, *Jacob's Room* does appear to me to be more complicated in voice, mood and structure than she allows.

In many ways it seems more successful in its tragi-comic form than *Night and Day*, not least because of its brilliant ending. The technique for which it has always been praised, that of creating presence out of absence, is still as much the strength of the novel's achievement as are the elements of parody contained within its form. One can see in this why Eliot admired the novel so much, though he must also have appreciated its imagistic narrative transitions. Unlike *The Voyage Out*, whose narrative unit is the chapter, and whose chapter endings are rounded and polished with dramatic flair, *Jacob's Room* relies on connecting the apparently disparate by setting up subtle trains of imagery which shift and modulate like a mirror of the narrative voice, creating a chain of perception wherein each new image reflects and contains the preceding one. To find an illustration of this, one has only to look at the opening section. Instead of beginning like the earlier novels with an external ironic viewpoint to give authority to the narrative voice, *Jacob's Room* opens with Betty Flanders's viewpoint, then modulates through the image of Charles Steele's paint-brush, trembling 'like the antennae of some irritable insect', into his view of Betty Flanders; then to Archer's view of Charles Steele—'the old gentleman in spectacles'—then to the impersonal narrator's view of Archer, placing him in the context of absence (of Jacob, whom he's calling unavailingly), disembodied purity and sadness (6–7).

It is this containing note of melancholy, introduced from the beginning and reinforced throughout by the imagery of absence and loss, which links the feeling of the book with Hardy's *Jude* and works against its Meredithian comic echoes to produce a contrapuntal effect, more successful because more rigorously

131

sustained than in *Night and Day*. The search to define an absence is continued on the formal level by the further depersonalizing of the narrator. The attempt to embrace and create 'what is outside [the] self and beyond', which Woolf criticizes Joyce for failing to undertake (in her essay 'Modern Fiction', written between *Night and Day* and *Jacob's Room* (*E*, ii, 108)) is clearly what she is after in her 'voicing' of *Jacob*. Yet this attempt, paralleled by Eliot's, as well as Yeats's, to remove 'self' or 'personality' from her writing, does not, I think, result in androgyny in Woolf's writing any more than it does in Eliot's use of Tiresias's voice in *The Waste Land*. Not, at least, androgyny in the sense in which Woolf praised it in *A Room of One's Own*: the achievement of unconsciousness of sex in the writer. There are, after all, both male and female androgynes, and either sex might be capable of using androgyny as a myth to raise sex-prejudice to the level of received truth: that is, of adopting an androgynous mask which offers to speak impartially for both sexes, but which, somehow, still gives utterance to the viewpoint of one. To label Virginia Woolf's progress as a novelist a 'flight into androgyny', as Elaine Showalter does in *A Literature of Their Own* (Princeton, 1977), is a misinterpretation in more ways than the obvious one of giving too much weight to one particular work (*A Room of One's Own*). For if she was in flight at all, it was a flight away from such easy certainties as were offered by inherited voices of authoritative masculine omniscient narration, or even of ironic feminine 'knowing' narration, towards a goal that was not so much the fusion of masculine and feminine perspectives, as the deconstruction of the opposition between them.

It is entertaining to observe the reactions of some eminent critics to gender-conscious criticism of Woolf's novels. Hillis Miller in his latest book makes elaborate obeisance to the idea of the author's female presence informing narrative voice, while at the other extreme James Hafley (author of *The Glass Roof: Virginia Woolf as Novelist* (Berkeley, 1954)), becomes quite vehement with indignation on the subject in a recent essay:

> How far the mark is a reading that identifies (often without thought) the 'I' with a woman because a woman wrote the story—or worse with Virginia Woolf because she wrote it—and

then looks to the voice's subject as to some revelatory 'idea' or 'message'. Nothing, evidently—not even the explicitly male narrator of *Orlando*—will stop this kind of misreading.[18]

My reply to Hafley would be to remind him that George Eliot showed us long ago that a male narrator-persona can yet convey, chiefly by the tone of his ironies about women, the gender-consciousness that betrays a female perspective. It is surely a mistake, too, to avoid the subtext of such teasing statements as this from *Orlando*: 'As that is not a question that can engage the attention of a sensible man, let us, who enjoy the immunity of all biographers and historians from any sex whatever, pass it over, and merely state . . .' (199). What this passage reveals, of course, is not the inconsequence of gender, but the absolute necessity for considering it as a factor in any discussion of narrative voice in Woolf's work. However attracted she felt to the possibility of escaping from the boundaries of one sex's perceptions, it is my view that she never did or could escape from the knowledge of her own femaleness. Perhaps it is simply that gender-consciousness, like class-consciousness, is easy to efface from one's mind only if one feels in the superior position.

In *Jacob's Room*, Woolf's technique deconstructs the whole notion of an integrated self as a unifying principle either for characterization or for narration. Gender critique has been largely submerged, subsumed into form, in the sense that there is no longer any female character to give cheerful voice to the debunking of patriarchal mythologies, as Mary Datchet does in *Night and Day* ('Men are such pedants—they don't know what things matter, and what things don't' (88)), and as the ironic narrator in the same novel can do as well: 'like most insignificant men he was very quick to resent being found fault with by a woman' (88–9). Miss Julia Hedge, the feminist in the British Museum reading room, functions only as a sly intrusion; even those shifts in narrative focus which temporarily personalize the narrator ('Often have I seen them' (95) are less important as a factor in the parodic role of the novel than is the gender-consciousness that inwardly informs all of its narration.

As Harvena Richter points out, the narrating presence in

Jacob's Room 'seems to take the position of the reader, who injects his own subjectivity, inventing where the author has left silences and spaces for just this purpose'.[19] Yet, are we really left so free? Or is this freedom itself strictly controlled, its spaces shaped? In one sense, Jacob himself withholds credence from 'his' novel—he doesn't believe in novels after Fielding. This point gives significant indication of the mixture of affection and combativeness with which the 'room' for Jacob is created. While it is possible to read the book as a perfectly sympathetic account of a young man who is in many ways full of promise, whose life is pointlessly thrown away, it is also possible to read it, as Judy Little does, as a parody of entrenched masculine prejudices. If one searches the novel for what Jacob has to say on his own behalf, one emerges with a list of utterances that make highly comic reading: blurted, arrogant, aborted. And yet—it is not as simple as that. The novel does embody a subtle questioning of all kinds of assumptions about male values, masculine superiority: 'Sandra would hear time accumulating, and ask herself, "What for? What for?" . . . Jacob never asked himself any such questions, to judge by the way he laced his boots . . . He was young—a man' (160–61). Yet, at the same time, there is a larger vision contained in the recognition of the price Jacob pays for his privilege:

> Like blocks of tin soldiers the army covers the cornfield, moves up the hillside, stops, reels slightly this way and that, and falls flat, save that, through field-glasses, it can be seen that one or two pieces still agitate up and down like fragments of broken match-stick. (155)

Likewise, the detailing of Jacob's struggle against mutability, 'kisses on lips that are to die' (152), as much as his evident power to affect other characters deeply, gives a resonance to his being which reaches beyond mere parody. Woof urges the reader's complicity here in seizing that very 'unseizable' life force which, whatever the 'men in clubs and Cabinets' (154) may say, animates all her fictions. She does this of course partly by the technique of showing its effects, by leaving the empty shoes to speak their own story. But more than this, it is by the enormously creative skill with which she varies, modulates, divides and joins the narrating voices of these fictions, in such a way that each voicing gives utterance not only to itself, and to its subject of discourse, but to a different relation between private and public vision, that Virginia Woolf can indeed, it seems, persuade many readers to accept her female perspective as the norm.

NOTES

1. See, for instance, 'The Laugh of the Medusa', transl. Paula and Keith Cohen, in *Signs*, 1 (1976), 875–93, and 'Castration or Decapitation?', transl. and introduced by Annette Kuhn, in *Signs*, 7 (1981), 36–55.

2. De Beauvoir's famous statement in *The Second Sex* (1949), 'One is not born a woman, one becomes a woman', is still a focal point in this debate. Julia Kristeva, for instance, has argued that the term 'woman' cannot be defined, since it is a social and not a natural construct. See the 1974 interview with her repr. in *New French Feminisms*, ed. Elaine Marks and Isabelle de Courtivron (Brighton, Sussex, 1981), pp. 137–41.

3. For instance the definition offered by the editors of *New French Feminisms*: 'an awareness of women's oppression-repression that initiates both analyses of the dimension of this oppression-repression, and strategies for liberation' (p. x).

4. That Woolf resented such treatment is testified both by her diary entry for 10 September 1928 (*D*, iii, 195) and by the way in which she introduced this criticism (omitting the reference to herself) into *RO* (113).

5. *Fiction and Repetition* (Oxford, 1982), p. 176.

6. See Woolf's review of Richardson's *Revolving Lights*, repr. *CW*: 'She has invented, or, if she has not invented, developed and applied to her own uses, a sentence which we might call the psychological sentence of the feminine gender' (124). Because of its particular reference to Richardson's dramatized first-person narrator, this comment cannot properly be applied to Woolf's own work.

7. I have taken this term from an article by Ann Banfield, 'Narrative Style and Direct and Indirect Speech', *Foundations of Language*, 10 (1973), 1–39. Banfield argues cogently for the use of this term to indicate the presence of an 'I' as expressor of point of view, since unlike James's 'centre-of-consciousness', 'subject-of-consciousness' is a '+human noun'.

8. 'Point of View in *The Waves*: Some Services of the Style', in *Virginia Woolf*, ed. Thomas S. W. Lewis (New York, 1975), p. 106.

9. Phyllis Rose, *Woman of Letters: A Life of Virginia Woolf* (1978), p. 190.

10. *Virginia Woolf's First Voyage: A Novel in the Making* (1980). See especially her concluding chapter, 'Fiction as Masquerade'.

11. *The World Without a Self* (Yale, 1973), pp. 27, 242.

12. Fleishmann, *Virginia Woolf: A Critical Reading* (1975), p. 5.
13. *Women in Fiction: Feminism and the Novel 1880–1920* (1979), p. 233.
14. *Virginia Woolf's Lighthouse: A Study in Critical Method* (1970), p. 59.
15. 'Enchanted Organs, Magic Bells: *Night and Day* as Comic Opera', in *Virginia Woolf: Revaluation and Continuity*, ed. Ralph Freedman (1980), pp. 97–122.
16. *ND*, 348. Cf. Tennyson's *Ulysses*:

> Death closes all; but something ere the end,
> Some work of noble note, may yet be done . . .
> One equal temper of heroic hearts,
> Made weak by time and fate, but strong in will
> To strive, to seek, to find, and not to yield;

and Arnold's *Dover Beach*:

> Ah, love, let us be true
> To one another! for the world, which seems
> To lie before us like a land of dreams,
> So various, so beautiful, so new,
> Hath really neither joy, nor love, nor light,
> Not certitude, nor peace, nor help for pain.

17. Leaska, *The Novels of Virginia Woolf from Beginning to End* (1977), p. 84; Little, '*Jacob's Room* as Comedy: Woolf's Parodic *Bildungsroman*', in *New Feminist Essays on Virginia Woolf*, ed. Jane Marcus (1981), pp. 105–24.
18. 'Virginia Woolf's Narrators and the Art of "Life Itself"', in *Virginia Woolf: Revaluation and Continuity*, p. 35.
19. *Virginia Woolf: The Inward Voyage* (Princeton, 1970), p. 137.

7

Mourning and Modernism

by JOHN MEPHAM

Why did Virginia Woolf feel that it was so important for fiction to escape from the tyranny of conventional form?[1] Why did she reject the conventions of plot, character, narrator and verisimilitude? What was the motivation for modernism?

In those essays where she tries to unravel her reasons for feeling that conventional form was falsifying, Virginia Woolf emphasizes above all two aspects of experience: density of meaning, and instability. In a passage that must have been written with Proust in mind she said that the novel must develop the means

> to dramatize some of those influences which play so large a part in life, yet have so far escaped the novelist—the power of music, the stimulus of sight, the effect on us of the shape of trees or the play of colour, the emotions bred in us by crowds, the obscure terrors and hatreds which come so irrationally in certain places or from certain people, the delight of movement, the intoxication of wine. Every moment is the centre and meeting-place of an extraordinary number of perceptions which have not yet been expressed. Life is always and inevitably much richer than we who try to express it.[2]

Conventional form, which is based on the definition of character and which encourages rapid judgement as to the meaning of an experience, is not equipped to explore, slowly and without prejudice, the 'tumultuous and contradictory emotions' (ii, 228). Conventional form is linearity and closure. Experience is of instability (of emotion, of values, of meanings) and endless ramifications of meaning. 'The commonest actions, such as going up in an elevator or eating cake, instead of being discharged automatically, rake up in their progress a whole series of thoughts, sensations, ideas, memories which were apparently sleeping on the walls of the mind', she says, again with Proust in mind.[3] Her emphasis is on what is ungovernable in experience, as with Proust's involuntary memory. The centrality of the involuntary undermines the confidence on which conventional form is based and points to areas of life which make that confidence seem foolish and cruel. For the moderns 'the point of interest lies very likely in the dark places of psychology'.[4]

Conventional form is personified in the figure of a 'powerful and unscrupulous tyrant' (ii, 106), because the choice of conventional form is not simply a benign mistake. It results in reproducing within the novel a relationship of power and subordination with which Virginia Woolf was very familiar in life. The novel, most particularly the English Edwardian novel,[5] tried to construct something orderly out of the chaos of fragmentary experience, involuntary memory, and obscure, ambiguous emotion. One of the most masterly devices for achieving this order was the symbiotic pair, the narrator and the fictional character. The character might be full of ambiguity and conflict, struggle and incoherence, but there always stood close at hand and observing with a judicious eye that tyrant, the narrator. The narrator's authoritative pronouncements made things intelligible for the reader: the narrator summed up, defined, forced things to stand still in the clear light of his language. The narrator's lucid discourse is the one in which judgements are pronounced, explanations are provided, praise and blame are apportioned, moral worth is estimated. The narrator's function is to say, 'This is what she really meant', 'This is what he was feeling', 'These are the real reasons why they acted so', 'This is how we are to interpret the event.' The narrator acts like Bernard's old nurse in *The Waves*, who turns the pages of the picture-book and stops and says 'Look. This is the truth' (204).

It takes an unhealthy sense of self-importance to have such confidence in one's judgements, such trust in one's powers. What may seem supremely healthy in the strong man is really a sickness. For Virginia Woolf, as for Nietzsche, the genealogy of these muscular morals leads one back into the dark recesses of the mind. For fiction to explore this 'dark country'[6] we need a transvaluation of values. Unlike Nietzsche, Virginia Woolf thought of this as a change to a woman's vision:

> It is probable, however, that both in life and in art the values of a woman are not the values of a man. Thus, when a woman comes to write a novel, she will find that she is perpetually wishing to alter the established values—to make serious what appears insignificant to a man, and trivial what is to him important. (ii, 146)

Virginia Woolf found confident judgement both foolish and horrifying. There are many men in her novels who proudly and ludicrously reduce things to their kind of order. In *To the Lighthouse* there is Mr. Ramsay with his heroic effort to get from A to Z. In *Mrs. Dalloway* there is Hugh Whitbread, who writes letters to *The Times*, 'drafting sentiments in alphabetical order of the highest nobility' (122). In *Jacob's Room* the connections between the conventions of the novel and the supposed virtues of male decisiveness are made explicit. Fiction must deal in ambiguity, the impossibility of judgement; it must avoid the formulaic definition of character. 'It is no use trying to sum people up. One must follow hints, not exactly what is said, nor yet entirely what is done' (153). But men of the world dismiss this as women's nonsense. Civilization depends upon confidence and the effort that is required to maintain confidence. Powerful men are impatient with subtlety and ambiguity. 'So we are driven back to see what the other side means—the men in clubs and Cabinets—when they say that character-drawing is a frivolous fireside art, a matter of pins and needles, exquisite outlines enclosing vacancy, flourishes, and mere scrawls' (*JR*, 154–55). Like the soldier Gerald Dawes in E. M. Forster's *The Longest Journey*, such men cannot stand unhealthiness (Ch. 4). They take health to be the uncomplicated exercise of the will to power, and the ability to wage war.

> The battleships ray out over the North Sea, keeping their stations accurately apart. At a given signal all the guns are trained on a target which . . . flames into splinters. With equal nonchalance a dozen young men in the prime of life descend with composed faces into the depths of the sea; and there impassively

(though with perfect mastery of machinery) suffocate uncom-
plainingly together. Like blocks of tin soldiers the army covers
the cornfield, moves up the hillside, stops, reels slightly this way
and that, and falls flat, save that, through field-glasses, it can be
seen that one or two pieces still agitate up and down like
fragments of broken match-stick.

These actions, together with the incessant commerce of banks,
laboratories, chancellories, and houses of business, are the
strokes which oar the world forward, they say. . . .

It is thus that we live, they say, driven by an unseizable force.
They say that the novelists never catch it; that it goes hurtling
through their nets and leaves them torn to ribbons. This, they
say, is what we live by—this unseizable force. (*JR*, 155)

The most bitterly drawn portrait of the prosaic mind at its
oppressive work is that of Sir William Bradshaw, the psychiatrist in *Mrs. Dalloway*. He pronounces Septimus Warren Smith
mad and drives him to suicide. He cannot listen as Septimus
tries to speak, for Septimus talks a kind of incipient poetry: 'He
was attaching meanings to words of a symbolic kind. A serious
symptom to be noted on the card' (106). Sir William Bradshaw's confidence is a sinister and destructive power. It
derived from 'his thirty years' experience of these kinds of
cases, and his infallible instinct, this is madness, this sense'
(110). Virginia Woolf was drawing directly on her own experience in writing these scenes.[7]

Here again, the connection between her denunciation of
tyranny and her choice of fictional technique is clear. In *Mrs.
Dalloway* there is no independent narrative voice; there is no
judgement or interpretation imposed on characters by an
authority external to their own consciousness. The one exception to this is precisely in that lengthy passage in which
Bradshaw's pretensions are fiercely denounced (110–13).
Here, a distinct narrative voice detaches itself from the consciousness of the fictional characters and intervenes to make
an extended pronouncement of its own. It does so precisely in
order to provide a commentary on Bradshaw and to pronounce
a definite verdict on him: guilty. Guilty of deafness and
blindness and the violation of personality. It is a novelist's
revenge. He is subjected to his own treatment. The narrator
exposes him in strikingly Nietzschean terms. What masquerades

as a sense of proportion is revealed to be the will to power; what pretends to be scientific diagnosis is condemned as the crushing of Septimus's poetic imagination. The psychiatric interview is a battle between concept and metaphor in which the power is all on one side.

Prosaic judgement, whether by a psychiatrist or a narrator, is an attempt to freeze, to immobilize. It is a discourse in which questions receive answers, in which causes are identified, in which things stand still to have their proper names pinned upon them. It stifles any effort to find a language in which we might collect the fragments of our lives together. In the words of Eliot's Prufrock (*Prufrock and Other Observations* (1917), was, like Septimus's delirious writings, dedicated to a friend who had died in the Great War):

> And I have known the eyes already, known them all—
> The eyes that fix you in a formulated phrase,
> And when I am formulated, sprawling on a pin,
> When I am pinned and wriggling on the wall,
> Then how should I begin
> To spit out all the butt-ends of my days and ways?[8]

So this is the first answer to our question: what was Virginia Woolf's motive for modernism? Her rejection of the conventional narrator and his posture of self-confident pronouncement is the rejection of a tyranny which reproduces the tyrannies of real life. They are the tyrannies which she later analysed in *Three Guineas*, and they are embodied in the judge, the psychiatrist and the military man with his glamorous uniform which covers over his naked lust for power. Such men are blind to the richness and the swiftness of our experience. For as Bernard says, in *The Waves*,

> it is a mistake, this extreme precision, this orderly and military progress; a convenience, a lie. There is always deep below it, even when we arrive punctually at the appointed time with our white waistcoats and polite formalities, a rushing stream of broken dreams, nursery rhymes, street cries, half-finished sentences and sights . . . that rise and sink even as we hand a lady down to dinner. (181)

Modern fiction must reject the military conventions of the novel in order to make contact with the deeper, darker waters of our experience.

Within this general perspective, a more specific theme emerges: the theme of mourning. In Virginia Woolf's own life as an author there was a strong connection between writing and mourning, perhaps most dramatically so in the case of *To the Lighthouse*. The writing of this novel seems to have allowed her to terminate her very protracted work of mourning for her parents.

> Until I was in the forties . . . the presence of my mother obsessed me. I could hear her voice, see her, imagine what she would do or say as I went about my day's doings. . . . Then one day walking round Tavistock Square I made up . . . *To the Lighthouse*; in a great, apparently involuntary, rush. One thing burst into another. . . . I wrote the book very quickly; and when it was written, I ceased to be obsessed by my mother. I no longer hear her voice; I do not see her.
>
> I suppose that I did for myself what psycho-analysts do for their patients. I expressed some very long felt and deeply felt emotion. And in expressing it I explained it and then laid it to rest. (*MB*, 80–1)

The connection between the mourning and the literary form is explicitly made in a well-known note in her diary. When she was writing *To the Lighthouse* she wrote: 'I have an idea that I will invent a new name for my books to supplant "novel". A new — by Virginia Woolf. But what? Elegy?' (iii, 34).

If *To the Lighthouse* is fiction as elegy, *Jacob's Room* is fiction as epitaph, for her brother Thoby. As for *The Waves*, it can be seen as a kind of shrine to Thoby's memory. A character in Julio Cortazar's *Hopscotch* (New York, 1967) cleverly remarks that *The Waves* is 'a cinerary piece of lace' (p. 332); it is like a highly decorated, commemorative artefact. A cinerary vase was a sepulchral urn in which, in ancient times, were preserved the ashes of the dead. Another well-known diary entry reads:

> I must record, heaven be praised, the end of The Waves. I wrote the words O Death fifteen minutes ago, having reeled across the last ten pages with some moments of such intensity & intoxication that I seemed only to stumble after my own voice, or almost, after some sort of speaker (as when I was mad). I was almost afraid, remembering the voices that used to fly ahead. Anyhow it is done; & I have been sitting these 15 minutes

142

in a state of glory, & calm, & some tears, thinking of Thoby & if
I could write Julian Thoby Stephen 1881–1906 on the first
page. (iv, 10)

So these three novels might be viewed as lamentations for
the dead, as elegies. Why did Virginia Woolf think that
writing about the dead demanded a literary form that is in
some ways more like song than story, in which image and
rhythm supplant plot and commentary as the basic archi-
tectonic devices? It would be a mistake to assume that these
interests and these connections were the result only of some
idiosyncrasy of her personality. Certainly, it is possible to
pursue these questions psycho-biographically, as a game of
psycho-detection, interpreting clues that she scattered in her
letters and diary, tracking down her infantile traumas, and so
on.[9] But it seems more fruitful to treat her insight into the
connections between literary form and forms of mourning not
as a symptom but as an achievement, an achievement which
has cultural and historical rather than purely personal significance. For Virginia Woolf's obsession with mourning
reflected a general cultural malaise. Many people no longer
felt at ease with traditional forms and ceremonies of mourning.
Many people felt bereft of a traditional public language for the
expression of grief. The rise of modernism is related to the
disintegration of very long-standing cultural traditions.[10]

If we return to the essay 'Modern Fiction', with which we
started, we note that Virginia Woolf selects two works as
exemplary of the virtues of modernism. They are both funereal.
One of these is 'Goussiev', a short story by Chekhov, in
which ill soldiers are being transported by ship back to Russia
from the Far East. They lie in their hammocks and they talk.
One of them dies and is buried at sea. Another is Goussiev,
whose mind is full of strange, troubled thoughts and images.
He thinks of his children. He has a haunting vision of an
eyeless bull's head and black smoke. He also dies and is sewn
into a sailcloth shroud and ceremonially tipped into the ocean.
The strange solemnity of the story does not derive from the
description of the funeral ceremony, for it is a banal affair.

Goussiev in his shroud, looking 'like a carrot or a radish',[11] is placed on a plank propped on an old box. What makes the story so appealing for Virginia Woolf is its uncommitted tone ('it is impossible to say "this is comic", or "that is tragic"') and the fact that no message is extracted from the fictional events (the story is 'vague and inconclusive' (*E*, ii, 109)). While it conveys a strong sense of Goussiev as a person, it offers no definition of his character. It leaves his essential mystery intact, and pronounces no judgements upon him. The narrator offers no interpretation of the images that haunt Goussiev. It is as though the story itself, precisely because it is 'vague and inconclusive', is his most appropriate epitaph.

The other work selected by Virginia Woolf as exemplary (though she deplores its indecency (*E*, ii, 107)) is the cemetery chapter from Joyce's *Ulysses*. Bloom attends the funeral of an acquaintance. His mind roves far and wide, but certain themes and preoccupations are uppermost. The funeral revives Bloom's mourning, for his father and for his infant son. Bloom remains detached from the official forms and ceremonies of the funeral. His interior monologue provides a fragmented, disturbed, sour commentary on the public languages of remembrance, on the service, the gravestones, the flowers.

> Mr Bloom walked unheeded along his grove by saddened angels, crosses, broken pillars, family vaults, stone hopes praying with upcast eyes, old Ireland's hearts and hands. More sensible to spend the money on some charity for the living. Pray for the repose of the soul of. Does anybody really? Plant him and have done with him. Like down a coalshoot. Then lump them together to save time. All souls' day. Twentyseventh I'll be at his grave. Ten shillings for the gardener. He keeps it free of weeds. Old man himself. Bent down double with his shears clipping. Near death's door. Who passed away. Who departed this life. As if they did it of their own accord. Got the shove, all of them. Who kicked the bucket. More interesting if they told you what they were. So and so, wheelwright. I travelled for cork lino. I paid five shillings in the pound. Or a woman's with her saucepan. I cooked good Irish stew. Eulogy in a country churchyard it ought to be that poem of whose is it Wordsworth or Thomas Campbell.[12]

Bloom's scepticism at the pieties of the gravestones has led him to a half-hearted interest in the revival of the epitaph. He laments the passing of the elegy. The gulf that separates him from those funereal traditions is the same gulf that separates Joyce and Virginia Woolf from the traditional conventions of fiction. For we are all separated from the belief and the confidence that allowed an epitaph to sound honest or a gravestone in a country churchyard to offer consolation. Whereas for Thomas Gray the grave and the epitaph focused the mind upon truth and surviving values, in modern fiction they are more likely to occur, as in *Ulysses*, as icons of falsehood and decay.

In Virginia Woolf's work it is *Jacob's Room* that is most directly concerned with traditions of celebrating the dead. Jacob's dead father, Seabrook Flanders, has his own dishonest epitaph:

> 'Merchant of this city,' the tombstone said; though why Betty Flanders had chosen so to call him when, as many still remembered, he had only sat behind an office window for three months, and before that had broken wild horses, ridden to hounds, farmed a few fields, and run a little wild—well, she had to call him something. An example for the boys. (14)

There is scarcely a page in the novel in which we do not find some mention of tombstones, epitaphs, requiems, lamentations, elegies, funeral practices, monuments, mourning emblems or skulls. But all these paraphernalia of death are thoroughly banal. They have no honest solemnity. They serve as curiosities for the visitors to St. Pauls, or to cloak the minor heroine Florinda in bogus mystery:

> As for Florinda's story, her name had been bestowed upon her by a painter who had wished it to signify that the flower of her maidenhood was still unplucked. Be that as it may, she was without a surname, and for parents had only the photograph of a tombstone beneath which, she said, her father lay buried. (76)

They are the mildly amusing relics of defunct traditions. They are represented ironically as contributing to civilized orderliness, part of the machinery used by society for holding mystery and muddle at bay:

> Dim it is, haunted by ghosts of white marble, to whom the organ for ever chaunts. If a boot creaks, it's awful; then the order; the discipline. The verger with his rod has life ironed out

145

beneath him. Sweet and holy are the angelic choristers. And for ever round the marble shoulders, in and out of the folded fingers, go the thin high sounds of voice and organ. For ever requiem—repose. (64)

But for the sceptical modern consciousness these contrivances do not work, and this is why Jacob's own life is recounted not as a story but as a series of fragments which leave the mystery of who and what he was unsettled. Jacob dies in the war and the book ends with his mother's unconsoling words, 'Such confusion everywhere!' Whatever has destroyed the force of traditional ways of burying the dead has also undermined traditional conventions of fiction.

The distance that separated the novels of Virginia Woolf from those traditions can be gauged by looking at Wordsworth's first 'Essay Upon Epitaphs'[13] in which he defines with admirable clarity the conditions that once made honest epitaphs possible. Epitaph, he argued, is based on the conviction that 'every man has a character of his own to the eye that has skill to perceive it.' It is not just that each individual is unique, but that this uniqueness consists in having a 'character'. The writer's skill enables him to convey to the reader 'sensations excited by a distinct and clear conception . . . of the individual whose death is deplored and whose memory is to be preserved. . . . The reader ought to know who and what the man was.' The dead person was also, of course, a human being who suffered from and was glorified in the general lot of mankind. His story will, therefore, illustrate general truths and can be used to remind us of enduring values. In writing epitaph, the author must, then, have command of 'the universal language of humanity'.

Confidence in the possibility of clear and distinct conceptions and of a universal language of humanity played a major role, of course, in underpinning the edifices of modern science and philosophy, and was a central element in Enlightenment humanism. It was also the foundation of literary conventions, not only of epitaph but also of the novel. Literary forms were trusted because they were believed to have secure epistemological foundations. Wordsworth's 'Essay Upon Epitaphs' makes it clear, however, that in the case of epitaph this secure

146

foundation was not only epistemological (justified trust in the
writer's knowledge of people and language, and trust in an
accepted framework of universal truths and values) but also
psychological. A trustworthy judgement can only be made by
someone who is in control of himself, who is not at the mercy of
emotional forces which might throw him off-balance and
destroy the clarity of his vision. Confidence in this possibility is
based on the belief that intense emotion, such as grief, is short-
lived and controllable. The writer's

> thoughts and feelings should be . . . liberated from that weak-
> ness and anguish of sorrow which is in nature transitory, and
> which with instinctive decency retires from notice. The passions
> should be subdued, the emotions controlled; strong, indeed, but
> nothing ungovernable or wholly involuntary. Seemliness requires
> this, and truth requires it also: for how can the narrator other-
> wise be trusted?

Jacob's Room could be read as Virginia Woolf's answer to
this 'Essay Upon Epitaphs'. Each of Wordsworth's premises is
denied. What pose as general truths and values, and the
institutions which embody them (the Church, the Cabinet, the
Army, Cambridge University, even the British Museum) are
mocked or reviled. Confidence in our judgements and knowledge of other people is shown to be misplaced: 'It seems that a
profound, impartial, and absolutely just opinion of our fellow-
creatures is utterly unknown' (70).

As for mourning and grief, they are very obscure, very long-
lasting, and beyond our control or even self-knowledge. Jacob's
life, unknown to himself or to those who think they know him
best, is lived in the shadow of his father's death. He suffers
from an ungovernable sadness; he is often overwhelmed by a
mysterious gloom. On holiday, in a boat off Cornwall, something strange invades him and dilutes his ecstasy:

> But imperceptibly the cottage smoke droops, has the look of a
> mourning emblem, a flag floating its caress over a grave. The
> gulls, making their broad flight and then riding at peace, seem
> to mark the grave.
> . . . Yes, the chimneys and the coast-guard stations and the
> little bays with the waves breaking unseen by any one make one
> remember the overpowering sorrow. And what can this sorrow
> be? (47)

147

Jacob is puzzled by his own instability of mood. He is aware of its connection with the loss of that faith that had sustained British society and Empire, though he does not identify that 'something solid, immovable, and grotesque' that is at the back of it with the 'solid piece of work' which is his father's tombstone (13).

> This gloom, this surrender to the dark waters which lap us about, is a modern invention. Perhaps, as Cruttendon said, we do not believe enough. Our fathers at any rate had something to demolish. So have we for the matter of that, thought Jacob, crumpling the *Daily Mail* in his hand. He would go into Parliament and make fine speeches—but what use are fine speeches and Parliament, once you surrender an inch to the black waters? Indeed there has never been any explanation of the ebb and flow in our veins—of happiness and unhappiness. (137–38)

That other modern invention, modern fiction, is based not only on the rejection of an old epistemology and alienation from social and cultural traditions, but also on a new self-consciousness about the activity of writing itself. Wordsworth's essay suggests that truth and emotional balance are to be acquired prior to writing, in preparation for it. First the author knows, then he puts his knowledge into words for the benefit and consolation of others. For Virginia Woolf, provisional truth and temporary stability are attained not prior to writing but by means of it. Truth is not a presupposition of writing but its achievement. It consoles not because it expresses clear and distinct conceptions but because it articulates ambiguities and contradictions that otherwise, being unvoiced, retain their power to hurt us. Writing 'gives me, perhaps because by doing so I take away the pain, a great delight to put the severed parts together' (*MB*, 72). Wordsworth's basic metaphor for writing is transcription; Virginia Woolf's is therapy.

The themes of death and mourning, grief and its expression, trauma and recovery, are central not only to *Jacob's Room* but also to *Mrs. Dalloway*, *To the Lighthouse* and *The Waves*, and are in each case connected with originality of literary form. In these three later novels there is a common dramatic pattern of bereavement followed by more or less successful recovery (the deaths of Evans, Mrs. Ramsay and Percival; the mourning of Septimus Warren Smith, Lily Briscoe and the Ramsay family, and the six 'characters' of *The Waves*). In the case of *Mrs. Dalloway* we can add that Clarissa Dalloway also suffers from a kind of bereavement, the loss of her own past youth, rapture and sexuality; her 'mourning' is her attempt to come to terms with this. We can appreciate how Woolf escapes from the constraints of conventional form by looking at how she treats this common pattern of trauma and recovery.

It is striking, for example, that death is never incorporated into plot and never functions as the termination of a story. Though we indirectly learn of Jacob's death at the very end of *Jacob's Room* we come to realize at the same time that the narrative has not been the story of Jacob's life but an attempt to assemble fragmentary knowledge of him after his death. In this sense Jacob's death does not close the action of *Jacob's Room*; when Jacob dies we have arrived at the point at which the narrator begins: there is no closure. In *Mrs. Dalloway* it is not Evans's death that is the subject of narrative treatment, but Septimus's response to it. Mrs. Ramsay's death, and also those of her children Prue and Andrew, are narrated in the 'Time Passes' section of *To the Lighthouse* as events of no greater significance than the falling of a leaf or the passing of a cloud. Percival is central to *The Waves* but he is himself never directly presented; he exists only as an echo in the minds of his friends, and we learn of his death only from their reactions to it. In each case the crucial death takes place 'off-stage', away from the scene of the fiction. It is never directly dramatized as it is in the famous death-bed scenes in Dickens's novels, scenes which centre on the display of innocent virtue or the intensity of religious vision. Death is never the culmination of the action, the event around which closure is achieved, as it so often is in Elizabethan drama. Death is always an event in the lives of the living. It is in itself without sense and it renders the living speechless with grief or rage. It is pure contingency which can more or less permanently dislocate every construction which we put upon ourselves and the world, 'for there is neither rhyme nor reason when a drunk man staggers about with a club in his hand' (*TW*, 188).

149

Recovery from this shattering blow is not always possible. Septimus Warren Smith is incapacitated by Evans's death because he cannot assimilate it into any stable system of meaning. He is unbalanced. He swings wildly from one extreme to another. Sometimes he exults in the discovery that every experience, however tiny, is filled to overflowing with meaning, with messages from the dead, with a 'great revelation'. At other times he despairs because 'it might be possible that the world itself is without meaning' (*MD*, 98). He sees only two possibilities—meaning is everywhere or it is nowhere; our experience is full or it is empty; exultation or desolation. This way lies insanity. On what terms then is recovery possible?

Lily Briscoe, in *To the Lighthouse*, does not suffer from Septimus Warren Smith's delusions. For her 'The great revelation had never come. The great revelation perhaps never did come. Instead there were little daily miracles, illuminations, matches struck unexpectedly in the dark' (249). She grieves for Mrs. Ramsay (whereas Septimus was unable to feel grief) but she knows that she cannot mourn directly in words, 'for how could one express in words these emotions of the body?' (274) Recovery is like bringing the lips of wounded flesh back together. It is like the process of suture, the covering over of a wound. A common image for it in Woolf's novels is the repair of torn fabric. One moment in Clarissa Dalloway's struggle to recover her self-composure is captured in a remarkable vision of her relaxing her body and mind in the task of mending a torn silk dress.

> Quiet descended on her, calm, content, as her needle, drawing the silk smoothly to its gentle pause, collected the green folds together and attached them, very lightly, to the belt. So on a summer's day waves collect, overbalance, and fall; collect and fall; and the whole world seems to be saying 'that is all' more and more ponderously, until even the heart in the body which lies in the sun on the beach says too, that is all. Fear no more, says the heart. (44–5)

At a similar moment of peace after a storm of memory and regret, Lily Briscoe looks out across the bay towards the lighthouse, her paroxysm of grief over:

The sea without a stain on it, thought Lily Briscoe, still standing and looking out over the bay. The sea is stretched like silk across the bay. Distance had an extraordinary power; they had been swallowed up in it, she felt, they were gone for ever, they had become part of the nature of things. It was so calm; it was so quiet. The steamer itself had vanished, but the great scroll of smoke still hung in the air and drooped like a flag mournfully in valediction. (289)

Recovering from grief involves recovering, calling back again, the dead. It is necessary to recall the dead in order to let them go. It is necessary to feel their presence within you before it is possible to release them to the earth. But it is also necessary to establish a distance from them, to externalize them and to say farewell to them. If the dead remain too close they stay to haunt us as Evans haunts Septimus, speaking to him from behind the bushes, walking towards him across the park. The burial of the dead, covering them over, is also a covering over of our wounds with a stretched and fragile skin, for life can now go on even though we can never be sure that the dead will not 'leap out on us at street corners, or in dreams' (*TW* 194). In mourning one closes around oneself a protective covering of incantation ('fear no more the heat of the sun' chants Clarissa Dalloway). One performs valedictory ceremonies, if one can find the right form of words. Recovery is an indirect and inexpressible form of healing. The most appropriate form for conveying it in fiction is neither the external narrator nor direct speech. It is that very particular style of indirect discourse that is so characteristic of Virginia Woolf's novels.[14]

Virginia Woolf's novels end with the sense of the completion of a rite. *To the Lighthouse* ends with Lily's painting achieving a kind of visual suture, a scar-like line in the centre covering the place where Mrs. Ramsay had been. *Mrs. Dalloway* ends with a similar gesture of achievement. Clarissa has not been pinned down or judged, but she has somehow been depicted in words. She has been *shown*: 'For there she was.' *The Waves* ends not with a conclusion, a final resting place, the victory of despair over exultation, for the ebb and flow of happiness and unhappiness that had puzzled Jacob does not stop, but with the achievement of a moment of provisional rest, a fine balance which contains both Bernard's defiance

(' "Against you I will fling myself, unvanquished and un-yielding, O Death!" ') and the italicized reassertion of the inevitable rhythm of doom (*'The waves broke on the shore'*).

At the end of *Jacob's Room*, from the point of view of the surviving characters (Jacob's mother and his friend Bonamy) and of the first-time reader, Jacob's death comes as a sudden shock. The novel ends with the wound of grief wide open, mourning scarcely begun. On the other hand, from the point of view of the narrator a rite has been accomplished. The narration, we now see, has mimed the process of mourning. The reader can now re-read the novel and this time will understand the appearance (which before might have seemed rather arbitrary) of the war-lords and the politicians, will be sensitive to the force of the emblems of death that occur throughout the book.

We can conclude this study of the connections between the forms of mourning and the forms of fiction by looking at an essay in which Virginia Woolf wrote about them directly, the essay 'On Not Knowing Greek', which was written in 1924 at the time when she was writing *Mrs. Dalloway*. Her central idea in this essay is that it was possible for the Greeks to directly express intense emotion in poetic and dramatic language, whereas in our age we suffer, in the stress of emotion, from a separation between body and voice. Typical of our age is Lily Briscoe's discovery, at the height of her grief: 'Little words that broke up the thought and dismembered it said nothing. "About life, about death; about Mrs. Ramsay"—no, she thought, one could say nothing to nobody. The urgency of the moment always missed its mark. Words fluttered sideways and struck the object inches too low' (274). The Greeks, by contrast, could give voice to things directly which we can only approach fearfully and obliquely. 'It was safe for them to step into the thick of emotions which blind and bewilder an age like our own. . . . [They] could march straight up, with their eyes open; and thus fearlessly approached, emotions stand still and suffer themselves to be looked at' (*E*, i, 10). The system of public ceremonies, public myths and public values provided a stable framework of meaning within which the individual voice could be direct. The individual character could directly embody and express 'heroism itself, fidelity itself'. The words of Sophocles' Electra are 'bare; mere cries of despair, joy, hate' (*E*, i, 3).

For us, in contrast, our separation from these traditions means that we have available only 'a heap of broken images' as Eliot says in 'The Burial of the Dead' (the first section of *The Waste Land*). We cannot create characters as the embodiments of public virtue and vice, and we have no language in which to directly define our emotions. Our experience and our literature are based on indirectness and displacement. As Virginia Woolf said in 'The Narrow Bridge of Art', 'It is as if the modern mind, wishing always to verify its emotions, had lost the power of accepting anything simply for what it is' (*E*, ii, 223). In this sceptical age modern literature must be a matter of 'hints, repetitions, suggestions' (*E*, i, 3). The burial of the dead in Greek drama is the burial of heroes killed in battle. The Greeks could say what we cannot say: ' "Yet being dead they have not died." ' They could say, ' "If to die nobly is the chief part of excellence, to us out of all men Fortune gave this lot." ' The public lament celebrates public heroic action. But for us, 'In the vast catastrophe of the European war our emotions had to be broken up for us, and put at an angle from us, before we could allow ourselves to feel them in poetry or fiction' (*F*, i, 10).

It is precisely a symptom of desperate delusion in Septimus Warren Smith that he translates his friend Evans, dead in the war, into a Greek hero: 'The dead were in Thessaly, Evans sang, among the orchids' (*MD*, 78). For being dead, Evans has not died, and Septimus hears this message, from an age remote from our own, that in mourning we are to celebrate life:

> A sparrow perched on the railing opposite chirped Septimus, Septimus, four or five times over and went on, drawing its notes out, to sing freshly and piercingly in Greek words how there is no crime and, joined by another sparrow, they sang in voices prolonged and piercing in Greek words, from trees in the meadow of life beyond a river where the dead walk, how there is no death. (28)

In *Jacob's Room* many characters tend to see themselves and their lovers as Greek heroes and heroines, but in this novel this

153

is not a symptom of individual madness but of cultural presumption and foolishness. Much fun is made of the fact that women sentimentalize and trivialize their relationships with Jacob by viewing him as a Greek hero. Fanny sees Jacob specifically as Ulysses: 'To reinforce her vision she had taken to visiting the British Museum, where, keeping her eyes downcast until she was alongside of the battered Ulysses, she opened them and got a fresh shock of Jacob's presence' (170; cf. 79). The inauthenticity of these fantasies of the warrior Jacob is brutally highlighted eventually by his death in the trenches. For Ulysses could no more walk the streets of London than of Dublin.

The young Cambridge men are themselves obsessed with Greek culture. The suggestion is that these highly educated young men could be extremely silly. As Jacob and his friends, drunk from a party, walk the streets of London, they boastfully proclaim their allegiance to Greece. It 'seemed to him that they were making the flagstones ring on the road to the Acropolis, and that if Socrates saw them coming he would bestir himself and say "my fine fellows", for the whole sentiment of Athens was entirely after his heart' (75). Florinda ('Wild and frail and beautiful she looked, and thus the women of the Greeks were, Jacob thought' (77)) is sarcastically depicted as a debased modern Electra, with her 'I'm so frightfully unhappy!' and 'I'm awfully happy' (73, 79). When Florinda betrays Jacob, causing him a terrible shock, it does not surprise us to see where the author has chosen to have this occur. 'Then he saw her turning up Greek Street upon another man's arm' (93).

Florinda was no Greek heroine and Jacob was no Greek hero. For Virginia Woolf there are no heroes. She resolutely refused to celebrate the death of men in war, whether in her life or in her fiction. She saw no public virtue which inspired war as noble, nor any cause as glorious.[15] Public death is not at all more significant than are the 'anonymous' deaths of women. In *To the Lighthouse* Andrew Ramsay's death in the trenches is no more notable than the domestic deaths of his mother and sister. Percival, in *The Waves*, dies as a young man in the service of the Empire; he has a uniform and the prospect of a public career before him. Yet any temptation that his friends might feel to romanticize his death is quickly dispelled. The pure non-sense of his death is that he fell from his horse into the mud.

When the dead are buried they are covered not with glory but with words. Percival is mourned only in 'the little language'. Bernard goes to the National Gallery to mourn alone, to find some comfort in the paintings.

> Behold, then, the blue madonna streaked with tears. This is my funeral service. We have no ceremonies, only private dirges and no conclusions, only violent sensations, each separate. Nothing that has been said meets our case. (111–12)

This, for Virginia Woolf, is the dark country where fiction operates: the burst of violent emotion, the private dirge. What is discovered, and woven into the fabric of lament, are fragments of memory, snatches of conversation, haunting images, little tags of poetry or song. These are the materials from which the text is to be built: hints, repetitions, suggestions. Bernard hums 'Come away, come away, death' (a song from *Twelfth Night*) under his breath as he walks down the street (184). In moments of panic Woolf's characters conduct little private ceremonies of incantation. In the story 'The New Dress', Mabel finds herself chanting a phrase, and she

> repeated the phrase as if she were crossing herself, as if she were trying to find some spell to annul this pain, to make this agony endurable. Tags of Shakespeare, lines from books she had read ages ago, suddenly came to her when she was in agony, and she repeated them over and over again. (*MDP*, 58)

Little tags like this are used by Woolf in *Mrs. Dalloway* as foci around which feelings crystallize, and as the poetic points around which the text circulates. It is anchored in two points, in the rapture of Othello's 'If it were now to die, 'twere now to be most happy', and the beautiful dirge from *Cymbeline*, magically soothing,

> Fear no more the heat o' the sun
> Nor the furious winter's rages.

There is an important reversal of values revealed in Virginia Woolf's novels, for the shape that emerges is a fundamentally poetic one. They are not primarily held together by a framework of socio-historical, moral or psychological concepts, nor by the literary forms with which these were traditionally associated. 'I am writing . . . to a rhythm not to a plot', she noted when she was writing *The Waves* (*D*, iii, 316). She wrote fiction based on 'metaphors, rhythm, repetitions', invested with the power of 'the incantation and the mystery . . . rhyme and metre'.[16] Everything is subordinated to poetry and to its mysterious healing power, to its power to draw together, if only temporarily, the echoes and fragments with which our experience reverberates.

NOTES

1. 'Modern Fiction', *E*, ii, 106.
2. 'The Narrow Bridge of Art', *E*, ii, 228–29.
3. 'Phases of Fiction', *E*, ii, 83.
4. 'Modern Fiction', *E*, ii, 108.
5. See especially 'Mr. Bennett and Mrs. Brown', *E*, i.
6. 'Women and Fiction', *E*, ii, 146.
7. See Roger Poole, *The Unknown Virginia Woolf* (Cambridge, 1978).
8. T. S. Eliot, 'The Love Song of J. Alfred Prufrock', *Collected Poems 1909–1935* (1958), p. 13.
9. See for example Mark Spilka, *Virginia Woolf's Quarrel with Grieving* (1980).
10. See Philippe Ariès, *The Hour of our Death* (1981).
11. Anton Chekhov, 'Goussiev' in *Plays and Stories* (1937), p. 341.
12. James Joyce, *Ulysses* (New York, 1961), p. 113.
13. Wordsworth, *Prose Works*, eds. W. J. B. Owen and Jane Worthington Smyser (Oxford, 1974), vol. ii; all quotations from pp. 56–60.
14. See John Mepham, 'Figures of Desire: Narration and Fiction in *To the Lighthouse*' in *The Modern English Novel*, ed. G. D. Josipovici (1976); J. Hillis Miller, *Fiction and Repetition* (Oxford, 1982), Ch. 7.
15. See *Three Guineas* and also the memoir that Virginia Woolf wrote on the death of Julian Bell in the Spanish Civil War in 1937, printed as Appendix C in QB, ii.
16. To John Lehman (*L*, v, 422); 'The Narrow Bridge of Art', *E*, ii, 226.

8

The Life of Monday or Tuesday

by TONY DAVENPORT

'Life is not a series of gig lamps symmetrically arranged'—
who ever thought that it was? Virginia Woolf's most often
quoted sentence has become so familiar that one has forgotten
what it first meant; now even critics who are still using
'Modern Fiction', the essay from which it comes, to provide a
framework of theory tend to avoid it as a cliché. It is an odd
non-comparison, in literal terms absurd. The two lamps at
either side of a two-wheeled one-horse carriage may have
lodged in her mind's eye as the necessary illumination for the
characters of Wells, Bennett and Galsworthy trotting along
the road of life, or be taken, as Hermione Lee says, to 'suggest
the material as well as the methods of the Victorian and
Edwardian novel'.[1] Perhaps also memory of her and her
sister's 'social' evenings, when George Duckworth insisted on
dragging them off to dinners and dances, left an association
between the evening appearance of a horse-drawn vehicle, or
an oncoming line of them, and the idea of life's false façades,
artificially lit and arranged. Or is there some more suggestive
connotation still?—a memory of Froude perhaps: 'Fireflies . . .
with two long antennae, at the point of which hangs out a
blazing lanthorn. The unimaginative colonists call them gig-
lamps.'[2] More probable is the slang sense of 'spectacles', as
used, for example, in answer to a question from Dr. Thorndyke

157

about the appearance of one Schonberg: ' "Like?" interrupted the resident. "He's like a blooming Sheeny with a carroty beard and gold giglamps!" '[3]

In context its sense is sharpened by antithesis, of course, and by the whole preceding passage, which acts as a rhetorical centre in 'Modern Fiction', and as a definition of what the conventional, materialist novel fails to communicate and how it constrains life within a rigid habit:

> Look within and life, it seems, is very far from being 'like this'. Examine for a moment an ordinary mind on an ordinary day. The mind receives a myriad impressions—trivial, fantastic, evanescent, or engraved with the sharpness of steel. From all sides they come, an incessant shower of innumerable atoms; and as they fall, as they shape themselves into the life of Monday or Tuesday, the accent falls differently from of old; the moment of importance came not here but there; so that, if a writer were a free man and not a slave, if he could write what he chose, not what he must, if he could base his work upon his own feeling and not upon convention, there would be no plot, no comedy, no tragedy, no love interest or catastrophe in the accepted style, and perhaps not a single button sewn on as the Bond Street tailors would have it. Life is not a series of gig lamps symmetrically arranged; life is a luminous halo, a semi-transparent envelope surrounding us from the beginning of consciousness to the end.[4]

As a model for the 'incessant shower of innumerable atoms' received by the 'ordinary mind on an ordinary day' clearly gig-lamps are ill-fitted; the myriad impressions which the mind receives contain us, as if our attempt to perceive is a message, and sanctify us in light divine, very different from the oil-lamps or the glasses that mundane observers need to enhance their benighted vision.[5] The imagery contrasts not only outer and inner life but also a manufactured means of observation, limited and artificial, with the medium through which images are passively received, images which are brighter and truer, even if blurred.

This famous passage was written somewhere between August 1923, when Virginia Woolf began to revise the old articles which she intended to include in *The Common Reader*, and April 1925, when the volume of essays was published. Her thoughts about modern fiction, first sketched in the essay's earlier version, 'Modern Novels',[6] were by this time coloured by Arnold Bennett's criticism, in the article 'Is the Novel Decaying?', 28 March 1923, of her own alleged failure in *Jacob's Room* and that of the younger generation of novelists in general to create characters who 'survive in the mind'.[7] Her reactions to his criticism formed the two versions of 'Mr. Bennett and Mrs. Brown'.[8] Because Bennett's main point was that 'the foundation of good fiction is character creating, and nothing else', the emphasis in Woolf's response is on the representation of people. In the first version she actually takes time to assess the quality of character-portrayal in nineteenth-century novels, recognizing how in Thackeray, for instance, 'the whole society is revealed to us, and revealed always . . . through the astonishing vividness and reality of the characters', but concluding that 'the undeniable vividness of so many' nineteenth-century characters 'is the result of their crudity'. As elsewhere, she turns to Dostoyevsky for her contrary instance of complexity and depth: 'These are characters without any features at all. We go down into them as we descend into some enormous cavern.' Finally she introduces the figure of Mrs. Brown, a flickering, tricksy embodiment of the human nature which the novelist is trying to catch or pin down: 'it is from the gleams and flashes of this flying spirit that he must create solid, living flesh-and-blood Mrs. Brown.' Thus the antithesis in this version is between two aspects of the actual subject of the novelist's art, life itself—an antithesis between insubstantial and solid, between light, movement, spirit and flesh and blood. In the later, more familiar, more wide-ranging and polished version of 'Mr. Bennett and Mrs. Brown' the antithesis has become that between a wrong and a right way of expressing or describing 'life itself', which is now explicitly personified in a much developed Mrs. Brown, who appears as a constant, eternal traveller in the train-carriage of literature: 'Mrs. Brown changes only on the surface, it is the novelists who get in and out.' The imagined advice of the Edwardian novelists on descriptive method here acts the part of the despised gig-lamps:

How shall I begin to describe this woman's character? And they said: 'Begin by saying that her father kept a shop in Harrogate.

Ascertain the rent. Ascertain the wages of shop assistants in the year 1878. Discover what her mother died of. Describe cancer. Describe calico. Describe —' But I cried: 'Stop! Stop!' . . . for I knew that if I began describing the cancer and the calico, my Mrs. Brown, that vision to which I cling though I know no way of imparting it to you, would have been dulled and tarnished and vanished for ever. (*E*, i, 332)

'Mr. Bennett and Mrs. Brown' shares a group of ideas with 'Modern Fiction': criticism of Wells, Bennett and Galsworthy, commendation of Russian novelists for their inclusiveness, and a plea for tolerance of contemporary experiment for the sake of the banishing of outworn conventions and the occasional brilliant gleam of truth to life, despite the uncertainties of 'the spasmodic, the obscure, the fragmentary, the failure'. One essay confirms the other, and the shift in 1924, while *Mrs. Dalloway* was being written, between the two texts called 'Mr. Bennett and Mrs. Brown', links significantly both with this novel and with 'Modern Fiction' and its shift from 'Modern Novels'. Woolf moves from emphasis on the different *forms* of life (which are difficult to capture) represented by Mrs. Brown (spirit/flesh, insubstantial/solid) to stress on the different *versions* of life found in the various treatments of Mrs. Brown (English, French, Russian; Wells, Bennett, Galsworthy; Edwardians, Georgians). This shift helps to explain the mental process whereby, in the antithesis of gig-lamps and halo/ envelope in 'Modern Fiction', she fuses the thing perceived with the means of perceiving. The shift also seems to me akin to the movement in her fiction from stress in *Jacob's Room* on the different forms of life (which are difficult to capture), contemplated inadequately and incompletely by the narrator and the other observers, to the division in *Mrs. Dalloway* between the different versions of life represented by Clarissa and Septimus.

Another influence upon Virginia Woolf's thinking about fiction at this period may explain why in 'Modern Fiction' she visualized her symbolic gig-lamps symmetrically arranged in a series. In mid-1922 she read Percy Lubbock's *The Craft of Fiction* (1921), and the review she wrote of it, under the title 'On Re-reading Novels', was one of the essays she considered including in *The Common Reader*; she was therefore revising this article in September 1924.[9] It is also obvious from several references in the diary and letters that, though she disagreed with Lubbock, she became more conscious of novelistic form after reading his book. Scattered through it are many statements that have a Woolfian ring, as, for example:

> It is clear that if we wish to see an abundance and multitude of life we shall find it more readily and more summarily by looking for an hour into a memory, a consciousness, than by merely watching the present events of an hour, however crowded. (118–19)

Equally suggestive is the summing-up of *Madame Bovary* ('The book is not a row of facts, it is a single image' (p. 62)) or the description of the process in *The Ambassadors*:

> The world of silent thought is thrown open . . . so the novelist, dealing with a situation like Strether's, represents it by means of the movement that flickers over the surface of his mind. (157)

However, it was the things she disagreed with, rather than these confirmations of her own creative impulses, which Woolf seems to have found most stimulating. She particularly resisted Lubbock's idea that novelists deliberately devised forms or predetermined methods for their works and recorded with some sense of triumph the contradiction of Lubbock by her own experience.[10] She writes of *Mrs. Dalloway*:

> It took me a year's groping to discover what I call my tunnelling process, by which I tell the past by instalments, as I have need of it. This is my prime discovery so far; & the fact that I've been so long finding it, proves, I think, how false Percy Lubbock's doctrine is—that you can do this sort of thing consciously. (*D*, ii, 272, 15 October 1923)

The particular instance that is likely to have struck her is Lubbock's citing of James's *The Awkward Age* as a novel in which the author 'followed a single method throughout', never drew upon 'the characteristic resource of the novelist' and offered 'no insight into anybody's thought'. Lubbock almost seems to be offering a challenge to Woolf when he writes:

> Has anyone tried to write a novel in which there should be no dialogue, no immediate scene, nothing at all but a diffused and

purely subjective impression? Such a novel, if it existed, would be a counterpart to *The Awkward Age*. Just as Henry James's book never deviates from the straight, square view of the passing event, so the other would be exclusively oblique, general, retrospective, a meditation upon the past, bringing nothing into the foreground, dramatizing nothing in talk or action. (195)

One reason why Lubbock's discussion of *The Awkward Age* would have made an impression, I think, is that it was James's idea for a pattern for this novel that had seemed to Woolf of particular interest when she had reviewed J. Warren Beach's *The Method of Henry James* in 1918. She had been struck by his sending to the periodical in which the novel was to be serialized an actual drawing of his design:

> . . . the neat figure of a circle consisting of a number of small rounds disposed at equal distance about a central object. The central object was my situation, my subject in itself, to which the thing would owe its title, and the small rounds represented so many distinct lamps, as I liked to call them, the function of each of which would be to light with all due intensity one of its aspects.[11]

At the time of her review she seems to have found this an interesting key to the quality of James's late novels where one has to look for 'not a plot, or a collection of characters, or a view of life, but something more abstract, more difficult to grasp, the weaving together of many themes into one theme, the making out of a design'.[12] Three-and-a-half years later she has come to dislike the idea of such consciously designed form and it seems to me that James's symmetrical circle of lamps, each lamp 'the light of a single social occasion', has joined the horse-drawn carriage in 'a series of gig-lamps symmetrically arranged'.

The 1925 version of 'Modern Fiction' thus represents, in my reckoning, a rejection of material realism, of the smooth falsity of contemporary middlebrow fiction and also the idea of artificial form. The antithesis between gig-lamps and the halo/envelope conjunction expresses a clear dichotomy and a definite choice. The point of interest is that this choice coincides with the composition of *Mrs. Dalloway* and marks the break between the tentative, 'experimental' feeling that the author had at all stages of *Jacob's Room* and the confidence— amounting at times, as in the treatment of Bradshaw, almost to aggression—of the later novel. With *Jacob's Room* she thought first of the design, with no idea of the material:

> happier today than I was yesterday having this afternoon arrived at some idea of a new form for a new novel. Suppose one thing should open out of another—as in An Unwritten Novel— only not for 10 pages but 200 or so—doesn't that give the looseness and lightness I want . . . no scaffolding; scarcely a brick to be seen; all crepuscular, but the heart, the passion, humour, everything as bright as fire in the mist. . . . conceive mark on the wall, K.G. [Kew Gardens] & unwritten novel taking hands & dancing in unity. What the unity shall be I have yet to discover: the theme is a blank to me; but I see immense possibilities in the form . . . I suppose the danger is the damned egotistical self. (*D*, ii, 13–14, 26 January 1920)

With *Mrs. Dalloway* it was the other way round:

> Mrs. Dalloway has branched into a book; & I adumbrate here a study of insanity & suicide: the world seen by the sane & the insane side by side—something like that. . . . —& to be more close to the fact than Jacob: but I think Jacob was a necessary step, for me, in working free. (*D*, ii, 207–8, 14 October 1922)

In one the expression is excited, doubtful but spirited, with a sense of nebulous light fancy. But for the saving grace of 'something like that', the other sounds rather too rigidly earnest, even complacent; the mind has settled into divisions.

There were several reasons for Virginia Woolf's greater assurance. It came partly from the freedom from the need to submit her writings to a publisher which the establishment of the Hogarth Press had brought, partly from the sense of having several published books behind her, and partly from simultaneous work on *Mrs. Dalloway* and *The Common Reader*, which created a useful variety in her work and came to seem a protection against criticism, since if the two were published close together (as they were) reactions of friends and foes would be diffused and disarmed. 'Modern Fiction' was revised during a period not only of greater confidence but also of greater positive desire for change on her part. She was particularly irked by living in Richmond, confined in a suburban place associated with the need to be careful about her health, cut off from London, forced to waste time travelling:

> This may be life; but I doubt that I shall ever convert L. & now sit down baffled & depressed to face a life spent, mute & mitigated, in the suburbs, just as I had it in mind that I could at last go full speed ahead. For the capacities in me will never after 40, accumulate again. And I mind missing life far more than he does, for it isn't life to him in the sense that it is life to me. . . . Always to catch trains, always to waste time . . . when . . . I might . . . go adventuring among human beings. (*D*, ii, 250, 28 June 1923; see also p. 249)

By the time she took Bennett on in print, Leonard had relented and they had moved to Tavistock Square. However, though she found the train journey from Richmond to Waterloo tedious in fact, she found railway travel fruitful in imagination, since she used it not only as the central image of the writer's encounter with 'life' in 'Mr Bennett and Mrs. Brown' but had previously explored the relationship between observer and the 'stranger on a train' in *Jacob's Room* (28–9) and in 'An Unwritten Novel'.[13] The latter provides another comparison from which one can judge the development of the author's ideas and attitudes.

The emphasis in 'An Unwritten Novel' falls on the author as observer and interpreter in a dramatic situation; the story consists of a sort of dramatic monologue, acting out the desire to compose in relation to the writer's material—'life'. Life is represented first in external terms (what she observes of her fellow passengers and what little she learns from polite conversation); then, as the writer embellishes the scanty material, the terms become those of an imagined literary biography of 'Minnie Marsh', including quick dashes, almost satirical in effect, into Arnold Bennett materialism of setting and into the clichés of situation and feeling which appearances suggest; finally life resists and the writer is disconcerted when the scene at the station fails to confirm her imagined idea. The disparity between appearance and actual vagary is the main point and it survives the sentimental ending: 'if I open my arms, it's you I embrace, you I draw to me—adorable world!' This is a story in which one senses real experience being converted to representative image; the casual encounters of daily life become the material for meditation on the writer's relationship to actuality and so the train journey itself becomes an image for the current of life which the novelist attempts to catch and hold still. Another repeated image with similar sense is that of walking in the city streets, 'seeing life, as I walk about the streets, an immense opaque block of material to be conveyed by me into its equivalent of language' (*D*, i, 214, 4 November 1918). Woolf's concern in the composition of the *story*, however, as opposed to the fictional attempt to imagine the life of the stranger in the train, is to express the writer's uncertainty and comic unreliability when faced with the variety of life. This is a different stance from the one she took up in 1924; by then she can cut out the sentimentality and be more suggestively unspecific about Mrs. Brown than about Minnie Marsh, but she has also moved away from exploring the writer's task to justifying her own view of things. 'Mr. Bennett and Mrs. Brown' still recognizes that Mrs. Brown has 'an overwhelming fascination, for she is, of course, life itself', and its author takes up the historical and argumentative position suited to an address, as in her bold assertion that 'in or about December 1910, human character changed', but the rhetorical bite of the piece is in the rejection of, say, 'the cancer and the calico'.

It is with the period of 'An Unwritten Novel' that the passage with the gig-lamps has often been associated, because so many critics have quoted it as if it came from 'Modern Novels', of which 'Modern Fiction' was a revision. The usual critical purpose has been to represent this essay of 1919 as a manifesto in which Woolf expressed the theory of her own current practice and her future intentions: that is, that she was turning away from the plot-dominated, 'conventional' novel, exemplified in the recently completed *Night and Day* (1919), towards experimental methods which, so the argument runs, after unsuccessful try-outs in *Monday or Tuesday* (1921) and in *Jacob's Room* (1922), came to fruition in *Mrs. Dalloway* (1925). I've been guilty of saying so myself. However, the original essay was not clear-cut enough to fulfil the role of manifesto, nor to establish the scale of values by which the four works have often been judged. 'Modern Novels' was probably written, certainly completed, in the first days of April 1919, in the week when Woolf had taken the completed manuscript of *Night and Day* to her half-brother, Gerald Duckworth, to be considered for publication. The few references she makes to the article suggest that it was simply part of her current busy involvement with literature.[14] There is no suggestion of particular significance felt or intended in the essay, nor of anxiety about it. There are no gig-lamps and the expression is, in several key places, less definite and downright, though the essential condemnation of the lifeless representationalism of the Edwardian trio is already there. The explanation of the nature of the elusive life that, in Woolf's view, escapes the materialist is rather different. The original version of the 'gig-lamps' passage quoted earlier was as follows:

> Is it not possible that the accent falls a little differently, that the moment of importance came before or after, that, if one were free and could set down what one chose, there would be no plot, little probability, and a vague general confusion in which the clear-cut features of the tragic, the comic, the passionate, and the lyrical were dissolved beyond the possibility of separate recognition? The mind, exposed to the ordinary course of life, receives upon its surface a myriad impressions—trivial, fantastic, evanescent, or engraved with the sharpness of steel. From all sides they come, an incessant shower of innumerable atoms, composing in their sum what we might venture to call life itself; and to figure further as the semi-transparent envelope, or luminous halo, surrounding us from the beginning of consciousness to the end. (*T.L.S.*, 10 April 1919)

'Modern Novels' represents a puzzled searching; it is a journalist's assembling of some thoughts about novels, formulating, somewhat loosely, the problem of how best to register mental life, but not offering a solution or defining principles of composition.

What the early essay does show clearly are signs of the reading and reviews Woolf had undertaken in the preceding months, and it is fair to see it as a sort of 'work-in-progress' spill-over from the various kinds of writing arbitrarily presented to her reviewer's hasty eye. The criticism of Wells in the essay is a continuation of her review of *Joan and Peter*[15] in which she found Wells misusing fiction, producing a hybrid book in

166

which 'Fiction . . . must take care of itself', since his ideas on education were the real subject: 'He has run up his buildings to house temporary departments of the Government.' What made her link praise of W. H. Hudson to that of Hardy and Conrad in the essay, and to cite the three in her diary in February as each having 'an interesting mind', was expressed in her review of *Far Away and Long Ago*[16]; Hudson's fascinating feat of memory whereby he returned to childlike vision without the false colouring of adult perception sent through the mist 'chinks of pure daylight' and 'lantern-like illumination' which revealed 'the simple, unmistakable truth, the underlying reason, otherwise so overlaid and befogged'; like Russian writers Hudson preserved the 'true, fresh and original colours'. In February a book on Meredith's use of actual people as the basis of fictional characters stimulates some thoughts on this particular type of 'realism', thoughts which could hardly fail to touch on her own subject-matter. 'All depends, of course, upon what you do with your handful of fact' she says, and at least excuses Meredith of any 'mean, spiteful, or ugly realism'; indeed, in his later works, perhaps he 'looked upon life too little and made his men and women too frequently masks for his own face'.[17] Even more obviously the starting-point of some of the ideas in 'Modern Novels' is her review of Dorothy Richardson's *The Tunnel*, and her identification of the experimental qualities of the method might be taken in itself as a statement of Woolf's supposed revolutionary aims:

> So 'him and her' are cut out, and with them goes the old deliberate business: the chapters that lead up and the chapters that lead down; the characters who are always characteristic; the scenes that are passionate and the scenes that are humorous; the elaborate construction of reality; the conception that shapes and surrounds the whole. All these things are cast away, and there is left, denuded, unsheltered, unbegun and unfinished, the consciousness of Miriam Henderson, the small sensitive lump of matter, half transparent and half opaque, which endlessly reflects and distorts the variegated procession, and is, we are bidden to believe, the source beneath the surface, the very oyster within the shell. (*T.L.S.*, 13 February 1919)

But the rest of the review puts this in perspective, identifying the book's reality as that of a 'very vivid surface' seldom

communicating 'the reality which underlies these appearances'; she even feels that 'the old method seems sometimes
the more profound and economical of the two.'

These various strands suggest a mind in flux, rather than
one that had reached some significant crossroads. The period
when 'Modern Novels' and these reviews were written, late
1918 and early 1919, is not the great divide between old and
new, but a time of intellectual engagement with literature and
of imaginative fertility which shows continuity between the
novel which was coming to an end, the stories she was
already composing and the novel she was to begin in early
1920. There is considerable evidence of continuity and overlap
between *Night and Day* and the sketches and stories she was
writing. She had enjoyed writing the last chapters of the novel,
and, despite some apprehension that she might be accused of
'niggling with emotions that don't really matter', she felt
satisfied that it was 'a much more mature & finished & satisfactory book than The Voyage Out' and that 'English fiction
being what it is, I compare for originality & sincerity rather
well with most of the moderns' (*D*, i, 259, 27 March 1919).
Night and Day was, in one way, a venture in the Russian
mode,[18] an attempt to combine the trivialities of the actual
with blazes of insight, sincere feeling, clear-sighted penetration
into human verities about love and people's aims in life. She
concluded later that this attempt to deal with 'non-being' (the
'nondescript cotton wool' of ordinariness with which much of
most days is filled) and with 'moments of being' was a failure,
and that it did not win its place among the company she had
originally hoped it would keep:

> The real novelist can somehow convey both sorts of being. I
> think Jane Austen can; and Trollope; perhaps Thackeray and
> Dickens and Tolstoy. I have never been able to do both. I
> tried—in *Night and Day*; and in *The Years*. ('*A Sketch of the Past*',
> *MB*, 70)

Her judgement of 1939 is not necessarily the one we accept. If
Night and Day fails, it is not for the reason Woolf here presents;
it is the relationship between being and non-being in the
experience of Katharine and Ralph that is the most memorable
thing in the work. The novel may also be seen as a replay on

her own ground of the rivalries treated in Leonard Woolf's novel *The Wise Virgins* (1914) and a turning of aspects of herself and her husband, her sister and her aunt and others into fictional forms which could be arranged in a pattern of debate over issues and values. In these two aspects, the combination of being and non-being and the projection of her own personal experience into fantasized forms, *Night and Day* is very much in tune with the sketches and stories in *Monday or Tuesday*.[19]

The earliest of these, 'The Mark on the Wall' (1917), records the author's branching thoughts as she sits by the fireside; its interest is in the combination of an intimate, casual autobiographical flavour and the web of opinion, fantasy, impression and reflection that she conjures from the mark on the wall, which is 'something definite, something real' and yet, because unidentified, is a suggestive source for the indefinite and the unreal. The fluidity of mental life and the self-flattering tendency of thought are interestingly acted out and the looking-glass images that we make of ourselves are identified as the proper stuff of fiction:

> the novelists in future will realize more and more the importance of these reflections . . .; those are the depths they will explore, those the phantoms they will pursue, leaving the description of reality more and more out of their stories. (*HH*, 43)

But reality, in the form of Virginia Woolf's actual situation sitting at home in a chair with an anonymous Leonard going out for the paper and removing the snail from the wall, is the framework of the meandering thoughts; the present moment, the immediate place, the personal identity form the image that remains of the 'story'.

'Kew Gardens', thought of in 1917, revised in early 1918, published in May 1919, suffers, like 'The Mark on the Wall', from Woolf's tendency towards 'fine writing' in a belle-lettrist tradition, but, despite this and the too obviously typical instances of class and relationship in the figures who visit Kew, the story lodges images in the mind. The writer's interest again was in creating two layers of apprehension, one representing the place as an exotic, slow-moving and continuous world of plants and light seen on the scale of snails, and the other registering the immediate random presences of the human beings who come and go; the incomplete dialogues present instances of memory and feeling, fantasy and madness, meaningless ritual talk and social games, and the disparity between physical triviality or inadequate words and real excitement of feeling. Though brief, the dialogues are storehouses of possible situations and images of the 'variegated procession', and it is not difficult to see them both as the fruits of casual observations on the many visits the Woolfs made to Kew while they lived at Richmond and as emblematic representations of moments in Woolf's novels before and after. She noted that:

> To the general loveliness and freshness was added a sense of being out when we should have been at home; this always turns things into a kind of spectacle. It seems to be going on without you. We sat under a tree, & became a centre for sparrows & robins, & pestered by the attentions of a gigantic aeroplane. (*D*, i, 148, 6 May 1918)

Even more suggestive is the cryptic notation of: 'I sat by choice on a seat in the shade at Kew; I saw two Heath butterflies; willows, crocuses, squills all in bud & blossom. Black clothes look like dusty palls. As for fur, it makes one laugh. We met at Kew' (*D*, i, 127, 12 March 1918). In sensing such moments of the author's life behind 'Kew Gardens', one reads it as the turning of autobiography into imagery. I have suggested above that the other substantial story in the collection, 'An Unwritten Novel', works rather similarly: the literal observed facts provide a framework for and act as a check to the writer's fantasy. None of the three reads like an attempt to communicate the 'semi-transparent envelope'; there is more sense of the interplay between transient actual fact and the novelist's alternative patterned arrangements of reality.

The most suggestive of the pieces in *Monday or Tuesday* are three of the shorter ones, 'The String Quartet', 'A Haunted House' and 'Monday or Tuesday' itself; all three present a version of the two-layered fiction. In 'The String Quartet' the first layer is that of the physical realities of here and now, as people assemble for a concert, chatting and putting on their own façades; this becomes interleaved with the second layer, the sensory impressions and mental pictures created by the music. If the impressionistic prose of the musical sections, where Woolf cleverly mingles a kind of mimesis of sound with a sequence of association, may be called 'experimental', the subject is familiar: the relationship between art and the reality of the present moment (in which, among other things, the seeds of the pageant/audience relationship of *Between the Acts* may be seen). The final snatch of conversation:

> 'Good night, good night. You go this way?'
> 'Alas, I go that.'

skilfully welds together the 'non-being' of trivial dialogue and the sense of memory and loss brought by the echo of the direction at the end of *Love's Labour's Lost* and the subliminal thought that: 'The words of Mercury are harsh after the songs of Apollo.'

In 'A Haunted House', though the idea that the life (the pulse or heart) of the house continues from the love of one generation to that of another is sentimental, the images used to express the relationship between past and present are full of disturbing power. As the ghostly couple remember past happiness, they stoop 'holding their silver lamp above us' to look at those who lie sleeping with 'love on their lips'; the image reaches backwards to Helen and Terence stooping over Rachel in the forest, forwards to the raising of the lamp of day in *The Waves*. The house is an image of safety from which light goes out in a straight beam into the wild dark, but it contains the uncertain questioner, trying to find the secret of the past:

> the beam I sought always burnt behind the glass. Death was the glass; death was between us; coming to the woman first, hundreds of years ago, leaving the house, sealing all the windows; the rooms were darkened. He left it, left her. (*HH*, 10)

Woolf returned to this imaginative core many times. Already in 'A Haunted House' there is a brief expression of her resolution of the pain of childhood loss—the idea that the imagination (or even just the feeling) of the artist/inheritor can heal the wound, can join together what was broken, can remake the 'house'. (Woolf's frequent use in her fiction of empty rooms and houses is the other half of her use of the house as a metaphor for a novel or for the world a writer creates.) It is not the impression of 'the shower of innumerable atoms' that she is after in this story, but an expressive image for the relationship of then and now. 'Monday or Tuesday' is a very short piece of 'art prose' with heron and sky in the first and last paragraphs used as a framework of indifferent movement and alternation of dark and light for a series of sketched-in images of the author's own mind and phases of her experience: random sounds, movements, colours register people and the city; fragments of appearance and speech in a firelit room register a social, possibly political, discussion group; a series of participles and adjectives combine non-human and human images and suggest ebb and flow:

> Flaunted, leaf-light, drifting at corners, blown across the wheels, silver-splashed, home or not home, gathered, scattered, squandered in separate scales, swept up, down, torn, sunk, assembled—and truth? (*HH*, 12)

The seeker for truth, blown hither and thither by experience, becomes the recorder/reader by the fireside; 'the white square of marble' turns from the writer's tablet into the book:

> Now to recollect by the fireside on the white square of marble. From ivory depths words rising shed their blackness, blossom and penetrate. Fallen the book; in the flame, in the smoke, in the momentary sparks—or now voyaging, the marble square pendant, minarets beneath and the Indian seas, while space rushes blue and stars glint—truth? or now, content with closeness? (12–13)

This short sketch is an enigmatic, even in a sense an allegorical, statement of her own endeavour and uncertainty as a writer. Repeatedly at this period she is questioning: how should one write? how convey reality? how record the impressions of the day, activity, people, appearances, opinions? what is truer, to be swept along on some flight of the mind or to stay close to the particular moment, to observation?

The stories in *Monday or Tuesday* are held together by images of the writer as muser by the fire, as traveller in the train, as observer of random groups of people, as seeker, hearer, watcher. The 'life' of *Monday or Tuesday* is the author's own life, though she converts her own experience into symbols of the mind's attempts to interpret and to express.[20] 'Have I the power

of conveying the true reality?' she wondered after Arnold
Bennett's criticisms of *Jacob's Room*, 'Or do I write essays
about myself?' (*D*, ii, 248) *Monday or Tuesday* had its origin in
essays about herself and forms a shadowy outline of 'a
portrait of the artist', but in trying to get away from the
'damned egotistical self' Woolf turned the personal into
anonymous pictures, currents of thought, and sequences of
imagery.

In saying that she thought of a new form (for *Jacob's Room*) in
the combination of 'An Unwritten Novel', 'The Mark on the
Wall' and 'Kew Gardens', Woolf was thinking of putting
together a number of aspects of her life: the inability of the
writer to interpret intriguingly shifting life; the writer's random
musings, often wrong about literal facts; random snatches of
observation, exact but fragmentary, put into perspective by a
sense of continuity in nature. This is hardly a recipe for a truer
record of 'life itself'; or (to put it into the terms of the title of this
essay) there is a difference between the life of *Monday or Tuesday*
and 'the life of Monday or Tuesday', as the phrase is used in
'Modern Fiction'. Emphasis is on the arbitrariness of perception, the conventional nature of people's views of one
another; there is no insight into relationships (which tend to be
treated mock heroically or with a disingenuous naïveté). The
method comes to seem to have a particular appropriateness to
Jacob's Room because it is about absence and memory,[21] and it
was, in part at least, an elegy for a lost brother who left a room
empty. But, if we put this aside, we see a fulfilment also of
purely artistic impulses: to create a twentieth-century variation
on *Tristram Shandy* and to express a desired indefiniteness—
something true to the feeling in 'Modern Novels' of 'a vague
general confusion in which the clear-cut features . . . were
dissolved beyond the possibility of separate recognition'. At the
same time, the author looks for brightness and the clear, true,
childlike vision. In the combination of the attempt to observe
and to express and the hesitant, self-correcting estimate of the
validity of the experience, the writings of 1918–22 seem to me
particularly sensitive. The same qualities are to be found in
some of the letters and passages in the diary, as in Virginia
Woolf's record of the life of one particular Monday, Armistice
Day:

173

Monday 11 November

Twentyfive minutes ago the guns went off, announcing peace. A siren hooted on the river. They are hooting still. A few people ran to look out of windows. The rooks wheeled round, & wore for a moment the symbolic look of creatures performing some ceremony, partly of thanksgiving, partly of valediction over the grave. A very cloudy still day, the smoke toppling over heavily towards the east; & that too wearing for a moment a look of something floating, waving, drooping. We looked out of the window; saw the housepainter give one look at the sky & go on with his job; the old man toddling along the street carrying a bag out [of] which a large loaf protruded, closely followed by his mongrel dog. So far neither bells nor flags, but the wailing of sirens & intermittent guns. (*D*, i, 216)

NOTES

1. *The Novels of Virginia Woolf* (1977), p. 15.
2. *English West Indies* (1888), xv, 248.
3. R. Austin Freeman, *The Moabite Cipher* (1909), repr. in *The Rivals of Sherlock Holmes*, ed. Hugh Greene (1970), p. 230.
4. *The Common Reader* (1925), p. 189; repr. *E*, ii, 106.
5. The sense of limited enhancement is clear in a reference (pointed out to me by Isobel Grundy) to F. L. Lucas and his wife: 'He is single eyed though; paces through life between blinkers, seeing only the high road. Perhaps Prudence serves as giglamp. She works for him in libraries' (*D*, iv, 180, 23 September 1933).
6. *T.L.S.*, 10 April 1919.
7. *Cassell's Weekly*, repr. M and M, pp. 112–14.
8. First version in *Nation and Athenaeum*, December 1923 (repr. M and M, pp. 115–19), later developed as an address to the Cambridge Heretics in May 1924, published under the title 'Character in Fiction' in *Criterion*, July 1924, and under the title 'Mr. Bennett and Mrs. Brown' as a Hogarth Press pamphlet, October 1924; the later version was included in *The Captain's Death Bed* (1950), and in *E*, i, 319–37. The question of Woolf's fairness to Bennett is not my concern here, but see Samuel Hynes, 'The Whole Contention between Mr. Bennett and Mrs. Woolf' in *Edwardian Occasions* (1972), pp. 24–38.
9. *T.L.S.*, 20 July 1922; *D*, ii, 261–62, and letter to Roger Fry, 22 September 1924 (*L*, iii, 132–33), where the footnote reference to 'Modern Fiction' is misleading: the words 'emotion put into the right relations' come from 'On Re-reading Novels', which in the event Woolf did not include in *The Common Reader*.

174

10. See *D*, ii, 249, 19 June 1923, for evidence that this view too had developed slowly; then she found 'the design is so queer and masterful'.
11. Preface to *The Awkward Age*, New York ed., vol. ix (1908).
12. *T.L.S.*, 26 December 1918.
13. First published July 1920; included in *Monday or Tuesday* (1921), repr. *HH*, 14–26.
14. See *D*, i, 247, 5 March 1919; i, 262, 10 April 1919.
15. *T.L.S.*, 19 September 1918.
16. *T.L.S.*, 26 September 1918.
17. *T.L.S.*, 13 February 1919.
18. My colleague Robert Hampson pointed out to me that there are similarities between passages in *Night and Day* and passages in Constance Garnett's translations. See R. Rubinstein, 'Virginia Woolf and the Russian Point of View' in *Comparative Literature Studies* (1972).
19. The six *Monday or Tuesday* stories discussed in this essay were included in *A Haunted House* (1944); the two others in the original volume, 'A Society' and 'Blue and Green', have not been reprinted. Woolf could well have included 'Solid Objects', published in The Athenaeum, 22 October 1920, a variation on the debate in *Night and Day* about private/public senses of what is of value in life; this story is in *HH*.
20. True to a lesser degree of 'A Society', a satirical reflection of the discussion-group aspect of her life, and 'Blue and Green', perhaps stimulated by the chemist's glass jars she obtained in 1918 (*D*, i, 170, 199; 23 July and 7 October).
21. See Allen McLaurin, *Virginia Woolf: The Echoes Enslaved* (Cambridge, 1973), pp. 125–26.

9

The Tunnelling Process: Some Aspects of Virginia Woolf's Use of Memory and the Past

by SUSAN DICK

In August of 1923, while at work on *Mrs. Dalloway* (then called 'The Hours') Virginia Woolf noted in her diary: 'I should say a good deal about The Hours, & my discovery; how I dig out beautiful caves behind my characters; I think that gives exactly what I want; humanity, humour, depth. The idea is that the caves shall connect, & each comes to daylight at the present moment' (*D*, ii, 263). She dug these caves using her 'tunnelling process'. 'It took me a year's groping', she wrote in October 1923, 'to discover what I call my tunnelling process, by which I tell the past by instalments, as I have need of it. This is my prime discovery so far' (ii, 272). Virginia Woolf had found a new way to use memory in her fiction, memory as both the faculty of remembering and the repository of the past. In the novels that preceded *Mrs. Dalloway* she had told the pasts of her central characters, as she had presented their thoughts and feelings, using conventional fictional methods. In *Mrs. Dalloway* she used on a much larger scale the narrative techniques she had recently been experimenting with in her short fiction. What I wish to explore first in this essay are the steps which led Woolf to her discovery. I shall begin by looking at the novels and short stories that precede *Mrs. Dalloway* to see how they may anticipate her new method, and then at *Mrs. Dalloway* and *To the Lighthouse*, the two works in which she developed her method and which foreshadow its use in the works that follow. My interest is in her dramatization both of memory as an aspect of consciousness, and of memories themselves, the particular fragments of the past which influence a character's perception of his world.

The reader looking at *The Voyage Out* from this perspective is immediately struck by how little specific detail is given about Rachel Vinrace's past. As the voyage which will take Rachel away from her familiar world begins, she muses about the life she is leaving behind. The narrator briefly describes Rachel's background and then tells us that her sketchy education 'left her abundant time for thinking' (33). She has often thought as she is thinking now, we are told, about her aunts and their way of life and she has come to see them and the other people in her life as 'symbols'. 'Reality dwelling in what one saw and felt, but did not talk about,' Rachel has decided, 'one could accept a system in which things went round and round quite satisfactorily to other people, without often troubling to think about it, except as something superficially strange' (35). Given this hazy perception of the world around her, it is hardly surprising that Rachel's mind is not filled with clearly differentiated memories. The past is for her a vague collection of impressions and feelings which she recalls as 'symbols' rather than as sharply defined people and events. Later in the novel when Hewet asks her to tell him about her life in Richmond, she does so by describing a typical day in her aunts' home (254). Her past is recalled as routine, a habit, which now that she has left it behind has little influence on her present experience.

What she does bring with her from her past, however, is the sense of reality described above. During the early stages of the voyage, she continues to feel that life is 'superficially strange', something 'very real, very big, very impersonal' and her place in it mysterious and tenuous. 'And life, what was that?' she wonders. 'It was only a light passing over the surface and vanishing, as in time she would vanish, though the furniture in the room would remain. . . . She was overcome with awe that things should exist at all. . . . She forgot that she had any fingers to raise' (*VO*, 144–45).

Hewet's love for her and hers for him alters her perception by giving solidity and purpose to the events and feelings which had seemed dreamlike and random. Hewet believes that 'there was an order, a pattern which made life reasonable . . . for sometimes it seemed possible to understand why things happened as they did' (366). Under Hewet's influence, Rachel achieves a new understanding of her past, an understanding which also marks an important change in her assumptions about the future. This occurs on the day following the dance at the hotel. Rachel is sitting with Hewet (who has fallen asleep) in the room where the dance was held. She has been watching the procession of people passing through the hall and her sense of 'the inevitable way in which they seemed to follow each other' is echoed in her thoughts about her own life, which next occupy her mind.

> She felt herself amazingly secure as she sat in her arm-chair, and able to review not only the night of the dance, but the entire past, tenderly and humorously, as if she . . . could now see exactly where she had turned. . . . Perhaps, then, every one really knew as she knew now where they were going; and things formed themselves into a pattern not only for her, but for them, and in that pattern lay satisfaction and meaning. (384–85)

Rachel's recognition of a pattern giving meaning to her random experiences anticipates Woolf's assertion twenty-five years later in 'A Sketch of the Past' that a pattern can be discovered beneath the 'cotton wool' of everyday life.[1] When reviewing the past and coming to this conclusion, Rachel does not isolate particular scenes as luminous 'moments of being' such as later characters will recall, for her perception of reality as strange and vaguely symbolic has not led her to have sharply defined experiences.[2] The meaning she now finds in her past she understands only as being 'of some kind'. What is important for her and for the development I wish to trace is the recognition that the present is part of a continuum leading from the past into the future. The pattern she discerns gives new significance to her memories and provides present events with a context of anticipation.

Rachel soon falls ill and under the strain of illness loses contact with both past and future. Hewet's presence becomes at times an irritation for he would force her to remember when pain compels her to exist only in the present. Her death releases her from these conflicts and establishes her as a memory in Hewet's mind. His sad cry, 'Rachel, Rachel', embodies for the reader too all that she was.

The Voyage Out is an unusual *Bildungsroman*. Late in the narrative Rachel realizes that her past has a pattern, but the reader's knowledge is restricted to that part of the pattern which occupies the time of the narrative.[3] Rachel's life before the novel begins seems a kind of pre-existence, a quiet and secure life of routine. Like Isabel Archer, Rachel seems only to begin to live when she is removed from her world of habits and is introduced to people and places that awake her to the potentialities in herself. In discovering a pattern in her life, she is endorsing the present by seeing its origins in the past. Her death fixes that pattern, making it for Hewet wholly the past and now a memory, just as Mrs. Ramsay, looking back on the successful dinner, sees that event as something complete that the others will remember in years to come.

In many ways Katharine Hilbery in *Night and Day* is Rachel Vinrace's opposite. Katharine is in danger of being engulfed by the past. She lives at home where she is surrounded by relics of her famous grandfather, Richard Alardyce. Each day she must help her mother try to impose order on the chaos of memories and manuscripts that Mrs. Hilbery is drawing upon as she attempts to write a biography of the famous writer. Katharine's attitude toward this rich inherited past is ambivalent. At times she feels that the present is insignificant when compared to the past in which lived the 'giant men' from whom she is descended (8). At other times, however, she fears that she is being stifled and 'that it was necessary for her very existence that she should free herself from the past' (38). This past not only dominates her present, but it also invades her memories, for she can recall being aware as a child that the rooms in her home were full of the past. When she feels that same presence of the past now, she is recapturing a former state of mind as well as experiencing it again (114).

Thus Katharine's inherited past and her personal past are

interwoven. As the narrative develops, Katharine's inherited past becomes less a part of her consciousness as her personal past, the past that the novel dramatizes, is placed in the foreground. Woolf emphasizes at the opening of the novel the dominant role that Katharine's family history has played in her life in order to establish the special context in which Katharine will develop her own history.

The need Katharine feels to free herself from the past complicates her relationships with the people around her. When the claims of her mother's world of fragmented memories become too great, she retreats to her room where she takes refuge in timeless impersonal mathematics. Similarly, when her feelings are touched by the demands of everyday life, she escapes into an imaginary world which, like her rich family past, sometimes overshadows the present. This second retreat is marked by a forgetting of the self as Katharine becomes to her mind 'another person'. Her imaginary world is an ideal world in which 'dwelt the realtities of the appearances which figure in our world'. The 'furniture' of this world, we are told, is 'drawn directly from the past, and even from the England of the Elizabethan age' but Katharine's own past plays no direct role in it (*ND*, 145). This dream world exists for her as a memory, however, for she repeatedly envisions it and it influences, in the way of memories, the things she says and does. As she emerges from her meditation in the passage quoted above, for example, her vision of the 'magnanimous hero' whom she loved in her fantasy suddenly prompts her to accept William Rodney's unwelcome proposal of marriage.

This habit of shifting her attention from the ordinary world to her imaginary one makes Katharine curiously distanced from her own life. When she becomes emotionally involved with William Rodney and then with Ralph Denham the liabilities of this habit become clear. When Rodney challenges her to tell him why she agreed to marry him, she cannot do so. The narrator reports her unspoken thoughts: 'Why indeed? . . . she could only recall a moment, as of waking from a dream, which now seemed to her a moment of surrender' (254). Again, when she meets Ralph Denham, with whom she is falling in love, she cannot, under the pressure of the moment, recall what she and Mary Datchet had recently been saying about him (309). The night and day of the title functions as a metaphor not only of the contrasts between fact and illusion, action and contemplation, but also of the simple contrast between remembering and forgetting. When Katharine remembers what she has said or thought, she is coming to terms with the world of fact. When she forgets her past thoughts, as in these scenes, it is because the illusions of her imaginary world are more real to her than are her actions in the ordinary world. As she learns to deal with the factual world, her memory begins to function more efficiently and, like Rachel's, her understanding of her own past becomes more complete.[4]

An important change in Katharine's perception of her past takes place soon after the scene in which she cannot recall her thoughts about Ralph. She has been thinking about the way that her upbringing has provided her with traditional answers to all questions. 'Like all people brought up in a tradition,' the narrator says, 'Katharine was able, within ten minutes or so, to reduce any moral difficulty to its traditional shape and solve it by the traditional answers' (*ND*, 329). This is a useless convenience for her, however, for 'the only truth which she could discover was the truth of what she herself felt' (330). She rejects the 'visionary voices' of the past and follows her own 'frail beam' as she seeks to discover what action she should now take. She does not, however, move into her imaginary world, but rather remembers three vivid scenes: 'she thought of Mary sitting upright and saying, "I'm in love—I'm in love"; she thought of Rodney losing his self-consciousness among the dead leaves, and speaking with the abandonment of a child; she thought of Denham leaning upon the stone parapet and talking to the distant sky, so that she thought him mad' (331). Woolf anticipates in this brief passage a method which will become central to her dramatization of character in *Mrs. Dalloway* and the works that follow it. Katharine recalls three 'memory pictures' (as Leslie Stephen called them)[5] which help her to focus her own thoughts and feelings about the tangle of relationships in which she finds herself. Such 'scene making' will become in the later novels one of Woolf's central means of dramatizing a character's recollection of his most intense experiences.[6]

These remembered scenes, striking confirmations of the

world of fact, lead Katharine to a perception (which recalls Rachel's) of 'some symmetrical pattern, some arrangement of life, which invested, if not herself, at least the others, not only with interest, but with a kind of tragic beauty' (*ND*, 332). Imagination then supplements memory and a 'fantastic picture' of her friends takes shape in her mind. Transitions such as this from memory to vision will be dramatized in far more complex ways in Woolf's later works.

By the end of the novel Katharine is able to see her own life as part of this symmetrical pattern and to envision the present leading into a future filled with potential. 'The future emerged more splendid than ever', the narrator tells us, 'from this construction of the present' (537). Katharine's synthesizing vision confirms the continuum of time and ends the novel on a hopeful note that will not be heard so unambiguously again in Woolf's fiction until the conclusion of *The Years*.

The Voyage Out and *Night and Day* are apprentice works in which Woolf tries her hand at many of the conventions she had inherited from nineteenth-century novelists. One can find in these early books preliminary expressions of the themes and perspectives of the later works in which Woolf experiments boldly with conventions. In her first two novels the pasts of her characters, whether given sparingly or in detail, are reported to the reader by the omniscient narrator or disclosed by the characters in dialogue. The characters' thoughts are narrated or, at times, quoted by the narrator, but seldom is the movement of their thoughts shaped by the process of recollection. The functions of memory and the presence of the past are important themes in *Night and Day*, but they do not inform the methods of characterization as they will do in later novels.

Woolf began to explore the potentialities of memory as an aspect of a new method of creating character in some of the short fiction published in *Monday or Tuesday* in 1921. This volume contained 'The Mark on the Wall' (first published in 1917) and 'Kew Gardens' (1919), two works which foreshadow Woolf's mature narrative method.

'The Mark on the Wall' is an extended memory in which the narrator recreates the train of thought initiated by her inability to identify a small mark on her wall. 'Perhaps it was the middle of January in the present year that I first looked up and saw the mark on the wall', she begins. 'In order to fix a date it is necessary to remember what one saw' (*HH*, 40). Her mind ranges from the look of the room in which she was sitting to considerations of the nature of life and of the self. The process she records here is like that which Mrs. Dalloway, Peter Walsh, Mrs. Ramsay, Lily, and others will experience, a process of reflection in which memories become so vivid that they seem for a time to usurp the present. The intense reality of such memories is suggested here, for example by the shift midway through the piece from past to present tense: 'I must jump up and see for myself what that mark on the wall really is', the narrator says, seeming to forget for the moment that she already knows (*HH*, 46). Katharine Hilbery's imaginary world bears some resemblance to the thoughts the narrator of 'The Mark on the Wall' has about an alternative world in which she might have been born, but the method of narration which shapes this short work—a process of association initiated by a single memory—is not used in *Night and Day*. It would be several years before Woolf would discover a way to dramatize in her characters, rather than in her narrator, the dark paths the mind follows (as Neville puts it) when it enters the past (*TW*, 128).

In 'Kew Gardens' one sees Woolf coming closer to this discovery. The narrator in this short work observes a series of people pass by a flower bed in Kew Gardens. The first of these is a man who is remembering an earlier visit to the garden when he proposed marriage to a woman who refused him. The return to the scene of his proposal sparks a vivid memory of it which the narrator, able to overhear his thoughts, quotes. After recalling the scene he turns to his wife and tells her that he has 'been thinking of Lily, the woman I might have married. . . . Do you mind my thinking of the past?' he asks. Her surprising reply is spoken from the perspective of one to whom the past is more than personal memories. 'Doesn't one always think of the past, in a garden with men and women lying under the trees?' she wonders. 'Aren't they one's past, all that remains of it, those men and women, those ghosts lying under the trees, . . . one's happiness, one's reality?' (*HH*, 33).

In this brief scene Woolf both dramatizes the process of

recollection and introduces an attitude toward the past which she will develop in later works. The sense of an individual's past as both personal and impersonal is present in *Night and Day* in that Katharine's knowledge of her family history is based on hearsay rather than on direct experience. In *Jacob's Room* and later in *The Waves* and *Between the Acts*, the impersonal past which the wife in 'Kew Gardens' perceives in the scene around her, expands to global proportions.

In *Jacob's Room*, the focus is almost exclusively upon the impersonal past for the narrator excludes herself for the most part from the mind of her central character. We know from her diary that Woolf conceived *Jacob's Room* as an extension of the method she had used in 'The Mark on the Wall', 'Kew Gardens', and 'An Unwritten Novel', in which 'one thing should open out of another' (*D*, ii, 13–14). What worried her about this method was the intrusion of 'the damned egotistical self' which she felt 'ruined' the works of James Joyce and Dorothy Richardson. This concern with the presence of the author's ego in his work may be in part what led her to insist on the great distance separating her narrator from her central character. The narrator refuses to indulge in 'character-mongering' for this would be to assume in fiction an ability to know another person denied us in life (*JR*, 153). Thus although *Jacob's Room* is a *Bildungsroman*, we do not know how Jacob remembers the experiences we see him having. Jacob's memory, like that of the other people in the novel, remains part of his unexplored and unexpressed inner life. 'Each had his past shut in him like the leaves of a book known to him by heart'; the narrator says of the people riding down Oxford Street, 'and his friends could only read the title . . . and the passengers going the opposite way could read nothing at all—save . . . "a young man in grey smoking a pipe" ' (63).

Though the narrator does not dramatize Jacob's sense of his past, she does present a view of human history which he seems to share. In a much later work, the essay 'Anon' which was left unfinished at the time of Woolf's death, she expresses a view of what I have called the impersonal past. 'There never was, it seems, a time when men and women were without memory', she says, speaking of Malory's *Morte Darthur*, 'There never was a young world. Behind the English lay ages of toil and love.

That is the world beneath our consciousness; the anonymous world to which we can still return.'[7] This anonymous world is what the narrator of *Jacob's Room* glimpses when she tries at one point to define the cause of Jacob's sorrow. 'It is brewed by the earth itself', she says. 'It comes from the houses on the coast. We start transparent, and then the cloud thickens. All history backs our pane of glass. To escape is vain' (47). Jacob feels this past impinging on him in Cambridge where the sound of the clock conveys to him 'a sense of old buildings and time; and himself the inheritor' (43). The narrator sees it in the 'enormous mind' contained in the British Museum (107), in London where the old man crossing from the Surrey side to the Strand seems to have been 'crossing the Bridge these six hundred years' (112), and in the ancient moor where Betty Flanders's lost darning needles and garnet brooch are kept safe beside the Roman skeletons (133).

Early in the novel the narrator teases us with the promise that Jacob has a future. 'Oh, far away they'd remember it,' she says of the hours the young men at Cambridge spent talking in their rooms, 'and deep in dulness gaze back on it, and come to refresh themselves again' (39). His death in the war cuts him off from these memories, of course. But Bonamy's cry on the last page, 'Jacob! Jacob!', like Hewet's cry to Rachel, fixes Jacob as a memory himself now, as one of the 'ghosts' from the impersonal past which influences the present and opens into the future.

In *Mrs. Dalloway*, the broad restless external perspective of the narrator of *Jacob's Room* gives way to a narrowly focused internal one. The span of twenty-some years is reduced to the time of a single day. Instead of a young central character, as we have had in the three earlier novels, we find a middle-aged one. And in place of an omniscient narrator who assumes, and even in *Jacob's Room* asserts, her distinction from her characters, we have a narrator whose voice is so similar to that of her main characters that we can scarcely distinguish it from theirs. As we have seen, Woolf considered her 'tunnelling process' the most important discovery she had made while writing *Mrs. Dalloway*. She later recalled that she had thought Clarissa 'tinselly' until she invented her memories (*D*, iii, 32). In discovering a new way to use a character's memories Woolf

185

was able to build upon her growing recognition of the central role that memory—both as a process and as a storehouse of experience—plays in human consciousness.

No doubt her reading of Joyce and Proust helped her to make this discovery. Her diary account, in which she refers to 'a year's groping' leading up to her new method, suggests that their influence was largely an unconscious one, though she had wondered in February of 1923 if her 'next lap' would be influenced by Proust, and had noted in November of 1924 that she could not read Proust while she was correcting *Mrs. Dalloway*, 'so persuasive is he'.[8] The opening of the novel, in which the sound of the door hinges triggers in Clarissa the memory of a scene at Bourton where she often heard a similar sound, recalls the way the characters of Joyce and Proust remember scenes from the past when stimulated by particular sensations. The continual blurring in the minds of characters in *Mrs. Dalloway* of the border separating present from past also resembles the interaction between the two in the works of Joyce and Proust. Though similar in these ways (and others) to the monumental novels of Woolf's two influential contemporaries, *Mrs. Dalloway* is vastly different from them in scale. Not only does Woolf tell the past 'by instalments' as she has need of it, she also uses a rigorous process of selection in presenting her characters' pasts. One could write detailed biographies of Bloom and Marcel, but the reader attempting to reconstruct Clarissa's life would soon realize how little he actually knows about it.

Though Clarissa's thoughts turn continually toward the past, they do not highlight random events, but rather centre around memories of the time when she was a young woman living with her family at Bourton. These memories seem to represent an idyllic past which continually looms behind her present life. We learn little from her memories about other periods in her past. She does not recall the terrible scene of her sister's death, for we learn of this from Peter Walsh's memory of it, not Clarissa's.[9] Similarly, she does not reflect in any detail on her marriage to Richard. She recalls that she has failed him at Clieveden, 'then at Constantinople, and again and again', but does not remind herself of how she has failed (36). Her recent illness is recalled by her, and probably underlies her frequent thoughts about death, but the nature of that illness is disclosed only in passing through Peter's memory. Her daughter Elizabeth's birth and childhood are not recalled by Clarissa at all. The paths of the mind lead habitually (on this day at least) to a brief time at Bourton. The other characters who radiate around Clarissa in the narrative—Peter Walsh, Richard, Sally Seton—all share memories of this time and their recollections expand and enrich Clarissa's own.[10]

The action of the novel is shaped by anticipation. 'Remember my party', Clarissa calls to Peter and to Elizabeth (*MD*, 54, 139). She spends her day preparing for the party which will be her 'offering' as she sees it to life. She celebrates life when she goes out to buy flowers, turning her mind from the past to the present. 'But every one remembered,' she tells herself, 'what she loved was this, here, now, in front of her; the fat lady in the cab' (11). Everyone in *Mrs. Dalloway* does remember and one of the dominant rhythms in the novel is the continual shift in the characters' minds from thoughts of the past to impressions of the present moment. 'For why go back like this to the past?' Peter complains to himself. 'Why make him suffer, when she had tortured him so infernally? Why?' (48). Had Clarissa answered this unspoken question she might have said, because we must. In this novel the present is inseparable from the past. The achronological memories of the characters function as a second tier of narrative which develops in tandem with the chronological action of the present.

This continual return to the past emphasizes the characters' awareness of the fugitive present. When Clarissa insists to herself that she wants to enjoy what is here and now, she is attempting to break free of her habitual orientation which is, as the opening page shows, toward the past. To remember is to confirm one's mortality. This is the darker side of memory, the side that Clarissa tries to ignore. When she thinks of her death she assures herself of a kind of immortality by assuming that she will be remembered. As she continues to live in her memory as a young girl at Bourton, so will she live on after her death in the memories of her friends and in the places where she has lived. 'Somehow', she tells herself, 'in the streets of London, on the ebb and flow of things, here, there, she survived, Peter survived, lived in each other' (*MD*, 11). Her assumption recalls the comment made by the wife in 'Kew Gardens' and reflects the notion Woolf will develop far more fully in *The Waves*, that we are all in some way a part of one another and that our memories confirm that unity.

Clarissa's admonition to 'Remember my party' can be read not only as a simple reminder that her party is that night, but also as a plea to remember it in the more distant future. Heard in this second way, Clarissa's command becomes associated with her thoughts about her own death. The party seems to mark the limit of her anticipation of the future. Beyond that she seems only to foresee her death.[11] Peter anticipates this too after he has met her again, for his thoughts move swiftly from a vivid memory of her to a vision of her sudden death (56).

Peter has returned to London to see about the divorce of the young woman he plans to marry, but once he has met Clarissa again his emotions are so deeply and fully engaged by her that this future life with Daisy grows as dim as her face in the photograph. Clarissa irritates him with her affectations and her parties, yet as a memory she still has the power to fill him with 'extraordinary excitement'. 'No, no, no!' he insists. 'He was not in love with her any more! He only felt, after seeing her that morning . . . unable to get away from the thought of her' (*MD*, 85). Woolf sums up the perspective of the entire book in the final two lines.

> It is Clarissa, he said.
> For there she was.

The present tense of Peter's moment of recognition (which is said in his mind we assume since it is not placed within quotation marks) is juxtaposed with the past tense of the narrator's statement. Clarissa both *is* and *was*, and Peter's final vision of her fuses these two identities into one. For Clarissa, Peter, and Sally Seton the past has been recaptured and contained in the present moment, and it has no future beyond this moment.[12]

The other characters in *Mrs. Dalloway* whose minds the narrator enters are also dominated in various ways by thoughts of the past. Clarissa's 'double' (as Woolf called him in her 'Introduction') Septimus Warren Smith cannot escape from the voices of the dead. In Septimus's distorted consciousness his friend Evans, killed in the war, continues to live. During moments of lucidity Septimus can remember why he married Rezia and how he relinquished control of his life, but these memories give him no stability now. Rezia's memories of their past accentuate her present misery and offer her little hope for the future. From Septimus's point of view his reluctant suicide is an affirmation of life for in death he escapes the memories which have isolated him in the present and given him only a mad vision of the future.

The one exception to the retrospective orientation of the characters in *Mrs. Dalloway* is the Dalloways' daughter Elizabeth, the youngest character in the book. Elizabeth is enmeshed for the moment in a relationship with the grim Miss Kilman, but we see as soon as we are given access to Elizabeth's thoughts that Clarissa has no need to worry about Miss Kilman's influence. Elizabeth is all potential. When she escapes from the stuffy Army and Navy Stores and from Miss Kilman's self-pitying company, she boards a bus and rides up Whitehall to the Strand. She is breaking new ground, 'For no Dalloways came down the Strand daily; she was a pioneer, a stray, venturing, trusting' (152). We feel that Elizabeth will do what she wishes with her life and will find her family less inhibiting than Katharine Hilbery does. Elizabeth plays a minor role in this novel, but her freshness and her spontaneity provide a significant if small counterpoint to the tug of the past felt by the other characters.

Young people abound in *To the Lighthouse*. Here Woolf expands and refines the narrative method of *Mrs. Dalloway* and her use of memory, like so much else, is far more subtle and varied here than in her earlier narratives. The ways that the characters remember the past, the things they remember, and in Part III the relation between the process of remembering and the creation of a work of art, are all aspects of *To the Lighthouse* that I wish briefly to explore.

The central characters in *Mrs. Dalloway* draw their memories from a common pool of memories. Woolf will use this device again in *The Waves* where her six speakers share a common childhood. In *To the Lighthouse*, however, she does not link characters in this way. Nor does she dramatize her central

189

character, Mrs. Ramsay, by using her personal memories as the background against which her present life is placed. The silent question Mrs. Ramsay asks herself as she sits down to dinner, 'But what have I done with my life?'[13] does not initiate a train of memories as it would have done in Mrs. Dalloway's mind. Mrs. Ramsay's past is drawn in sketchily and the events which have made her what she is are not disclosed. 'What was there behind it—her beauty and splendour?' the narrator wonders, echoing the curiosity of others. 'Had he blown his brains out, they asked, had he died the week before they were married—some other, earlier lover, of whom rumours reached one?' (*TL*, 46). Mrs. Ramsay's thought that 'she had had experiences which need not happen to every one (she did not name them to herself)' is as close as she comes to recalling the specific events which might be grounds for these rumours (92). When she thinks of her marriage, her thoughts centre around general memories of things her husband has done or said and on general regrets or concerns, and she recalls only two specific scenes from her early life (132, 150). The first of these is prompted during dinner by Mr. Bankes's reference to her old friends the Mannings. 'Oh, she could remember it as if it were yesterday—going on the river, feeling very cold' (132). This recollection becomes for her that 'dream land, that unreal but fascinating place, the Mannings' drawing-room at Marlow twenty years ago; where one moved about without haste or anxiety, for there was no future to worry about' (140). She sees this memory as she will later see the successful dinner party, as something 'immune from change' (158). Mrs. Ramsay links memory and the escape from mutability in a way that recalls Clarissa's thoughts about immortality and foreshadows Lily's about art.

The other scene Mrs. Ramsay recalls from the past gives us a glimpse of Mr. Ramsay as he was when 'she had first known him, gaunt but gallant; helping her out of a boat, she remembered; with delightful ways' (*TL*, 150). Perhaps she has told Lily of this scene or perhaps it is coincidence that leads Lily to imagine one like it ten years later as she attempts to recapture the past and complete her painting (295).

Lily and Mr. Bankes function as a kind of chorus in Part I. They observe the Ramsays, discuss them, and recall particular scenes from the past which illuminate facets of their characters. Woolf's habit of marking the past through the process of 'scene making' is shared by Lily and Bankes. William Bankes's memory of the time when Mr. Ramsay pointed at a hen and her chicks and said 'Pretty—pretty', epitomizes for him both a moment when he gained an insight into Mr. Ramsay's character and the turning point in their friendship (34). Similarly, Lily's extended memory of Mrs. Ramsay's visit to her room, which seems to combine memories of several visits, helps Lily to explain to herself the intense combination of resistance and desire which she feels for Mrs. Ramsay (76–80). These memories function as mirrors which reflect both the character remembered and the character remembering.

By using memories of the distant past sparingly in Part I Woolf avoids the retrospective angle of vision which dominates *Mrs. Dalloway*. Her presentation of the thoughts and feelings of Mr. and Mrs. Ramsay makes it clear that what they do on this single day typifies their relationship. By contrast, Clarissa and Richard (like Clarissa and Peter) spend little narrative time together and we learn about their relationship mainly through their memories.

Though Lily and Bankes recall scenes from the past in which the Ramsays figure, their memories of their own pasts remain largely unexplored. Mr. Carmichael's thoughts are never given and all that we know of his past is conveyed through Mrs. Ramsay's memories. While at dinner Charles Tansley recalls his past, as Miss Kilman does hers in *Mrs. Dalloway*, in an effort to bolster his self-confidence by asserting to himself the superiority of his lower class background. His focus is on the future, however, for he will blow these 'mild cultivated people . . . sky high' he tells himself, when he becomes a leader of men (*TL*, 138). He has his dissertation just as Lily has her painting, Mr. Bankes his scientific experiments, Mr. Carmichael his poetry, Minta and Paul their marriage, Mr. Ramsay his lectures, Mrs. Ramsay her children, and her children their futures. The emphasis throughout Part I is on life as a process, with the present opening not only backward into glimpses of the past, but forward into a promising future.

This movement toward the future, like the use of memory,

191

changes radically in Part III. The characters who return to the summer house after a ten-year interval in which Mrs. Ramsay, Prue, and Andrew have died, return to a haunted house. The airs which stole through the empty house in 'Time Passes', testing its stability, are replaced by ghosts of the past who haunt the memories of Lily, Mr. Ramsay, Cam, and James. Lily faces those ghosts by returning to the painting she had left unfinished in Part I. Mr. Ramsay, Cam, and James complete the trip to the lighthouse, anticipated but (we assume) not taken ten years earlier. The two activities occur simultaneously and dramatize the influence that Mrs. Ramsay, now a memory, continues to have on some of those who love her.

Woolf has already linked the artistic process and memory in her earlier description of Lily who as she scrutinized her painting was 'subduing all her impressions as a woman to something much more general; becoming once again under the power of that vision which she had seen clearly once and must now grope for among hedges and houses and mothers and children—her picture' (82). In Part I Mrs. Ramsay is there to serve as model and to help Lily recapture her vision. In Part III Lily must call upon her memory not only of her earlier vision (for she intends to paint the same picture) but also her memories of Mrs. Ramsay, who is part of her design. Thus as she begins to paint, she is preoccupied simultaneously with both her picture and the past. The reader may feel that Woolf is straining her fiction here somewhat, that she is so interested in exploring the process by which life is transformed into art that she becomes more discursive than dramatic and that the 'bolts of iron' (255) come rather too close to the surface. One may also feel that Woolf faces a difficulty she doesn't completely overcome in relating Lily's memories of scenes from the past to her creation of an abstract painting. It is clear from her treatment of Lily's struggle that Woolf is more interested in the process than in the product and that this is where the reader's attention is directed, too. Woolf will move closer to her own craft in *Orlando*, *The Waves*, and *Between the Acts*, where her artist figures must remake their visions in language, not paint.

The scenes that Lily recalls as she goes on 'tunnelling her

way into her picture, into the past' (258) are new to us, though they involve characters we know. The detailed 'memory pictures' Lily creates of Mrs. Ramsay, Tansley and herself on the beach illustrate for her Mrs. Ramsay's ability to make 'of the moment something permanent' (241). In recalling scenes in which Mrs. Ramsay seemed to say 'Life stand still here', Lily is experiencing again moments of heightened perception which were at the time, as she says, 'of the nature of a revelation'. By providing her with evidence in life of the order and value she would express in art, the memory of these 'moments of being' plays a central role in her effort to complete her painting.[14]

As Lily works on her canvas her mood swings from extreme grief when Mrs. Ramsay's absence overwhelms her to moments of elation when she succeeds in calling Mrs. Ramsay back. Eventually she reaches a point in this painful process when she must forget instead of remember. 'But what she wished to get hold of was that very jar on the nerves,' the narrator reports, 'the thing itself before it has been made anything' (*TL*, 287). When she stops soliciting the past for help, she feels isolated in the present moment, as if 'everything this morning was happening for the first time, perhaps for the last time' (288). Lily is allowing what Woolf elsewhere calls the 'under-mind' to do its work as she stands 'with all her faculties in a trance, frozen over superficially but moving underneath with extreme speed'.[15] The vision of Mrs. Ramsay that now comes to her seems more a resurrection than a memory. For a moment Mrs. Ramsay actually sits at the window. Lily's simple acknowledgement of her presence—'There she sat'—recalls Peter Walsh's recognition of Clarissa. Life does stand still for a moment as past and present fuse in a fleeting revelation.[16]

The scenes in the boat, which interrupt the description of Lily on the lawn four times and which take up roughly one-third less narrative space than do Lily's sections, function as counterpoints to Lily's activity in several ways. The two events are linked by shared memories. Like Lily's memories, those of Cam and James take the reader's mind back to Part I so that he too becomes engaged in a process of recollection. Their memories also increase the reader's knowledge of the Ramsays by giving new glimpses of them. There are some major differences between the dramatization of the functions of memory in the two scenes, however. Unlike Lily, whose memories are those of an adult and extend into the more recent past, the recollections of Cam and James are early childhood memories recalled now in adolescence. Further, except for her final vision of Mrs. Ramsay, the realistic scenes from the past which Lily remembers are summoned up by her deliberate effort to remember. By contrast, memories enter the minds of Cam and James without their seeming to call them forward. The return to the house they have not visited in ten years, the struggle with their father, and the deeper implications of this trip to the lighthouse combine to initiate in the minds of them both the process of recollection. The memories that surface in their minds lack the dramatic completeness and sharp visual definition of Lily's memories. Cam and James recall impressions and emotions from childhood which are associated with but not always circumscribed by detailed scenes. The language in which their recollections are presented is poetic and reflects the image-making power of a child's mind, something Woolf would explore again in the opening passages of *The Waves*.

Perhaps because one of the functions of the scenes in the boat is to dramatize Cam and James changing their attitude toward their father from hostility to sympathy, the memories of James, who most resents Mr. Ramsay, are given in more detail than those of Cam. Cam's memories are less painful and less intense than James's. As she looks back at the receding house the images and rhythms of her thoughts remind us of the words Mrs. Ramsay used to soothe her to sleep. Though Cam cannot forget her father's imperiousness 'which had poisoned her childhood and raised bitter storms, so that even now she woke in the night trembling with rage and remembered some command of his' (253), her memories of visits to his study and of the security he and the other elderly men in her childhood offered her softens her resistance to him and makes it much easier for her to offer him the sympathy he doesn't ask for, but clearly needs.

James's memories are fragments of past scenes given form in his mind by the images and symbols he makes for them: the knife, the black-winged harpy, the footprints in the snow, the foot crushed to purple by the wheel, all make concrete in metaphor the emotions he felt as a child, and continues to feel. He seems to see in his past a re-enactment of the intrusion of evil into Eden. 'Everything tended to set itself in a garden,' he thinks, 'where there was none of this gloom. . . . It was in this world that the wheel went over the person's foot' (275–76). The intensity with which he recalls his childhood hatred of his father confirms Mrs. Ramsay's thought that 'children never forget' (95). The process of remembering, however, leads him to see Mr. Ramsay as he has not done before, to move beyond his hatred of him as an enemy from the past to a new recognition of him as one who also feels 'that loneliness which was for both of them the truth about things' (301). James's realization that 'nothing was simply one thing' (277) helps him to achieve a new understanding of his father and a new perspective on his past.

The descent into memory enacted in Part III takes the characters into a past which for a time seems as real as the events of the present. Yet this descent also confirms the distance separating the present from the past. Lily, Cam, and James all reach a point when they must emerge from recollection and confront the present moment. Their excursions into the past lead them to see the present from new perspectives. To Cam and James Mr. Ramsay appears heroic and defiant as he springs 'lightly like a young man' on to the lighthouse rock (*TL*, 308). Lily turns from her vision of Mrs. Ramsay and her thoughts of the arrival at the lighthouse back to her canvas and in a moment of sudden clarity draws a single line down the centre of her picture. Her recognition that the process is complete ('I have had my vision', she thinks), like Carmichael's succinct benediction ('It is finished'), draws the two scenes together and brings the novel to a resonant close. Like an elegist, Lily has called forth memories of the dead and has found in these memories a way to answer her initial question, 'What does it mean then, what can it all mean?' (217). The answer is her vision, for like the trip to the lighthouse it seems for the moment to bring to rest the ghosts of the past. The movement of the narrative is completed with this final return to the present. The anticipation of the future felt so strongly in Part I is felt again, in a muted form, at the end of Part III. We are not invited to speculate about what will become of these characters, but we do feel an impetus toward the future in them, an impetus which we do not feel at the close of *Mrs. Dalloway.*

In the novels that follow *To the Lighthouse—Orlando, The Waves, The Years, Between the Acts*—the functions of memory continue to be central to Woolf's dramatization of the complexities of human character.[17] The new method that she discovered while writing *Mrs. Dalloway*, the 'tunnelling process', led her to explore with increasing profundity the ways that the memory brings to mind fragments of past experience and the potential it has to tap memories of the impersonal past buried more deeply in the unconscious. This latter function of memory, which Woolf alluded to in *Jacob's Room* but did not explore in *Mrs. Dalloway* or *To the Lighthouse*, becomes a central concern in her later novels. Through the artist figures in her later works—Orlando, Bernard, Neville, Isa, Miss La Trobe—she dramatizes the special role that memory plays in the writer's struggle to create something that captures his private vision and yet transcends the limitations of his private experience. The need which Lily understood for the artist to 'subdue' himself as he confronts his blank canvas or paper becomes associated in *The Waves, Between the Acts*, and Woolf's later diary and letters with the goal of anonymity. She must have admired her disreputable Miss La Trobe who brays from the bushes a 'megaphontic, anonymous, loud-speaking affirmation' (*BA*, 218).

In her late memoir, 'A Sketch of the Past', Woolf finally allowed herself to begin to write the autobiography she had suppressed in her fiction. She feels free in this work to speak directly of the particular events in her life which have had a special meaning for her. The process of calling these events into her mind leads her to consider too the relationship between the present and the past and the power that memory has to call back that which has been forgotten. This memoir contains some of Woolf's most poetic evocations of the past and some of her most searching reflections on the mind and on what she called 'reality'. It also demonstrates, as I hope this discussion has too, the striking continuity in her work. Though unfinished, this remarkable memoir can be read as Virginia

The Tunnelling Process

Woolf's final summing up. I would like to conclude by quoting from it her eloquent description of her 'first memory'.

If life has a base that it stands upon, if it is a bowl that one fills and fills and fills—then my bowl without a doubt stands upon this memory. It is of lying half asleep, half awake, in bed in the nursery at St. Ives. It is of hearing the waves breaking, one, two, one, two, and sending a splash of water over the beach; and then breaking, one two, one two, behind a yellow blind. It is of hearing the blind draw its little acorn across the floor as the wind blew the blind out. It is of lying and hearing this splash and seeing this light, and feeling, it is almost impossible that I should be here; of feeling the purest ecstasy I can conceive. (*MB*, 64–5)

NOTES

1. *MB*, 72. In *The Years*, Eleanor Pargiter toys with the same idea: 'Does everything then come over again a little differently? she thought. If so, is there a pattern; a theme, recurring, like music; half remembered, half foreseen? . . . a gigantic pattern, momentarily perceptible?' (398)
2. 'Moments of being' is Woolf's term for 'exceptional moments' in one's experience. For her description of the role these played in her life see 'A Sketch' (*MB*, 70–3).
3. In her analysis of the various manuscript drafts and revised versions of *The Voyage Out*, Louise DeSalvo discusses the ways that Woolf altered her presentation of the pasts of her main characters as she revised the novel. Apparently one of her main reasons for removing details about Rachel's past was a desire to make the novel less autobiographical. See *Virginia Woolf's First Voyage: A Novel in the Making* (1980), pp. 112ff.
4. The contrast between Katharine and Mary Datchet, who deals competently with the world of facts, is dramatized in part by the contrasting ways they remember. Mary sees her past as 'various stages . . . which made her present position seem the culmination of successive miracles' (*ND*, 44). Katharine comes closer to this perspective at the end of the novel. See M. Rosenthal, *Virginia Woolf* (New York, 1979), pp. 72–3.
5. Sir Leslie Stephen, *Mausoleum Book*, with an Introduction by Alan Bell (Oxford, 1977), p. 10.
6. 'A Sketch of the Past', *MB*, 122.
7. Brenda R. Silver, ed., ' "Anon" and "The Reader": Virginia Woolf's Last Essays', in *Twentieth Century Literature*, 25 (1979), 385. See also 'The

String Quartet' (1921): 'I too sit passive on a gilt chair, only turning the earth above a buried memory, as we all do, for there are signs . . . that we're all recalling something, furtively seeking something' (*HH*, 28). Louis in *The Waves* and Isa in *Between the Acts* feel burdened by their memories of a buried past.

8. *D*, ii, 234 and 322. Useful discussions of the relationship between Woolf and Proust can be found in Floris Delattre, *Le Roman Psychologique de Virginia Woolf* (Paris, 1932); Margaret Church, *Time and Reality: Studies in Contemporary Fiction* (Chapel Hill, 1963); Ruth Temple, 'Never Say "I": To the Lighthouse as Vision and Confession' in *Virginia Woolf: A Collection of Critical Essays*, ed. Claire Sprague (Englewood Cliffs, N.J., 1971), pp. 90–100; and Harvena Richter, *Virginia Woolf: The Inward Voyage* (Princeton, 1970), 1978. Woolf discusses Proust's work in 'Phases of Fiction', *E*, ii, 83ff.

9. *MD*, 87. Clarissa's feeling of apprehension which is mixed in with many other emotions as she anticipates her day ('feeling as she did, standing there at the open window, that something awful was about to happen' (5)) may be caused in part by a suppressed memory of this traumatic event.

10. Sartre's comment on the way 'emotional constellations' shape the memories of the characters of Faulkner and Proust could be applied to the dramatic use of memory in *MD*. 'The order of the past [is] the order of the heart. It would be wrong to think that when the present is past it becomes our closest memory. Its metamorphosis can cause it to sink to the bottom of our memory, just as it can leave it floating on the surface. Only its own density and the dramatic meaning of our life can determine at what level it will remain.' Jean-Paul Sartre, 'On *The Sound and the Fury*: Time in the Work of Faulkner', transl. Annette Michelson, in *Aspects of Time*, ed. C. A. Patrides (Manchester, 1976), p. 206.

11. Woolf later wrote that in the first version Mrs. Dalloway was 'to kill herself, or perhaps merely to die at the end of the party'. 'Introduction' to the American editon of *Mrs. Dalloway*, included in the Modern Library edition (1928), p. vi.

12. J. Hillis Miller discusses this passage and the 'tunnelling process' in *Mrs. Dalloway* in *Fiction and Repetition* (Harvard, 1982).

13. *To the Lighthouse* (New York, 1955), p. 125. Hereafter, in this essay, the abbreviation *TL* refers to this edition.

14. Lily's thoughts here anticipate Woolf's later discussion of the role that 'moments of being' have played in her life and art. See notes 2 and 6, above.

15. *TL*, 298. 'Unconsciousness, which means presumably that the under-mind works at top speed while the upper-mind drowses, is a state we all know. . . . Do we strain Wordsworth's famous saying about emotion recollected in tranquillity when we infer that by tranquillity he meant that the writer needs to become unconscious before he can create?' ('The Leaning Tower', *E*, ii, 166).

16. *TL*, 301. There is not room here to explore the ways that this scene resembles Proust's depiction of the operation of 'involuntary memory'.

See Ruth Temple's commentary on this in 'Never Say "I"' and Harvena Richter's analysis in *The Inward Voyage*.

17. For a discussion of memory in *The Waves* see S. Dick, 'I Remembered, I Forgotten: Bernard's Final Soliloquy in *The Waves*', *M.L.S.* (Vol. III, No. 3). Harvena Richter discusses memory in *The Waves* and *The Years* in *The Inward Voyage*, pp. 162–79.

10

'Words Without Meaning— Wonderful Words': Virginia Woolf's Choice of Names

by ISOBEL GRUNDY

'Directly I'm told what a thing means,' Virginia Woolf wrote to Roger Fry, 'it becomes hateful to me.' This is not wilful obscurantism, but a statement to be taken seriously, related to other important opinions: that words live not in dictionaries but in the mind, that not 'a single word has the same meaning for two people', that the writer has to take one thing and let it stand for twenty (*L*, iii, 385, 201–202; *E*, ii, 249).

Nevertheless, we come to her fictions seeking meanings, seeking if we are wise, therefore, the elusive and the multiple. From the beginning (from, at any rate, the *Morning Post*'s review of her first novel, 5 April 1915)[1] readers have found something to pause over in her naming of her characters. In recent years volumes of comment have built round some of these names, much of it illuminating; but no general account of her habits and procedures in giving names has been offered. Such an account is of course strictly impossible. 'The difficulty about criticism is that it is so superficial. The writer has gone so much deeper. . . . Our criticism is only a birds eye view of the pinnacle of an iceberg. The rest under water' (*D*, iv, 173).

I attempt to offer such a bird's-eye view, however, in the belief that the communicating, or withholding, or implication, of meaning in the names of characters may provide some glimpse into the larger, hidden workings of the author's creative imagination.

Virginia Woolf herself described how the associations of names affect the mind, taking for example the sign 'Passing Russell Square', designed to notify passengers on the tube which route the next train will take:

> 'passing' suggested the transiency of things. . . . 'Russell' suggested the rustling of leaves and the skirt on a polished floor; also the ducal house of Bedford and half the history of England. Finally the word 'Square' brings in the street, the shape of an actual square combined with some visual suggestion of the stark angularity of stucco. (*E*, ii, 247)

The emphases which Woolf brings to these words, two of them proper names, are particular to herself. 'Passing', perhaps combined with 'rustle', evokes (245–46) a Tennysonian autumnal mood. The rustle of a floor-length skirt was the sound by which the Angel in the House announced her presence, so that the word signifies a feminine as well as a ducal tradition. On the other hand a word which 'brings in the street' brings in for Woolf a whole train of ideas: anonymity, freedom of movement, the rich and varied flow of other people's lives. This neutrally-designed message can therefore be read as bearing on some of its recipient's central concerns; that is presumably why she chooses it as her example to argue that though words cannot be bound down to one meaning, their variable wealth in echoes, memories, associations, is still a difficulty to the writer as much as an asset.

Personal names are the most suggestive of words. Their lexical meaning is seldom uppermost in the mind of namer or user. E. G. Withycombe notes that the traditional elements in names 'seem, in most languages, to have been combined with no particular regard for meaning', as is shown by the compounds 'peace-wolf', 'war-peace', and others of which translations make nonsense.[2] Our surnames, received automatically, and given names, intended to mark a still unrealized individuality, have all been the property of thousands before us.

Virginia Woolf was more conscious than most people of names being held in common, either simultaneously or sequentially. Different blends of society, past and present, figure in her writings as 'our Freds & Wills', or 'Sylvias & Geralds & Roberts & Roses', or 'Fanshawes and Leghs, Verneys, Pastons, and Hutchinsons' (*D*, i, 191, iii, 71; *E*, ii, 14). Such lumping together of undifferentiated units, which occurs in almost every novel, signifies distance of one kind or another; the distance becomes vertiginous, terrifying, in a drafted passage early in what became *The Waves*, which has no equivalent in the finished novel, describing 'the steps of innumerable children. Merely to call them by their names would take too long. Consider how many thousand Helens there have been; & Toms & Marys.' Later, this scene of endless dying generations took shape with children emerging from the sea's edge:

> innumerable multitudes of little bald naked purplish balls. . . . There must have been many millions of Helens, Toms, Margs [*sic*], John [*sic*], Ellens, Dicks, Hughs, Charles [*sic*], Dorothys,— to call them by their names would be impossible. And how discriminate?

Here the names intended to distinguish have themselves become indistinguishable. From these swarms emerge the six characters gifted with 'this visible body, this name, this age, this label'; the undifferentiated others are reduced to the 'boasting boys. . . . Archie and Hugh; Parker and Dalton; Larpent and Smith—the names repeat themselves; the names are the same always.'[3]

A novelist, like a parent, chooses names as one instrument of discrimination, choosing with widely varying aims: euphony, or significance either etymological or still current—most people would discern a meaning in Lily, but not in Susan, which originally means the same—or association either close or remote—Thoby Stephen with an uncle, Vanessa, apparently, with an obscure, unhappy, short-lived eighteenth-century woman who loved a great writer (QB, i, 18), and Virginia Woolf's fictional Judith Shakespeare with her real-life niece, the poet's daughter—or freedom from association—most parents would fight shy of Salome; Woolf disliked Helen for her niece because of having a maid called Nelly, and rejected

202

Cynthia for her first heroine because it 'dont do. All fine ladies, ingenuous young ladies, with Meridithian blood in them, are called Cynthia' (*L*, ii, 339, i, 343). Recent comment on Woolf's naming has concentrated either on lexical meaning or on associations, often those most distant, learned, and obscure,[4] without sufficiently examining whether these were her most pressing concern. The 'Passing Russell Square' passage and the spoof on the etymology of 'spaniel' in the opening paragraphs of *Flush* (7–8) ought at least to give us pause.

We need first to distinguish between the source of a name and the motives for its choice. Virginia Woolf, when working on her first novel, scanned tombstones and shop-signs. She drew on place-names (Manresa Road is in Chelsea; Denham and Datchet, Thames Valley towns, are within six miles of each other; Mr. Bennett, Woolf said, would connect Mrs. Brown with Datchet); on her acquaintance (she early knew a Rezia, a Seton, a Gibbs; her husband, like Jacob Flanders, had a tutor called Mr. Floyd; Roger Fry had a charwoman called Mrs. Filmer in 1918); on literature and history (Sir John Denham, Thomas Otway, Sir Robert Filmer); and perhaps on contemporary literature (Bertha Ruck, a popular living novelist, gave her name *to* a tombstone in *Jacob's Room*).[5] To trace all such germinations would be neither possible nor much to the point: few tombstones, signboards, actual or reading experiences, yielded names that would 'do'.

Several sources show us Virginia Woolf in the process of choosing names: MS drafts, full of decisions and indecisions; her diary, which weighs names for characters, for novels, even for genres of fiction to replace 'novel'; and letters, first sketch-book of names for fiction, for Vanessa Bell's children, and for recipients of nicknames. A childhood composition humorously presents the difficulties of parental choice.[6] Her diary muses, 'Septimus Smith?—is that a good name?' and 'this book, that is, The Hours, if thats its name?' (ii, 207, 248). These glimpses reveal a good deal about what Virginia Woolf expected of names and how she chose them, and about her personal 'pool of names', regularly available when a choice was to be made.

After her niece's birth she sent her sister a list, confessedly incomplete: 'Clarissa. / Miriam. / Rachel. / Venetia. / Sabina. / Clara. / Sarah. / Sara. / Euphrosyne. / I think on the whole I prefer Clarissa' (*L*, ii, 308). In terms of either meanings or associations, this is a most heterogeneous collection. It includes three Jewish names (one in two forms), of Moses' sister, Jacob's wife, Abraham's wife; three Latinate names (one in two forms), descriptive, apparently geographical, and tribal; and a Greek name, that of one of the three Graces. It involves various English literary associations (most notably Clarissa with Pope and Richardson, Euphrosyne with Milton's 'L'Allegro' and with young men Virginia Woolf knew and mocked (QB, i, 205–6)) and meanings (Rachel means 'ewe', Sarah 'princess'). There are, however, certain elements in common. All these names employ liquid or sibilant sounds and end liltingly on an unstressed syllable; all except Sarah are fairly uncommon at this date and had never been central to the English tradition (no Marys, Ellens, Dorothys here, though Susan crept in a few days later (ii, 317)); and a majority later feature largely in Woolf novels. (She had already applied her preferred Clarissa to her sister and to a projected niece, as yet unborn and unconceived (*L*, i, 382, 366).) Soon she extended the list, to include 'Sidonia, Griselda, Leslie, Vashti', praising Sidonia for having 'distinct emerald' in it, Griselda for being 'light and fantastic' (ii, 318, 330, 337). She made no mention of the fact that Leslie (to which she later joined the usual feminine Lesley) was their father's name, nor of the English literary associations of Griselda or, when she adds it, Nerissa, nor the Hindu provenance of Vashti.

The whole sequence reflects delight in uncertainty and in multiplicity of choice. 'How is Griselda, Theresa, Bridget?' her aunt writes. Of nicknames, Owlina succeeds Anonyma after she sees the baby's father, Duncan Grant, as 'a white owl perched upon a branch and blinking at the light, and shuffling his soft furry feet in the snow' (ii, 310, 331, 335). When 'Angelica' is chosen, she at once claims to have chosen it herself independently: it 'has liquidity and music, a hint of green in it, and memories of no one except Kaufmann, who was no doubt a charming character.' She repeats her approbation more playfully: 'a lovely name; I wish it had been possible to include Moll Flanders though; or Roxana. If ever anyone reminded me of you it is Moll Flanders' (ii, 339, 349). What, with humorous regret, she relinquishes is the possibility of including in a single name *all* admired associations, no matter how contradictory; what she welcomes is poetic sound, a very general atmospheric impression ('a hint of green'), and freedom from limiting associations. Professor Quentin Bell tells me that Princess Angelica in Thackeray's *The Rose and the Ring* was remembered in this choice. Other associations are never raised—neither Congreve's heroine in *Love for Love*, nor a character who causes and suffers innumerable adventures in *Orlando Furioso*, nor the etymology 'angel-like' nor the irrelevant dictionary meaning of crystallized vegetable stalks. Presumably these evidences of the name's having 'been out and about, on people's lips, in their houses, in the streets, in the fields, for so many centuries' (*E*, ii, 248) would be invisible in daily use, just as Virginia Woolf no doubt used her sister's name without calling to mind either Jonathan Swift, or the red admiral butterfly, or—after 1933—the play by Hugh Walpole.

All in all, Woolf seems to have demanded from names what she found in words as distorted by illness: 'a mystic quality. . . . beyond their surface meaning . . . a sound, a colour, here a stress, there a pause' (*E*, iv, 200). But she saw names as important as well as problematical; so do her characters. When Terence Hewet asks ' "Mightn't we call each other Rachel and Terence?" . . . "Terence," Rachel repeated. "Terence—that's like the cry of an owl." She looked up with a sudden rush of delight' (*VO*, 265). Mrs. Hilbery finds William Rodney's such 'a nice, rich, English name' (*ND*, 146)—more for the sake of Shakespeare, one assumes, than of Admiral Rodney (d. 1792). Mrs. Hilbery, like her creator, is unwilling to relinquish *any* promising name: mention of Mary Datchet provokes from her 'Ah—I half wish I'd called you Mary' (325). The heroine of 'Lappin and Lapinova' (rewritten in 1938 from twenty years earlier (*AWD*, 308)), working at being Mrs. Ernest Thorburn, muses 'Ernest was a difficult name to get used to. It was not the name she would have chosen' (*HH*, 69)—ironically, since her husband turns out in the end to resemble the implications of his name, more than her idea of him. Mrs. Richard Dalloway, similarly ambivalent about her married title, is luckier: the novel which opens by naming her as Mrs. Dalloway closes by recognizing the terror and excitement of her being Clarissa. To name her is the only possible expression, however inadequate,

of her uniqueness, even in swarming London, which is indifferent to the 'fantastic Christian names like Septimus with
which their parents have thought to distinguish' young men
called Smith (13, 94).

The naming of Angelica Bell casts some light on the names of
Woolf's fictional characters, especially women. It encourages
us to believe that in switching Cynthia to Rachel in *The Voyage
Out* she would be less urgently concerned with origins—Greek
or Hebrew, moon-goddess, ewe-lamb, or Jacob's bride[7]—than
with contexts closer to home: the social milieu of Meredith
novels. This naming shows her to be selective in her openness to
associations, sometimes admitting and sometimes excluding
them. It suggests limited interest in etymology—though
Clarissa and Clara, like so many on James Hafley's list, signify
shining light—but great sensitivity to sound and texture, along
with a joking pretence that a name can convey a quite
impossible freight of meaning. All these qualities are epitomized in a commentary on her sister's name, in a consistently
elaborated, fanciful, virtuoso letter to Clive Bell:

> It contains all the beauty of the sky, and the melancholy of the
> sea, and the laughter of the Dolphins in its circumference, first
> in the mystic Van, spread like a mirror of grey glass to Heaven.
> Next in the swishing tail of its successive esses, and finally in the
> grave pause and suspension of the ultimate A breathing peace
> like the respiration of Earth itself. (i, 282)

It would take a mystic name indeed to incorporate all this
(reference to three of the four elements) and Moll Flanders
too! No wonder the dedication to *Night and Day* could find no
'phrase . . . to stand beside' this symbol. Among her fiction it
is only in *Orlando* (226, 231–34) that such resonance is ascribed
to names.

Liquidity and music are shared in the names of Rachel and
Helen (who began as Lucilla), Clarissa (who began as
Lettice)[8] and Rezia, Lily, Eleanor and Sara, but absent from
the traditional Katharine and Mary which *Night and Day* sets
against Cassandra, as *Mrs. Dalloway* sets Clarissa against
Daisy, who would look ordinary beside her (49). Mrs. Ramsay's
Christian name, which her husband utters 'for all the world
like a wolf barking in the snow' (*TL*, 307), is withheld from

us.[9] Not only the Marys in *A Room of One's Own*, but also Susan, Jinny and Rhoda in *The Waves* are all a little abrupt and solid after Clarissa. Isa and Lucy are both sibilant, and the latter resembles other Woolf names in connoting light; but each is a short form of something more liquid and euphonious. 'Isabella' is seldom used at length in *Between the Acts*, and Isa calls her daughter Caro, an abbreviation on the same lines as her own. The childhood appellation 'Cindy, or Sindy, for it could be spelt either way . . . short for Lucy' (28) tells us that the woman who is also called Mrs.—or 'old Mother'— Swithin, 'old Flimsy', and 'Batty' would be properly named— as she never is—Lucinda. Liquidity and music seem to be on the ebb.

Though Mrs. Swithin's Victorian mother deplored such playing on people's names, Virginia Woolf did not. She apparently welcomed the spread of nicknaming which Hermione Lee sees as 'downgrading . . . erosion of the grandeur of the past'.[10] It is true that people can be downgraded by the mangling of their names. The charwoman who transforms Jacob Flanders into Mr. Sanders (*JR*, 100–1), Peter Walsh transforming Mrs. Ellen Barnet into 'old Moody, old Goody' (*MD*, 67, 183), can neither of them see the individual on the other side of the class barrier. Professor Walter Raleigh seeks to demystify the poets as 'Bill Blake or Bill Shakespeare or old Bill Wordsworth' (*E*, i, 315). Clarissa Parry mistakes Richard Dalloway's name before she sees him as a matrimonial prospect, but indignantly prohibits playing on his name once she has fallen in love with him (*MD*, 68, 71). It is true that the Ramsays, whom as readers we never see as equals but always as members of a parent generation, have no Christian names, and that Susan, Jinny, Rhoda, Bernard, Neville, and Louis, whom we see almost *sub specie aeternitatis*, have names which are never added to or varied in form, though one is itself a pet-form. Nevertheless taking liberties with names can convey not solely a snub but a whole emotional repertoire. It is a favourite Woolf activity, increasing with time in her fiction but present from the very beginning in letters which dub her father 'The President', her brother Thoby 'Your Highness', 'your Mightiness', 'milord', 'My dear Grim' and 'My dear old Gribbs', and herself 'Miss Jan', 'Poor Janet' and 'your loving

Goatus Esquire'. Her basic convention of addressing Emma Vaughan as 'Toad' and signing 'Goat' proliferates into 'Goatus', 'Capra' or 'Il Giotto' writing to 'The Toadus St Albaniensis', 'My dear and ancient Toad', 'My dearest Todkins', 'my dear little swampy reptile', 'My beloved Todelkrancz', 'Dearest Toadlebinks' (*L*, i, 2–9, 19–170). This is not downgrading but a play of fancy over titles originally chosen in either mock-reverence or playful insult. The same process works in 'Friendships Gallery', Woolf's spoof biography of Violet Dickinson, which, typed 'with a violet typewriter ribbon and bound in violet leather', makes much of its subject's narrow escape from being called Mary, and the fact that her surname is *not* spelled with a 'y'.[11]

Nicknaming serves many purposes in mocking and questioning the grandeur or relevance of the past, or systems of naming and titling (not only paternal or fraternal status but also in 'Friendships Gallery' the fascinating but tyrannical 'history of Christian names' (p. 275)), or the career structures by which men 'get a name'. It recognizes the futility of trying to sum up an individual in a name, discussed by Allen McLaurin; it celebrates variety and the anarchic creative intelligence, contributing to what Joanna Lipking calls 'the enormous amount of mischief going on in the text'.[12] In *The Years* Colonel Abel Pargiter is Bogy to his mistress; the self-important Edward is Nigs to his elder sister; the liquidly-named Magdalena is usually Maggie, Sara often Sally or Sal (the lack of a short form may have been one reason why Woolf decided not to call her Elvira). Foreign names of rich symbolic meaning, Pomjalovsky 'fruitful' and René 'reborn', become English Brown and Renny. Jane Marcus sees these names as travestied to 'lifeless English puddings',[13] wrongly I think. Nicholas 'Brown', who can never get his speech made or his real name remembered, who drinks his toast to the human race (*TY*, 447–60), shares an elusive quality, transcending individuality, with the Mrs. Brown whom Woolf coupled with Mr. Bennett.

Sara the mocker and ironist, who institutes some of these changes, who calls her cousin North 'a lieutenant in the Royal Rat-catchers', calls another cousin 'Rose of the flaming heart; Rose of the burning breast; Rose of the weary world—red, red

Rose!' or 'Red Rose, thorny rose, brave Rose, tawny Rose!' (307, 177, 453). The name's range of poetic and mysterious associations is at odds with its handsome, pugnacious, masculine bearer, who was named after the mother she so little resembles. The devices of fiction are summed up in this novel as 'Comedy . . . Contrast . . . The only form of continuity' (372). So names and titles move towards dignity and recede from it: Dubbin, 'a slim young man in a boat', becomes Sir William Whatney, but to the younger generation he becomes the 'old Mock Turtle' (214, 220, 426).

In *Between the Acts* all who aspire to status have their names mangled, down to the pedigree cat. Miss La Trobe, director of events, becomes 'Bossy' as well as the persistent 'Miss Whatsername'. Old Mr. Oliver becomes Bart or Bartie, so that nicknames link him closely with his sister Mrs. Swithin (one of hers is Batty) while their surnames remain antithetical (Norman and Saxon; chivalric hero and priestly saint). Virginia Woolf's husband wrote of the period of 'wholesale revolution in society and manners' which coincided with the action of her first novels and much in the later ones, which enabled intimate male friends for the first time to move from surnames to given names: a change 'not entirely unimportant. The shade of relationship . . . is not exactly the same.'[14] These shades of relationship inform Virginia Woolf's naming. Flimsy or Bossy convey a kind of affection, though a different kind from Cindy or Bart, while honorific titles often make their bearers, especially married women, feel uneasy. Sally lives on in Lady Rosseter, Kitty in Lady Lasswade, widow of the Governor-General. The bestowers of nicknames—usually the younger generation, or women, or the lower classes—are surely closer to their author's mind than the bestowers of titles; names which question identities are more suggestive than names which prescribe them.

Woolf's later novels reflect acute awareness that one cannot live up to the meaning of a name like René or Rose, but they reflect an interest—often oblique or ironical—in meanings. Her choice of the synonymous Rose and Rhoda, and of so many names signifying light or purity (Helen, Katharine, Clarissa, Lily, Susan, Eleanor, Lucy), is rather surprisingly in tune with that of other name-givers over the generations: these are the qualities which our race has chosen to see in its daughters. Male names (Orlando from 'fame' and 'land', Bernard from 'bear' and 'stern', William from 'will' and 'helmet') originate from the opposite pole of sex-linked virtues, but also show even more clearly how names have unmoored themselves from their root meanings. In many complete male names—Ridley Ambrose, Hughling Elliott, St. John Hirst, Seabrook and Archer Flanders, Scrope Purvis, North Pargiter— the former element is indistinguishable in type from the latter, individual submerged in family character. These formal names are the very reverse of nicknames.

Hafley notes that Virginia Woolf gives the name William, which for Mrs. Hilbery is for ever Shakespeare, to the less than totally satisfactory Rodney, Bradshaw and Dodge (p. 24)— and, one might add, Bankes, Whatney and others. This is no surprise when William has for centuries remained second in popularity only to John. Names are aspects of social realism, class-linked as well as sex-linked. The passage in *The Waves* drafts, having wondered how to discriminate, goes on to note sardonically how Flora 'would be going to school in Switzerland about the same time that Florrie went out for the first time as kitchenmaid', as if the different forms of their related names had dictated their different directions (p. 67).

Virginia Woolf's relating of one name to another is, however, generally a great deal more subtle than this. In fact, none of her names should be seen in isolation, but each in relation to those which surround it. Ruth Gruber's 1935 study of Woolf observed (p. 25) the continuity or repetitiveness of sound among the names of *The Voyage Out*, the r's, s's, n's, and l's of Rachel, Helen, Clarissa, Vinrace, Ambrose, and the novel's original title, *Melymbrosia*. Terence, Richard and Ridley add a single plosive each. Rachel who comes from Richmond is first kissed by Richard; she becomes engaged to Terence, whose name strikingly resembles that of her dead mother, Theresa. In this novel names come to us obscurely linked by sound, before meaning or association is considered. The tangled interconnectedness extends to Evelyn's suitors Sinclair and Oliver, one echoing St. John, the other the name of Miss Allan's bottle of *crème de menthe* (311)! We first meet the young men Hewet and Hirst as a matched pair, alike in intelligence, unconventionality and university background. The next chapter reveals sharply distinguished Christian names: Terence liquid, borne by a Latin writer but currently rare outside Ireland; St. John 'pompous and aristocratic' (as Woolf said of 'Claudia' (*L*, ii, 317)), borne by an eighteenth-century statesman and an unsympathetic character in *Jane Eyre*. As the novel moves gradually into use of their Christian names it shows us they are less alike than different; in the same way *Night and Day* puts forward but then overrules the link between Denham and Datchet.

Meanings and associations reinforce the sense which sound gives of recurrence and pattern in *The Voyage Out*'s names. The twice-hinted 'ambrosia' suggests divinity and intoxication, made ominous by the prefix *mel-*, black, or scholarly by memory of the Ambrosian library at Milan (a town Virginia Woolf had very briefly visited (*L*, i, 393)). Vinrace sounds like a continuation of the second theme, using 'race' in the connoisseur's sense (though it is also the name of an actual family with a genealogy printed (1920?)). Louise De Salvo has shown (pp. 21–7) how a group of names with interconnected, recondite associations (reaching the bizarre with Geranium) gave way to a more usual group drawing on the Stephen family tree.

This first novel anticipates four names Virginia Woolf would suggest for her niece; it anticipates many more later novelistic choices. Mrs. Raymond Parry, named like a sister-in-law of the later Clarissa, is famed for her 'wonderful parties'; the Thornburys are conventional and prolific like the Thorburns in 'Lappin and Lapinova'; Mary Umpleby, delightful and brave, with her unexplained 'dreadful sorrows' and odd likeness to Terence Hewet, seems to stand outside the bourgeois norm as does old Miss Umphelby the Cambridge classicist in *Jacob's Room* (*VO*, 172, 130; *JR*, 40). Such recurrence continues to recur in the novels. The wife of pompous, uxorious Hugh Whitbread was once to have been Milly; Milly Pargiter marries Hugh Gibbs and becomes with him an instance of bovine family stability; Jasper was an early choice for the character who became Neville in *The Waves*, Bernard for the character who became Septimus Smith. Names, even more than actual characters, from one novel are regularly given walk-on appearances in another.[15]

211

Along with repetition, we sometimes find carelessness in continuity, which reflects the novels' long gestation, as well as consistent preferences. Rachel's two aunts between them retain four names: Lucy, Eleanor, Katie and Clara (*VO*, 33–4, 220, 255). (All figure in later novels; Lucy does for a maid in *Mrs. Dalloway*, a tutor in *The Years*, a central figure in *Between the Acts*.) Edward Pargiter's college friend is both Ashley and Ashton (*TY*, 55, 281). When Evelyn Murgatroyd first hesitates between Alfred Perrott and the dark, romantic Raymond Oliver, then is claimed by both Alfred Perrott and the beastly, passionate Sinclair (*VO*, 223, 301), the reader is hard put to it to know just how often the character has changed her mind.

Hirst and Hewet, Denham and Datchet, Ralph and Rodney, are followed by other pairings both direct and oblique. We have Clarissa and Rezia; we nearly had in *The Pargiters* Eleanor and Elvira; Mrs. Foxcroft, Lady Bexborough, Sir John Buckhurst and Lady Lexham represent the same ideal of *noblesse oblige*; Millicent, Lady Bruton, comes companioned by her unwilling, less privileged *alter ego*, Milly Brush (*MD*, 6, 7, 20, 185, 34, 114ff).

Jacob's Room, as Hermione Lee has written, goes further than other novels in presenting names

> which are ludicrously similar. It is not possible to distinguish carefully between Norman, Budgeon, Sturgeon, Masham, Bonham, Stretton, Gresham, and Sherborn . . . Helen Aitken and Helen Askew. No wonder that Jacob, introduced to an American called Pilcher, remembers him as Pilchard. Evidently there is more to this than mere paucity of invention. The motives are partly the same as those which inspired Dickens in *Bleak House* to call his politicians Boodle, Coodle, Doodle, and so on: their names don't matter, so long as they sound ridiculously interchangeable. (p. 87: page-references omitted)

Woolf goes further still. Names slip close to the irresponsibility of nursery-rhyme in 'courtly Mr. Wortley' and 'Miss Eliot in her velvet' (*JR*, 57). An obscure Mary Sanders makes a momentary appearance in a rural pub just before Jacob has the name Sanders fastened on him for his own. The charwoman who does this is a Mrs. Papworth, whose name chimes with that of Sopwith the eternally talking don, though their lives could hardly, within England, be more different (100, 39).

Virginia Woolf is up to something different from Dickens here: where he invents Boodle and Doodle according to a comically mechanical principle for indistinguishable human automata, she uses names as they occur in life: the same names hitched at random to the random swarms of people who might well be very different from each other if only we could get close enough to see them; similar names which accurately reflect the shared history of the race that lies behind individual difference.

To the Lighthouse presents a different version of earlier repetitiveness: the name Ramsay seems something like a norm to which other names aspire. Its stressed vowel is repeated in Bankes and Tansley, in the peripheral Langley and Carrie Manning, in McNab, Bast, McAlister, in the dog Badger, in four of the eight children's names: Andrew, Jasper (linked already in *Jacob's Room* (17, 20)), Nancy and Cam. As Tansley approaches Ramsay on one side, Rayley approaches it on another. Lily Briscoe, on the contrary, sounds nothing like it at all, and neither does Augustus Carmichael. The repetition of sound, and the different notes struck against it, do not convey any possible explicit message, yet they are suggestive. Sound and suggestion override the question of actual meaning. (Ramsay and Briscoe, both from place-names, indicate respectively 'wild garlic island' and 'wood of birches, or of the Britons'.) Ramsay, however, *suggests* rams' horns, battering rams; these and the *apparent* meaning of Briscoe (brought out by Mrs. Ramsay calling Lily 'her little Brisk' and recalled outside the novel when Woolf uses 'to brisk' about artistic bringing to life (*TL*, 81; *AWD*, 326)) are readily available to the reader, as sounds are and as the place-name dictionary's verdicts are not.

Woolf's sensitivity to 'the history of Christian names' and to associations, whether historical or imagined, is remarkable: she can make a central or even a peripheral name almost an *Iliad* in a nutshell. Evelyn Murgatroyd in *The Voyage Out* is a remarkable study: the child of her mother's romantic seduction, rebellious and dissatisfied, flirtatious and frigid. She bears a surname which (despite its homely significance of 'Margaret's clearing') suggests a moustachioed villain of Victorian melodrama, and a Christian name which, for readers

213

of Fanny Burney, encapsulates a sentimental story of a heroine whose wronged mother is dead and whose rich and un-approachable father at the very last relents and owns his daughter's legitimacy.

The cognate Christian names of Jacob Flanders and James Ramsay stamp them as being what their creator felt all intellectually and socially gifted young men to be: heirs to privilege of questionable title. The Hebrew name is thought to mean 'supplanter'; the Biblical Jacob was his mother's favour-ite, ousted his elder brother, received his father's blessing and prospered mightily as a patriarch; Virginia Stephen's own formidable family tree included an uncle James Fitzjames (whose baronetcy passed, after her death, to another James), a grandfather James on one side and a great-grandfather James on the other. 'Jacob' stands for ancient, 'James' for modern patriarchy. To this, Woolf's Jacob, whose privileged air many characters remark on, joins a surname which marks him out (after the kindness and admiration of old Miss Wargrave and Dick Graves (89, 110)) for ugly and futile death in the trenches, and which also, incongruously, suggests that vivacity and tenacity of Defoe's underworld which Virginia Woolf would have liked to include in naming her niece. Jacob's name proclaims him a focus of warring influences.

Clarissa Dalloway must owe less to Samuel Richardson, whom Woolf had not read when she created her (*D*, ii, 309, iii, 94–96), than to Alexander Pope. The Clarissa of Pope's *Rape of the Lock* (which she reviewed in 1925) is equipped to bequeath Mrs. Dalloway both her touch of tinsel ('to dance all night and dress all day') and her counterbalancing awareness of the swift approach of grey hair, wrinkles, and death. Dalloway, sur-prisingly, is absent from the London telephone directory, the British Library catalogue, the *D.N.B.*, and Woolf's hunting-ground Richmond cemetery. Woolf would have known of the early nineteenth-century scholar James Dallaway. Was she concealing her tracks?

Miss La Trobe's name combines several different concep-tions of the author's role, suggesting a star or diva (La Melba, La Callas), a maker of tropes, or a troubadour, whose art is by implication—*objets trouvés, ben trovato*—chancy. She also had an uncommonly versatile namesake: Charles Joseph La Trobe, who governed Victoria, Australia, gave his name to a university and to the Natural History Museum's prized La Trobe Gold Nugget, is buried near Eastbourne and had an ancestor who impressed Fanny Burney.[16]

Many names reflect Virginia Woolf's alertness to comic, undignified, or commercial associations. The pregnant implications of Pargiter (plasterer or whitewasher) have recently been well expounded; the novelist must also have enjoyed giving her epitome of the upper-middle classes the name of a left-wing working-class acquaintance, as she gave to Mr. Oliver of Pointz Hall a Christian name which was the surname not only of a housekeeper in *Orlando* but also of her own gardener and maid.[17] 'Bart Oliver' would comically suggest Bath Oliver biscuits (mentioned in her diary in 1935 (iv, 324))—her character, however, is never called by that particular combination of his names. Hugh Whitbread and Sir William Whatney conjure up, for the British reader, brewing firms. Sir William Bradshaw and the Rev. Edward Whittaker (whose preaching converted Doris Kilman) suggest long-established, impeccably accurate reference books. *Bradshaw's Railway Guide* has been shredding and slicing time to the minute since 1839 as punctiliously as Sir William and the clocks of Harley Street,[18] and associates him with what Woolf calls masculine 'railway lines of convention' or 'a formal railway line of sentence' (*D*, ii, 178; *L*, iii, 135). *Whitaker's Table of Precedency*, which lists exactly 'who follows whom', and the now better-known *Whitaker's Almanack* ('one of the most dispassionate of authors, but one of the most methodical') both enumerate inequalities and counsel submission, especially by women, as 'The Mark on the Wall' (*HH*, 46–7) and *Three Guineas* (83ff.) point out.

Woolf achieves a masterpiece of significant naming, generally unnoticed, in *A Room of One's Own*, when she introduces her lecturing, narrating self with 'call me Mary Beton, Mary Seton, Mary Carmichael or by any name you please—it is not a matter of any importance' (8). One cannot read this book aright without knowing the ballad that these names come from. It is not necessary to know that 'Friendship's Gallery' had specifically linked the popularity of the name Mary with the power of the Church, nor that this ballad has transferred itself from a Scots girl at the Court of Russia to the Maries of

215

Mary Queen of Scots; it *is* necessary to know the story: how female comradeship is about to be broken and the speaker ('me', Mary Hamilton) hanged for the murder of the baby who resulted from her seduction by the king.

> Yestreen the Queen had four Maries,
> The night she'll hae but three;
> There was Marie Seaton, and Marie Beaton,
> And Marie Carmichael, and me.[19]

Virginia Woolf assumes this knowledge in her readers. She takes the name Beton for the aunt who left her a legacy (56); she gives Seton (already used in *Mrs. Dalloway* for Sally) to an Oxford don and to her prolific, impecunious mother (28ff); she gives Carmichael (already used in *To the Lighthouse* for a highly delphic poet) to a novelist (120). In the ballad, these women were the lucky ones. She reserves unmentioned the name of the criminal/victim, Hamilton, whose suppressed story is a powerful, silent presence in the book. Taken literally it parallels that of Shakespeare's sister, or the newspaper report of the rape in *Between the Acts*. Taken allegorically, bearing and killing a royal child suggests the stifling of creativity.

Another fleeting presence in *A Room of One's Own* is 'Mrs. Martin, aged thirty-six, dressed in blue', representative of the woman of the past in 'fact' (66). The genesis of this name is revealed in Virginia Woolf's early 'Journal of Mistress Joan Martyn', where a modern historian meets the Martyns, John and Betty, owners of a precious MS which preserves a rare female voice from the past. It is Mrs. Martyn who 'drew my attention to the y. in their name'.[20] But of course the name is historically her husband's, not her own; and 'all my eye and Betty Martin' is proverbial for nonsense, poppycock. So we must not be surprised when Mrs. Martin of *A Room of One's Own* vanishes into insubstantiality.

The characters of *The Waves* draw life from many sources. Percival carries the Grail connotations, as has been pointed out.[21] Louis, name of eighteen French kings, reflects its owner's self-identification with Saint-Simon and the eighteenth-century French Court. Neville binds its bearer to the Cambridge tradition: in Neville's Court, Trinity College, Jacob Flanders has rooms, and there Leonard Woolf, Thoby Stephen, and

Clive Bell used to quote poetry and 'listen to the soaring song of innumerable nightingales'.[22] Susan, widespread from the seventeenth century onwards among all classes, is self-explanatory as a name suggesting tradition and stability. Rhoda, Greek for *rose*, is ironical when we compare red Rose, brave Rose Pargiter, with this character's associations with white, with violets, and with fear. About Jinny two things strike me as relevant: one is Leigh Hunt's rondeau 'Jenny kissed me', whose rapid spontaneous action is reproduced—with such different emotional consequences—as the first major event of the novel (9); the other is that it is a version of the author's own name. 'Jenny' is historically a pet form of Jane, not Jennifer, and has until fairly recent times been pronounced 'Jinny'; the novelist used 'Jinny' for her own childhood name, as well as 'Ginny', which she signed as late as November 1935 (*MB*, 84; *L*, v, 445). Critics have so regularly identified her with Rhoda—except when noting her presence in Bernard or in all six characters of *The Waves*—that it may redress the balance to notice this link with the gay, acutely sensuous, party-going, courageous Jinny.

The act of naming with which Peter Walsh closes *Mrs. Dalloway* is repeated in Virginia Woolf's work in novel after novel, in every conceivable mood from this exaltation to despair or feigned despair.[23] Orlando calls her husband, Marmaduke Bonthrop Shelmerdine, and the 'beautiful, glittering name fell out of the sky like a steel-blue feather', rapidly followed by its owner, leaping from his supernatural aeroplane (294–95). Rachel feels delight when she first calls Terence by name; just before she dies, when the 'curtain which had been drawn between them for so long vanished', they greet each other by name in matter-of-fact tones: ' "Hullo, Terence." . . . "Well, Rachel" ' (*VO*, 340). Mrs. Hilbery, sorting out the muddled lovers at the end of *Night and Day*, does it by naming them: ' "Katharine and Ralph," she said, as if to try the sound, "William and Cassandra" ' (526). Here names become an acceptable shorthand: by their confessed inadequacy, they earn the right to stand for their immensely complicated and changeable owners. Often, however, the speaking or crying of names signifies the failure of contact. The young Peter Walsh cries out Clarissa's name after he has lost her (*MD*, 72). When Terence

217

and Rachel walk together in the jungle and the others try to use his surname as a charm to bring them back, they hear only meaningless sound like 'the crack of a dry branch or the laughter of a bird' (*VO*, 346). The narrator's attempt to pin down and describe Jacob unrolls itself between his elder brother's thrice-repeated call 'Ja-cob! Ja-cob!' and his bereaved friend's repetition of it. It is the earlier cry, addressed to the living child, which has 'an extraordinary sadness. Pure from all body, pure from all passion, going out into the world, solitary, unanswered, breaking against rocks—so it sounded' (*JR*, 6–7, 176). But that is also how the names of the dead sound, when vainly called after them. Three times Lily calls 'Mrs. Ramsay! Mrs. Ramsay!'—the first time in grateful memory, but later in the anguish of loss, 'the old horror come back—to want and want and not to have' (*TL*, 250, 277–78, 310).

Virginia Woolf's people swing between two moods: delight in their named identity and desire to escape into 'the delight of having no name' (*O*, 97). Her diary often records these swings, as in 'Sydney comes & I'm Virginia; when I write I'm merely a sensibility. Sometimes I like being Virginia. . . . Now . . . I'd like to be only a sensibility' (ii, 193). Of *The Waves* at an early stage she wrote, 'Autobiography it might be called. . . . she. . . . But who is she? I am very anxious that she should have no name' (*D*, iii, 229). Neville contrasts the narrow limits marked by his name with his immeasurable self; even Louis, who signs his name with such satisfaction—'I, and again I, and again I. Clear, firm, unequivocal, there it stands, my name'—yet feels at Hampton Court 'Our separate drops are dissolved; we are extinct, lost in the abysses of time, in the darkness'; Bernard, who submerges himself again and again in the identities of his friends, resumes his 'I, I, I' both with exhilaration as inheritor and continuer, and with resigned acceptance as an elderly man, 'tired as I am, spent as I am' (*TW*, 152, 118, 160, 180, 210). In *Between the Acts* Woolf planned to present ' "I" rejected: "We" substituted' (*AWD*, 289). To escape altogether from one's name, as characters do when their consciousness reaches out to respond to the huge unknown stretches of past or future time, is to evade the danger of 'the damned egotistical self', to approach the condition of the writer, or the Greeks, or women before the eighteenth century, or of 'Anon', that early unidentified lyric

218

voice whom Virginia Woolf's last work celebrates.[24] In *Between the Acts*, after individual identity and theatrical identities have been many times sloughed off and re-assumed, after the audience, 'neither one thing nor the other; neither Victorians nor themselves', has listened to 'the voice that was no one's voice' (207, 211), names are firmly re-introduced by 'The Rev. G. W. Streatfield', 'calling himself Reverend, also M.A.'. And this is how the listeners react: 'O Lord, protect and preserve us from words the defilers, from words the impure! What need have we of words to remind us? Must I be Thomas, you Jane?' (221–23). Neither of these names is found in Woolf's usual word-pool. I have no doubt that this is another multiple allusion: to Lawrence's famous naming of our anonymous, unmentionable parts as 'John Thomas and lady Jane',[25] and to an even more famous cinematic naming (Virginia Woolf had discussed the film in her diary in 1932 (iv, 103–4)): 'Me Tarzan. You Jane.' Names are the end of innocence, the burden of the human.

NOTES

1. M and M, p. 51. My title comes from *BA*, 248.
2. *Oxford Dictionary of English Christian Names* (Oxford, 2nd ed., 1950), p. xiv. I have used this, P. H. Reaney, *A Dictionary of British Surnames* (1958), and Eilert Ekwall, *The Concise Oxford Dictionary of English Place-Names* (Oxford, 4th ed., 1960).
3. J. W. Graham (ed.), *Virginia Woolf, The Waves, The Two Holograph Drafts* (Toronto, 1976), pp. 10, 61–2, 11–12; *TW*, 33–4.
4. Useful are James Hafley, 'Notes on the Names of Virginia Woolf's Characters' in *The Glass Roof, Virginia Woolf as a Novelist* (Berkeley, 1954), pp. 168–69, and Beverly Ann Schlack, *Continuing Presences: Virginia Woolf's Use of Literary Allusion* (Pennsylvania, 1979).
5. *L*, i, 349, 14; *MB*, 84, 73; Leonard Woolf, *Sowing, An Autobiography of the Years 1880–1904* (1960), p. 60f; Virginia Woolf, *Roger Fry, A Biography* (1940), p. 215.
6. *A Cockney's Farming Experiences*, ed. Suzanne Henig (San Diego, 1972), p. 5.
7. Louise A. De Salvo, *Virginia Woolf's First Voyage: A Novel in the Making* (1980), p. 27ff.
8. De Salvo, pp. 13, 34.

9. See David Leon Higden, 'Mrs. Ramsay's First Name', *Virginia Woolf Quarterly*, i (1972–73), 46–7.
10. *The Novels of Virginia Woolf* (1977), pp. 212–13.
11. Ellen Hawkes (ed.), *Twentieth Century Literature*, 25 (1979), 272, 275–76, 279–80.
12. McLaurin, *Virginia Woolf, The Echoes Enslaved* (Cambridge, 1973), pp. 167–70; Lipking, 'Looking at the Monuments: Woolf's Satiric Eye', *B.N.Y.P.L.*, 80 (1976–77), 142.
13. '*The Years* as Greek Drama, Domestic Novel and Götterdammerung', *B.N.Y.P.L.*, 80, p. 282.
14. *Sowing*, p. 119.
15. Cf. Winifred Holtby, *Virginia Woolf* (1932), p. 143; Alice Van Buren Kelley, *The Novels of Virginia Woolf: Fact and Vision* (1973), p. 86.
16. Information from Dr. Evelyn Haller and the Natural History Museum; Burney, *Diary and Letters*, ed. Charlotte Barrett (1842–46), ii, 324, 333–34.
17. Mitchell A. Leaska, 'Virginia Woolf the Pargiter: A Reading of *The Years*'; Jane Marcus, '*The Years* as Greek Drama' (*B.N.Y.P.L.*, 80, pp. 172ff.; 280ff.); *D*, i, 39. 'I wish my name were Bartholomew. She has been mad, squints, and is singularly pure of soul' (1924, *L*, iii, 104). Duncan Grant's father's name was Bartle.
18. *MD*, 113, 137. Sir William owes his name also to the Bradshaw Lecture given at the Royal College of Physicians (Roger Poole, *The Unknown Virginia Woolf* (Cambridge, 1978), p. 124).
19. F. J. Child, *English and Scottish Ballads* (Boston, 1857–59), iii, 379; Antonia Fraser, *Mary Queen of Scots* (1970), p. 230 n. Leonard Woolf, also intrigued by this ballad, connected it with the romance of women's names (*The Wise Virgins*, 1914, p. 20).
20. Susan M. Squier and Louise A. De Salvo (eds.), *TCL*, 25, pp. 240–69.
21. E.g. Mitchell A. Leaska, *The Novels of Virginia Woolf from Beginning to End* (N.Y., 1977), p. 182; Schlack, p. 126ff.
22. *Sowing*, p. 167.
23. *TY*, 49. Cf. Jean O. Love, *Worlds in Consciousness: Mythopoetic Thought in the Novels of Virginia Woolf* (Calif., 1970), p. 138.
24. *D*, ii, 14. Cf. Maria DiBattista, *Virginia Woolf's Major Novels: The Fables of Anon* (New Haven, 1980), p. 59ff.; Nora Eisenberg, 'Virginia Woolf's Last Words on Words: *Between the Acts* and "Anon"' in Jane Marcus (ed.), *New Feminist Essays on Virginia Woolf* (1981), pp. 253–60.
25. *Lady Chatterley's Lover* (1960), p. 193.

Notes on Contributors

VIRGINIA BLAIN teaches nineteenth- and twentieth-century literature at Macquarie University in Sydney. She has edited R. S. Surtees, *Mr. Sponge's Sporting Tour* (1981), and is working with the editors of this volume on a *Feminist Companion to Literature in English.*

PATRICIA CLEMENTS teaches modern literature at the University of Alberta. She has published on nineteenth- and twentieth-century poetry and prose, and edited jointly with Juliet Grindle a previous volume in the Critical Studies series on Hardy's poetry.

TONY DAVENPORT, Senior Lecturer at Royal Holloway College, London University, is author of *The Art of the 'Gawain'-Poet* (1978), and *Fifteenth-Century English Drama* (1982), and has published on *To the Lighthouse.*

MARIA DIBATTISTA is author of *Virginia Woolf's Major Novels: The Fables of Anon* (New Haven, 1980). She is an Associate Professor of English at Princeton University.

SUSAN DICK teaches at Queen's University, Kingston, Ontario. She is editor of George Moore's *Confessions* and of the holograph *To the Lighthouse* (Toronto, 1982).

LYNDALL GORDON teaches at Jesus College, Oxford. She is author of *Eliot's Early Years* (1977). Her book on Virginia Woolf, *A Writer's Life*, will be published in 1984.

ISOBEL GRUNDY teaches at Queen Mary College, London University, and is joint editor with Robert Halsband of Lady Mary Wortley Montagu's *Essays and Poems* (1977). She has published on the modern period as well as the eighteenth century.

JOHN MEPHAM has taught both philosophy and English at the University of Sussex. He has translated works by Alexandre Koyré and Roman Jakobson, and edited *Issues in Marxist Philosophy* with David-Hillel Ruben. He is now a freelance writer.

221

SHIRLEY NEUMAN has published *Gertrude Stein: Autobiography and the Problem of Narration* (1979), *Labyrinths of Voice: Conversations with Robert Kroetsch* (with R. Wilson, 1982), *Some One Myth: Yeats's Autobiographical Prose* (1982), and articles on modern literature. She teaches at the University of Alberta.

S. P. ROSENBAUM teaches at the University of Toronto. He has edited *English Literature and British Philosophy* (1971), and *The Bloomsbury Group: An Anthology* (1975), and he is general editor of the University of Toronto's Bloomsbury Studies series.

Index

Index